JOB IDEAS FOR TODAY'S WOMAN

by

RUTH LEMBECK

PRENTICE-HALL Inc., Englewood Cliffs, N.J.

To the Memory of
Zena Brody
who was with me this time
around, too

Other Books by RUTH LEMBECK

380 Part-Time Jobs for Women
Teenage Jobs

Job Ideas for Today's Woman by Ruth Lembeck
Copyright © 1974 by Ruth Lembeck

Printed in the United States of America

Prentice-Hall International, Inc., London
Prentice-Hall of Australia, Pty. Ltd., North Sydney
Prentice-Hall of Canada, Ltd., Toronto
Prentice-Hall of India Private Ltd., New Delhi
Prentice-Hall of Japan, Inc., Tokyo

10 9 8 7 6 5 4 3 2

Library of Congress Cataloging in Publication Data
Lembeck, Ruth.
Job ideas for today's woman.
1. Vocational guidance for women—United States.
2. Woman—Employment—United States. I. Title.
II. Title: Ways to work part-time, freelance, full-
time at home, and as entrepreneur.
HF5382.5.U5L38   331.4'0973   73-8993
ISBN 0-13-510057-7

Contents

Book Remarks

1. Let's Get Down to Basics   1
2. Bon Appetit! Good Business!   19
3. The Social Life: Get It All Together   33
4. When Persuasion Pays Off   40
5. For Animal Lovers   61
6. Health: An Expanding, Vital Field   66
7. Fashion Is Fun   92
8. There's Always Plenty to Do with Kids Around   109
9. Library Work Can Be Dynamic   120
10. Go Back to Nature   124
11. Communications via Media and Muse   130
12. Office Work—Your Foot in the Door   146
13. Author! Author! (That Could Be You)   155
14. If You're a Go-Go Person, Try Travel Work   164
15. Help the Harried Homemaker   169
16. Handy Andys, Move Over!   174
17. Play Up Your Talents   179
18. Promotion Hints   213
    Appendix of Organizations   215
    General Index   220
    Job Title Index   223

Book Remarks

The examples of real-life women written up in these pages have been drawn largely from the East Coast area simply because this is where the author happens to live. They were more accessible However, all over the country equally dynamic women are equally involved in jobs just as fascinating and rewarding.

Any salaries stated herein represent the most recent available at publication time. Nevertheless, keep in mind that all are subject to change with time; best to check current rates before you job-hunt. Geography, individual employers, local supply and demand, and the extent of your skills, talent, knowledge, and experience are all salary-influencing factors.

If you wonder why there are so few professions in this text, the explanation lies in (a) space limitations (how much can a conscientious writer cram into only one book, anyway?), (b) training for most professions is long, costly, and not feasible for the greater number of women, (c) those who lean toward a particular profession strongly enough will follow through on that inclination without additional urging, and (d) help for such advanced, specialized spheres is to be found in other books and through continuing education counseling.

1

Let's Get Down to Basics

Somewhere in these pages, there's a job idea for you—one that's challenging, absorbing, full of promise. Whatever your interests, whatever your home schedule, whatever your age, education, personal circumstances, and reasons for wanting to work, dig into these chapters, and you're bound to come up with a plum, the answer to what-can-I-do. It could get you out of the house or keep you happily occupied under your own roof. It may take only an hour or so of your week until you're willing or able to give it more time, or it may be so totally absorbing, you can't drag yourself away from it and give it far more than the usual workday.

However, this is more than a book of job ideas. It's a handholding, step-by-step guide that tells you how to go about getting them, what you need (personally, materially, educationally), any costs involved, possible earnings, and most important of all—how to get started. Its purpose is to help you over the hurdles and soothe your preliminary anxieties by making you savvy to the tricks of your new "trade."

The first step is the hardest. It **always** is, but when you read the dozens of vignettes woven through these chapters of women who've taken that step and more to add new and often exciting dimensions to their lives, you'll be inspired to do likewise.

GETTING STARTED
If your confidence is nil or barely there, and you haven't the foggiest notion what you can do or how to go about finding out, relax! You're not alone. What's more, all kinds of help is at hand.

Counseling Everybody needs it. There's nothing like having a heart-to-heart with someone who's sympathetic, objective, and informed about the world of work—someone who can listen to all your facts, then guide you in making major decisions about everything that stands between you and a job. Sponsorship of counseling help is quite varied. It could be any of the following: your public school system's adult-education vocational-extension program; the local Y; the community arm of any national religious group or service club; women's clubs or business group; a community-action program; Community Chest or United Fund; an industrial union; a professional organization or trade association; individual employers; or a continuing education or noncredit workshop at a college or university. Then, again, it might be found at a service set up expressly to guide women in further education and job choices such as WOW (Washington Opportunities for Women), a nonprofit organization, or at a government agency such as Massachusetts' Women's Bureau, which conducts small-business workshops, offers job guidance, and publishes helpful pamphlets.

Catalyst, a New York based, nonprofit, privately funded organization, is aimed primarily at helping college-educated family women to find their way into challenging jobs or careers. It provides guidance on continuing education, publications and advice on where to go for direct counseling and placement. Address: Catalyst, 6 East 82nd Street, New York, New York, 10028.

Jewish Occupational Council (United States and Canada) has member agencies in key cities. It offers educational and job counseling, training, placement, and aptitude testing. Scholarship grants are available. Look under "Jewish Vocational Service" or a similar name in your local telephone book, or write to the parent organization at 114 Fifth Avenue, New York, New York, 10011.

Advocates for Women, largely the brainchild of a woman named Del Goetz, is a funded, nonprofit San Francisco organization that provides economic counseling to women setting up their own businesses. It also offers career counseling and help in overcoming employer discrimination. New York State and Massachusetts also give business guidance. New York City's Executive Volunteer Corps is made up of fully retired business people who advise others on setting up a broad variety of business enterprises. They help people from anywhere in the

United States—or the world, for that matter—providing they come to the office at 415 Madison Avenue, New York, New York, 10017. The federal government has SCORE (Senior Corps Of Retired Executives), an ACTION program that provides expert counseling in every phase of business for anyone either already running a small business or about to start one. It has 205 chapters scattered all over the United States (Note: They welcome qualified women volunteer counselors.) Local, state, regional, or federal, the list of counseling agencies is long and constantly changing and growing, so snoop around a bit to uncover some on your own.

Private counseling agencies These advise you and provide testing services at a wide range of fees. It's best to look into just how much experience they've had counseling mature women and whether their types of testing are valid for you. To learn costs and other particulars, look through DIRECTORY OF APPROVED COUNSELING AGENCIES, published yearly by the American Personnel and Guidance Association (APGA), 1605 New Hampshire Avenue, N.W., Washington, D.C. 20009. If it's not in your public library, write to the association.

Watch your newspapers for word of other vocational help available to women.

Education and Training Where did yours stop? After high school or college or somewhere before you finished either one? An incomplete formal education doesn't mean you're quicksanded, quagmired, stuck. The real question is—how much have you learned, either formally or through just plain living, that can be used for a job? How much refreshing, new training or further education will you need? Interestingly enough, women with college degrees are often as stymied about what to do or how to go about it as those who've never finished high school—sometimes even more stymied, because the college woman frequently has built-in feelings of status and considers many nonprofessional positions beneath her. This automatically rules out all sorts of fascinating brain-using and creative jobs.

So if you're college-bred, relax your approach, please. Yield to a fresh interest or trend, maybe one that's come along since school days as an outgrowth of your adult life. On the other hand, if you never reached the halls of higher learning or left midway, you may be suffering from an overblown sense of inadequacy. Has it occurred to you that college credits are only numbers on a filed record unless you breathe life into them by using what you've learned? Formal intellectual exposure is enriching, granted. But it doesn't necessarily channel you into the best vocation for your abilities or carry you through with all flags waving.

What this all boils down to is simply that there's absolutely no need to settle for nothing-to-do or any-old-job because of your education or lack of it. There's too much mind-stretching, talent-developing help around to make this anything like a valid excuse.

HOW YOU CAN LEARN

Read Constantly and omnivorously. Use your public library. It's stacked to the rafters with volumes on every imaginable subject, yours included. What's more, most libraries also offer slides, films, records, tapes, and all kinds of periodicals—government publications, as well.

On-the-Job Training Nothing can beat this as a way to learn, as a guide to what extra schooling or experience you need, if any, and as a means to determine where you go from there. It can take any of these forms: (a) Working at something other than your particular interest in a place where you can observe and learn about the job you really want to do. (b) Training in an organization program, paid while you learn. (c) Doing part-time clerical or other work in the field of your choice in conjunction with outside training, sometimes sponsored by your employer. (d) Serving apprenticeship with an expert at little or no pay until you're knowledgeable. (e) Learning while working because, in some instances, this is the only way you can learn.

Home-Study Courses These can solve the learning problem if you live too far from other opportunities or simply can't get out of the house to take desired training. They're the answer for close to five million people these days, many of them women. For a list of all accredited home-study schools, write to National Home Study Council, 1601 18th Street, N.W., Washington, D.C., 20009. To learn which accredited colleges and universities offer home-study courses, write to the National University Extension Association, Suite 360, 1 DuPont Circle N.W., Washington, D.C., 20036 (booklet, fifty cents).

Public School Adult Education Many cities and towns now offer job workshops in their adult-education programs, often with a wide choice of both academic and vocational courses and, with some, a fascinating roster of popular special-interest subjects, as well. These may be free or require a nominal registration fee. Call your board of education or write to your state education department for information about schools in neighboring areas.

Community Service Classes These are usually sponsored by local organizations such as Y's, community-action groups, and the like, teaching any of a variety of subjects at nominal fees.

Educational Television It offers vocational training, college credits, and even a college degree, depending on which channel is beaming classes into your area. Your local newspaper listings, TV GUIDE, or a telephone call to stations reaching your home screen should enlighten you. Contacting your board of education and state education department should also prove informative.

Privately Owned Vocational Schools These can be found in the classified pages of your telephone directory, through recommendations, and by writing to the national association of your chosen field. Sign nothing and hand over no money until you've checked out a school's qualifications thoroughly.

College There are any number of ways to get your degree and/or advanced training. Financial aid is usually available.

Two-Year Colleges Most are public and known also as junior or community colleges, city colleges, technical institutes, seminaries, and just plain colleges. Those which are public, charge relatively low tuition; the private schools are often church-related or supported. Yearly fees range from quite low to as high as many private, four-year liberal-arts colleges. Some now offer special programs for adult women. Admission requirements are more flexible than those for standard-term colleges, and some will admit adults of proven worth who are not high-school grads but can show ability to handle college-level material. For details and a list of member colleges, write to the American Association of Community & Junior Colleges, 1 DuPont Circle, N.W., Washington, D.C., 20036.

Extension Courses Given by a college or university with classes conducted in surrounding communities, as well as on campus, these take the form of lectures and workshops, study and discussion groups or weekend seminars, and are often tied in with the school's continuing-education program.

Continuing Education Was originally conceived to let Mama get back to school by scheduling credit-earning classes during her children's school hours. There's been all sorts of experimentation with time slots to try to work out the best plan. About 450 programs were in operation early in 1971; the number probably will have increased by the time you read this. As indicated earlier, most offer counseling assistance as well as various educational approaches, such as workshops, seminars, field work, etc. For full particulars and a state-by-state listing of programs, send seventy cents to Superintendent of Documents, U.S. Government Printing Office, Washington, D.C., 20402. They'll send you a copy of the booklet, CONTINUING EDUCATION PROGRAMS AND SERVICES FOR WOMEN, published by the Women's Bureau of the U.S. Department of Labor.

University Without Walls A learning plan that's unconfined by time or place, this allows students to integrate course work, travel, independent study, and field experiences into an undergraduate program, and permits them to tailor a program to their personal needs and interests. **Weekend College,** another learning schedule, is explained by its name. Both adapt admirably to a woman's need for schedule flexibility. To learn which colleges and universities offer these, write to Union for Experiment in Colleges and Universities, Antioch College, Yellow Springs, Ohio, 45387.

Commuter-Car Classes A unique teaching program under the aegis of Adelphi University in Garden City, New York, conducts classes each morning and evening in a commuter-train car equipped with blackboards, an audiovisual system, microphones, and—yes—desks and a teaching platform. Its first graduation ceremony was held, appropriately, in Pennsylvania Station. Plans are afoot (or arail?) to expand the program to include various degree studies. The idea could catch on country-wide, as inquiries have been coming in from around the United States from those interested in learning in initiating similar train classes.

Leisure Learning Centers Another new education idea that probably will spread. The first of its automated schools opened in Greenwich, Connecticut, in 1972 and allows students of all ages to drop in at any time for a lesson of programmed, concentrated instruction done with machines. Twenty-three courses are offered, ranging from speed reading to commercial flying. According to the center's president, one hour of this type of study equals four or five in a traditional classroom.

College Proficiency Examinations Given for credits in a wide range of subjects toward earning a college degree, these are geared to help (among others) the adult who has mastered a subject through self-study, on-the-job experience, industrial training, noncollegiate business or trade-school training, off-campus television courses, programmed or recorded lessons, correspondence courses, public-school adult education, and other noncredit study. For details, write College Entrance Examination Board, Box 592, Princeton, New Jersey, 08540. New York State has a similar program, also open to out-of-staters if they come to New York to take the exams. Write Director, College Proficiency Examination Program (CPE), State Education Department, Albany, New York, 12224; ask for their booklet, THE NEW YORK COLLEGE EXAMINATION PROFICIENCY PROGRAM.

High-School Equivalency Tests These are given in just about every state of the Union. Telephone your board of education for information. Your high-school records will tell which subjects you need for credit. TV High School ("Your Future Is Now") is a home-study course given on television, based on a curriculum developed by the Manpower Education Institute. It consists of sixty half-hour TV lessons covering subjects needed to take a high-school equivalency exam (GED tests), and uses three specially prepared textbooks (there's a nominal fee covering all three). Communities throughout the United States have been showing programs based on this curriculum. For information, write to Manpower Education Institute, 127 East 35th Street, New York, New York, 10016, or to Great Plains National Instructional TV Library, University of Nebraska, Box 80699, Lincoln, Nebraska, 68501.

GET CREDIT FOR WHAT YOU KNOW is a helpful question-and-answer brochure on education published by the Women's Bureau, Employment Standards Administration, U.S. Department of Labor, Washington, D.C., 20210. Send for it.

WHAT'S IT LIKE OUT THERE AT THE JOB SCENE?

This could be called a loaded question. At first glance all seems much as always. Scratch the surface a bit and, lo and behold! you discover a new awareness. Everyone has it. It relates to women as a group and their rights as individuals, and stretches from the boudoir to the ballot box. Here are some of the legislative breakthroughs that have changed or will be changing the status of women:

•The Equal Rights Amendment passed by Congress in March, 1972, prohibits discrimination based on sex by any law or action of federal, state, or local government. (It will become part of the Constitution when two-thirds of the states ratify it.)

•Title VII of the Civil Rights Act of 1964 added sex discrimination to the ban against race bias.

•Powers of the Equal Employment Opportunity Commission were strengthened for enforcing nondiscrimination in employment.

•Revised Order 4 (Department of Labor) requires companies having at least fifty employees and doing at least $50,000 in federal-government business a year to submit affirmative action plans to move women into job categories where they are underrepresented. Goals and timetables must relate to the number of women potentially available for these jobs.

•Extension of the Equal Pay Act of the Department of Labor provides additional economic benefits to an estimated 15 million executive, administrative, and professional employees. This benefits women because the new law requires the same pay for men and women doing the same or comparable work.

•New rules of the Equal Employment Opportunity Commission giving more rights to pregnant women employees say that to deny a woman a job because she is pregnant is a violation of the Civil Rights Act of 1964 and that pregnancy must be regarded as an illness—therefore, women who leave jobs to give birth must be eligible for sick pay.

The four-day week is gradually sneaking up on the work scene, and you just might point this out (when the time is right) in order to effect a better home-job workday balance.

Here and there, private employment agencies are tapping the too-long-fallow married-women's labor market. One such, New-time, Inc., in New York City, thinks in terms of five-day, twenty-five-hour-week jobs and although, due to the economy slump, it's had more applicants than spots to place them, its premise is certainly on target.

The tandem job is not a new idea, but it is one that deserves to spread, for two women working full steam at four hours (a half-day) each, can certainly accomplish more than one woman working eight. And how beautifully it adjusts for those with home responsibilities! Catalyst, for one, has placed women in tandem jobs successfully.

Many employers are adjusting their thinking to fit changing needs and attitudes. Two examples: Arthur Hoffer, president of Transvac Electronics, Inc., in Plainview, New York, lets many of his women employees work a 9 A.M. to 3 P.M. day so that they can see their small fry off to school and be home before they return. The company had to come up with an unusual technique for training people and then keeping them after training, so decided to be flexible about hours. It's been good for the employees, good for business.

Theodore Karger, president of The Nowland Organization, Inc., a consumer research company in Greenwich, Connecticut, feels the same way about the all-around success of his "customized schedules" for the organization's women, who virtually run the place for him on the administrative level. Mr. Karger feels that women should not think only in terms of standard jobs—they should look around at all the quiet, small organizations where they live, realize that their (the companies') problems parallel those of giant corporations, and get in there to bring fresh thinking and problem solving in different spheres. After all, he maintains, isn't the "gal Friday" often the acting boss?

These are just two aware employers. Search a bit and you could come up with one or two of your own right on home ground.

The all-male job bastions are falling and women are literally into everything, taking their femininity right along into the fray. To rattle off a few—they're now United States Army generals and Navy admirals (talk about brass!) and with just a few exceptions, in all noncombat armed-forces jobs, including missile repairer, gunsmith and aircraft maintenance specialist (WAFs). They are dynamite blasters, air-transport shuttle pilots, rabbis and ministers, bellhops, auctioneers, morticians, shipfitters, exterminators, automotive mechanics, welders, stevedores, cement finishers, FBI agents, dog catchers, and telephone-line repairwomen. The list is too long to complete here. And on the civilian professional and executive level, they're designing high speed auto-test tracks, developing a birth-control pill (for men!), directing ballistic-missiles research, heading up big-company labor and consumer relation groups, running huge retail and manufacturing businesses, holding important political offices, v.p.'ing major banks and brokerage concerns, and countless other high-echelon jobs in science and health, art, sales, the professions, and all the other spheres related to life in the 1970's. Not the least of these are the women involved in all the activities, social and political, that will ultimately make this a better world for women and all others in it.

As you climb to these heights, the going frequently gets tougher and resistance is stronger, for to make it, you must be at least as good as—usually better than—your male counterpart. But growing awareness and new legislation are on your side, no matter which field of work or level of achievement you aspire to. So get on with it!

VOLUNTEER WORK

Believe it or not, the world of unpaid work can be anything you want it to be. An eye-opener and mind expander. On-the-job training. A proving ground for your ability to get along with different kinds of people. A chance to try your administrative skills. A way to test your toe in the vocational mainstream or dive into the deep water of community involvement—which one is up to you. It can give you all the mental challenge and sociability you desire, and you can stop right there—or it can be a stepping-stone to a highly responsible, well-paid job.

Most of us have done some volunteer work, be it den mothering, making election phone calls, or ringing doorbells for health causes. Many have also been presidents of clubs, trustees of museums, nurse aides, teachers, ghetto workers. Or have initiated important community projects, e.g., senior-citizen groups, conservation programs, child-care facilities. Or worked for any one of dozens of different causes, including political. The possibilities for volunteer work are endlessly varied and right under our noses. Still, if you feel you need pointing in a special direction, search out the nearest volunteer service bureau (the title varies a bit from locale to locale) or write to the headquarters for all such bureaus: United Way of America, Inc. (United States, Canada, Mexico), 801 N. Fairfax Street, Alexandria, Virginia, 22314.

Other Sources for Volunteer Work Civic, church and temple groups, health organizations, hospitals, homes and similar institutions, and the youth groups listed in the index, among others. Large religious organizations can help to place you in volunteer work via local chapters or write to them: Federation of Protestant Welfare Agencies (Volunteer Bureau), 281 Park Avenue South, New York, New York 10010; National Council of Jewish Women, 1 West 47th Street, New York, New York, 10036; Catholic Charities (check your own diocese), and all other denominational groups.

Job Interest Volunteerism Some of your volunteer energies can be channeled to help you prepare for paid work. For instance, if you're a gardening buff and would like to earn with this interest, offer your help to a botanical garden, a nursery, a landscape architect, a florist—to anyone who's immersed in some facet of that world—in order to learn. There are women scattered throughout these pages who've done just this—they've learned their jobs as volunteers. All you need is one knowledgeable person to become his/her apprentice in the field of your choice.

SOME THOUGHTS FOR THE OVER-FIFTY-FIVE CROWD

Vitamin E, Yoga, and estrogen-replacement therapy have their place, but for doing away with those depressing, getting-older blahs, there's nothing—but nothing—like being all wrapped up in a fascinating interest or activity. It wards off the chills of loneliness and isolation, bolsters a sagging sense of identity, and bridges the biggest generation gap of all—the one between you and the rest of society. It's true that some women wilt on the vine very early and others lead dynamic, creative lives until they're way up there in the seventies, eighties, and even, sometimes, beyond. Maybe the difference in life span has something to do with being involved, for medical research has shown that continuing to work is vital in prolonging life. Not only that, but gerontologists strongly suspect that using your creativity to the hilt can help to keep you around until you're pushing one hundred. No matter where you sit in the age range, you can **stop** sitting, because it's never too late to discover a new exciting world of work or develop an intriguing interest.

Who wants to hire an older woman? These days, plenty of people and for good reasons. Study after study of the job performances of older workers has shown that absenteeism actually is lower among them than among younger workers, that the older worker is at least as productive as her younger counterpart—often more so. Also, the well-seasoned woman who's chalked up some years of living gives the employer a sense of security. He knows that she's generally more dependable, loyal, adaptable, has better judgment and often a greater sense of responsibility than the young woman fresh out of school who's distracted by personal concerns.

Besides following the general suggestions in this book, there are some special helps around for what are usually termed the aging. Don't let that word throw you—just use all the help you can get.

Membership in the American Association of Retired Persons This offers training and brushup in skills, trainees serving others while they learn. For information, write to them at 1225 Connecticut Avenue, N.W., Washington, D.C., 20036.

Personnel agencies catering to the mature citizen These can be found in many parts of the country. For example, Mature Temps, Inc. (offices in thirteen cities) specializes in temporary jobs on a contract basis and pays your salary, Social Security, and insurance. Others are localized, such as Retirement Jobs, Inc., of San Jose, California (five offices serving three counties). Over-60 Employment Counseling Service of Maryland, Inc., and Senior Personnel Placement Bureau of Norwalk, Connecticut. There's most likely one in your county; find it in the classified pages of your telephone book or inquire at your state employment office. Manpower, Inc., the giant national temporary-help service, also helps to get around some of the special obstacles of the Social Security crowd, so check with their nearest office. (Example: they handle the hiring, payroll, and paperwork of former employees of John Deere Tractor Company, now working as tour guides in that company's Waterloo, Iowa, plant so that retirement benefits are not affected.)

Forty-Plus Clubs Set up in at least six major American cities, these help unemployed executives aged forty and over to find jobs. They offer counseling, resumé help, an interview course, and a job-search plan. There's a membership fee, dues, and a minimum-previous-salary required for joining.

The United States government sponsors a number of programs These are aimed at low-income Americans aged fifty-five and over. Your state office on aging administers these. • **Green Light**—For rural residents who work as aides in health, education, and community-service agencies. In eleven states. Minimum federal pay rate. • **Senior Community Service**

Project—Work as aides in health or social-service programs. Training is given to do jobs such as home repairs, library help, community-center work, distribution of surplus food, organizing senior-citizen activities. • **Senior Aides**—These people work in public-service jobs in thirty-three communities. They're aides in schools, hospitals, day-care centers, and other community agencies. They also help other elderly folks, deliver meals to shut-ins, teach arts and crafts, provide information on Medicare and other senior needs. Twenty hours a week. Average, $2 per hour. • **Foster Grandparents**—For those aged sixty and over. Offers work with children in residential settings (institutions such as juvenile detention homes, industrial schools, homes for neglected and abandoned children, disturbed children, and the physically handicapped) four hours a day, five days a week for the federal minimum hourly wage. During this time, they extend love and companionship, and are repaid manifoldly with beautiful and enduring relationships and a sense of achievement and worth. (This is true for the other programs, too, in many instances.) • **RSVP** (Retired Senior Volunteer Program)—No pay, but transportation, and sometimes meals, are covered. Volunteers serve on a regular basis, where possible, for a minimum of once a week—in hospitals, museums, prisons, day-care centers, and a wide variety of youth organizations. The exact place is determined by local needs. Chores are also wonderfully varied, ranging from clerking or working with children to using special talents, skills, or knowledge. The volunteer has a choice of job spots. To learn more about this program, contact the RSVP Resource Specialist in your state's office on aging. • **The National Weather Service**—Uses paid and volunteer weather observers around the country. Write to them for information c/o National Oceanic and Atmosphere Administration, U.S. Department of Commerce, Silver Spring, Maryland, 20910.

AND FOR THOSE WITH HANDICAPS

There are a number of vital channels for receiving job help. Your own state's Office of Vocational Rehabilitation, in conjunction with the federal government, offers rehabilitation counseling, job training, and placement. The Social and Rehabilitation Service, Rehabilitation Services Administration, U.S. Department of Health, Education and Welfare, 330 Independence Avenue, S.W., Washington, D.C., 20201, will, on request, send you two important booklets: REHABILITATION

SERVICES ADMINISTRATION PROGRAMS, which outlines in detail all federal programs for the handicapped, and ACHIEVEMENT, inspiring real-life stories from the files of 2.5 million disabled Americans who, thanks to vocational rehabilitation, are leading productive lives. The Easter Seal Society, 2023 West Ogden Avenue, Chicago, Illinois, 60612, offers advice, information, and a referral service. Jewish Occupational Council is particularly involved in working with all types of handicaps through its member agencies in twenty-four American cities (see Counseling for location help). The Human Resources Center in Albertson, New York, is one of nine centers for the handicapped around the country participating in Projects of Industry, a pilot program sponsored by the U.S. Department of Health, Education and Welfare, to show private industry that individuals with all types of handicaps can work outside a sheltered situation. To this end, they give on-the-job training in either entry-level clerical work or industrial jobs, or basic-skills training to prepare them for job placement.

Human Resources Center also runs a program called Project Senior Abilities, geared to help those fifty-five and over (but not necessarily handicapped) to find work, and a tuition-free school for severely disabled children that's fully accredited by the N.Y. Board of Regents—the only school of its kind in New York State.

JOB (Just One Break) is a New York City-based organization that works at placing the physically handicapped in appropriate jobs. Address: 373 Park Avenue South, New York, New York, 10016.

HELPFUL READING

OCCUPATIONAL OUTLOOK HANDBOOK (latest edition). U.S. Department of Labor. Over eight hundred work categories described in detail. Find it in your public library or high-school counselor's office. $6.25 from U.S. Department of Labor Statistics, U.S. Department of Labor, 1515 Broadway, New York, New York, 10036.

TOWARD MATCHING PERSONAL AND JOB CHARACTERISTICS (Volume 15, Number 4). A free reprint from the Occupational Outlook Handbook, it charts 268 job categories, relating them to twenty-five occupational characteristics and requirements. From same address as above. Also ask them for a free CATALOG OF PUBLICATIONS.

SELECTED UNITED STATES GOVERNMENT

PUBLICATIONS. Free biweekly listing of for-sale publications. Request it from: Superintendent of Documents, U.S. Government Printing Office, Washington, D.C., 20402.

Small Business Administration Publications. Send for HANDCRAFTS AND HOME BUSINESSES, Pamphlet No. 1. Bibliography of government and nongovernment publications that can help you to plan, organize, direct, coordinate, and control a handcraft or home business. Gives sources of help available state-by-state, including assistance for the handicapped in making and selling their own products, and reading suggestions for each work category. BASIC LIBRARY REFERENCE SOURCES, a guide to reference books that can help the small business woman. DISCOVER AND USE YOUR PUBLIC LIBRARY, a primer for making the most of this information archive. FOR-SALE BOOKLETS (most are considerabley under one dollar). FREE MANAGEMENT ASSISTANCE PUBLICATIONS (includes list of all SBA field offices, as well).

JOB-FINDING TECHNIQUES FOR MATURE WOMEN, Pamphlet No. 11. (Women's Bureau, U.S. Department of Labor.) How to do a self-inventory job hunt and prepare resumés and letters of application, guides to an effective interview, training opportunities, reading suggestions, and a listing of agencies and organizations that can be helpful. Send thirty cents to Superintendent of Documents, U.S. Government Printing Office, Washington, D.C., 20402.

PUBLICATIONS OF THE WOMEN'S BUREAU, Leaflet No. 10. Listing of printed material available, broken down by subjects, with costs, if any (small).

URBAN BUSINESS PROFILES. A relatively new series from the U.S. Department of Commerce has been created to assist small-business ventures. Each profile is twenty to thirty pages long, costs from twenty to thirty cents. For a title listing, write to Superintendent of Documents (address above).

MADEMOISELLE magazine (College and Career Series). Though aimed at young women, this series is equally informative and inspirational for those thirty on up. Detailed, fun to read, helpful, the series covers dozens of job categories as well as such titles as GOVERNMENT JOBS (Civil Service), PUBLIC SERVICE JOBS, MARKETING YOUR TALENTS, and YOUR OWN BUSINESS. For current title listing, address: MADEMOISELLE, Box 3389, Grand Central Station, New York, New York, 10019.

Alumni Advisory Center, geared to college-level women, publishes job fact sheets, booklets, and cassette tapes on special-interest fields and how-to techniques, plus guides and bibliographies. Send for free listing: 541 Madison Avenue, New York, New York, 10022.

Catalyst Publications. Series aimed at college-educated women: SELF-GUIDANCE SERIES, EDUCATIONAL OPPORTUNITIES SERIES, CAREER OPPORTUNITIES SERIES, YOUR JOB CAMPAIGN, and PLANNING FOR WORK. They also publish HOW TO GO TO WORK WHEN YOUR HUSBAND IS AGAINST IT, YOUR CHILDREN AREN'T OLD ENOUGH & THERE'S NOTHING TO DO, ANYHOW, a put-down, tongue-in-cheek title for a book outlining types of employers, job prospects, and educational requirements for entry-level jobs in over fifty fields. Inquire Catalyst, 6 East 82nd Street, New York, New York, 10028.

A BUSINESS OF YOUR OWN IN MASSACHUSETTS. Guide booklet that's also useful for anyone not a Massachusetts resident. Touches on all elements involved in starting a new business. Free from Women's Bureau, Department of Commerce and Development, 100 Cambridge Street, Boston, Massachusetts, 02202.*

THE LITERARY MARKETPLACE, Directory of American book publishing. R.R. Bowker, publishers. Includes material helpful to many of the jobs in this book—art, some communications skills, photography, translating, direct mail and promotion, selling, etc. In your public library, of course.

BACK TO WORK AFTER RETIREMENT (No. 2900-0130). This spells out what a retiree can do with her time, explains Social Security and age discrimination rulings, lists job suggestions, and gives details on government-sponsored or approved work programs. In your library, or sixty cents from Superintendent of Documents, U.S. Government Printing Office, Washington, D.C., 20402.

SUGGESTIONS NOT USUALLY FOUND IN JOB-HUNTING GUIDES

•The functional type of resumé (one that paragraphs by type of work experience rather than by companies or dates of service) is preferable for the woman over thirty or thirty-five. It can be written with more "sell" for your abilities and skirt that old bugaboo, time.

•Decide where you'd like to work. Make a list of

*Please include a long, stamped, self-addressed envelope.

the specific companies or organizations and go directly to the person at each who is in charge of your special interest. Telephone and make an appointment first. Consider any place a possibility until you get a firm and final "no" from the right person.

•Approach job-hunting with a sense of adventure and play long shots with a gambler's spirit. This applies equally to any venture of your own. The job that seems unlikely for you before you really look into it thoroughly and/or have an interview may be the one that changes your whole life in a positive way.

•Remember, the classified section of your telephone book can help you to find just about anything, and is a goldmine of companies and organizations for any need. Your local telephone office can also supply directories for areas surrounding your own.

•You can go the personnel-agency route and sign up with as many as you wish, but don't depend on them to pursue you until you're placed in a job. Once you sign up with them, they might never call you at all (it happens!). Best that you check in with them by phone periodically in between job-hunting on your own.

•Don't let officious or overly-protective office help throw you off the scent in reaching your party. You're more likely to run into this if you come on too meekly; the trick is to sound just authoritative and important enough without seeming overbearing or hostile—even if you're feeling anything-but inside. It's a fact of life (and you must know it, too) that nothing inspires confidence as much as someone's self-confidence.

•Determining how much money you should ask for can be ticklish. Whether you're selling your handiwork or any other abilities (and your time), don't underestimate your worth. Far too many women do. In most instances, it's easier to come down a bit in asking price than to go up.

•Before you start looking for a job or a venture of any kind that will eat into your daily schedule, streamline your life on paper. Figure out all your possible expenses (estimate your transportation, clothing needs, lunches, etc.), whether it pays (monetarily) for you to work and whether to work, per se, is more important than the money, housekeeping shortcuts, child care, if any (solution and cost), among others. To balance both your worlds: • Start your day earlier • Get things set up for the morning rush the evening before • Ideally, all members of the family should help; it's a lesson in community living • Look for the wash-and-wear label in whatever soft goods you buy (chances are, you already do), you won't have time for much ironing • Market once a week and keep your supply closet stocked for nibbles and emergencies (e.g., those too-tired-to-cook nights) • Plan ahead—meals, must-do's. Make lists. Cook for more than one day; freeze the rest • Save social telephone chats for after-work hours (particularly if you work at home); they devour time • Certain time-work-saving appliances pay for themselves. In the long run, so might a once-a-week house-worker.

2

Bon Appetit!
Good Business!

When you tie on your apron and make things come
alive in the kitchen, is every meal a marvelous challenge, a call
to creativity? If food is your forte, you've practically got it
made for a successful business, for just one smashing specialty
can send you on your way to fame and fortune. The beauty of
it all is the tiny cash outlay needed to start. You already have
your kitchen and basic equipment. All you require is the food.

The Four Main Types of Caterers • The Food
Specialist who prepared her specialty, provides no other service,
and quotes her prices on quantity. • The Prepared Meal Expert
sells all or part of an entire meal to order—casseroles, boxed
lunches, salads or buffet foods and dinner-party specialties—
does preparation and delivery only, and usually quotes her rate
per portion. • The Special-Occasion Caterer makes meals for
large affairs, working at her home or where the job is. She
supervises service and may or may not supply equipment,
figures prices per person. • The Director is the major domo,
queen of fine catering. Her specialties are outstanding, she
knows all the tricks of her dynamic trade and can, if necessary,
cope admirably with every detail—invitations, decoration,
menus, service, and entertainment. She can dream up party
themes and quite possibly provide party space. She quotes a
flat, coverall fee.

What You Need Personally • Love of cooking.
When you're not up to your elbows in actual ingredients, you're
reading, planning, or buying food • Ability to manage and
organize. Your kitchen, menus, and time must be scheduled in
advance for maximum economy and efficiency • A high panic

threshold and a philosophic approach. If the soufflé falls in, you can't cave in, too • Know-how in working with people. Party giving and special occasions breed their own brand of personal tension for host and hostess. Your sense of humor, patience, and tact help keep it all on an even keel • A flair with food. Whatever you make, make it delicious—pleasing to the eye as well as the palate. Once established, don't rest on your laurels. Experiment and add to your menus; new dishes help win new customers, hold old ones.

What You Need Materially • A kitchen. Naturally! Yours need not be model pretty or complete to the last corkscrew, as long as it has the utensils you'll need. (I know one woman who began a highly successful catering business in a fourth-floor walkup apartment with one of those closet-sized kitchens) • Good help. You may start out as a one-woman business but become so busy, you need extra pairs of hands. When hiring, consider abilities first, but also gauge disposition, appearance, and experience. Line up your workers ahead of time.

What You Need Educationally • Excellent cooking ability, of course. Many women seem to be born cooks; others, if the interest in food is there, are made, either by self-training or outside instruction from skilled practitioners. For you who dream of chef-ing it for fine hotels, motels, and restaurants, there is the Culinary Institute of America in Hyde Park, New York, the only private, nonprofit post high-school educational institution in the United States where a student, male or female, can get this advanced, specialized training) • Learn your community's catering potentials. Is there much at-home social-izing? Are there enough clubs and other groups that could use your help? Check with your chamber of commerce. College towns, for instance, have faculty affairs and other on-campus catering needs. Resorts will be receptive to a box-lunch and picnic business • Bone up on accepted social procedures and correct etiquette for a variety of occasions, from small formal dinners to weddings.

Hours You Work Weekends are usually your busiest times, but if you cater to businesses, organizations, and women's groups, it can fill up the week. Take only as many assignments as you can do well.

How Much You Earn This will be affected by the type of service you provide and the demand for it. A rule of thumb has been to multiply all costs by three to determine your charges, but a marketing expert has suggested you make this four times your costs, if you take into consideration additional expenses of promotion, packaging and containers, and expansion planning. Since your profits will be proportionate to your investment, if your initial costs are small, your profit will be likewise, and it's best to work this way, limiting yourself, until you master all the pitfalls. You may make less initially, but you pay less for your errors, too. For guidance on pricing, send for PROFIT IN THE PANTRY, an excellent free booklet on catering that includes a cost-analysis chart and record-keeping suggestions. Write to Women's Bureau, Massachusetts Department of Commerce and Development, 100 Cambridge Street, Boston, Massachusetts, 02202.

How You Get Started Perfect at least one specialty. You really needn't be another Escoffier to do this—just an average cook who loves to fuss with food can work up a genuinely superior and delicious dish. Get all the facts down pat—tools, exact ingredients, quantities, time it takes to make. From this, you'll be able to figure larger quantities and costs for customer estimates. (Don't forget to include the value of your time—very important.)

Food Specialty Suggestions • Canapes and hors d'oeuvres • Sandwiches (from dainty tea-size to oversized heroes) • Special-occasion cakes, including wedding • Casserole dishes and meat pies • Home-baked breads (very big these days—include health loaves, low-sodium bread); rolls, cookies • Slow-cooked stews • Seafood specials: deviled crabs, bouillabaisse, oyster stew • Soufflés, crêpes, omelets • Continental pastries • Fruit cakes and others, such as lepküchen, kipfel (rugelach), and that ilk • Candies: hand-dipped chocolates, old-fashioned favorites • Holiday pies: pumpkin, apple, mince • Ethnic specialties, international cuisine, regional dishes (Soul, Jewish, Creole, French, Greek, American Indian, New England, etc.) • Healthfood cooking (natural or organic foods) • Wine dishes, curry dishes, herb specialties • Brandied fruits and pickled vegetables • Hearty soups and finger food • French pastry • Smorgasbord delights • Picnic food and box lunches and suppers

Food Service Suggestions • Hot-meal delivery • Telephone-order box lunches for offices • Camper specials (overnight-hike foods) • Basket meals or snacks in resort areas for summer residents opening their homes over weekends • Food baskets mailed to prep school and college students •

Sunday brunch dishes to relieve that breakfast monotony • Buffet platters

Whatever you make, make it special As the song went, "T'aint what you do, it's the way that you do it!" e.g., a picnic can be anything from conventional but good sandwiches, with their own mouth-watering touches and some surprise goodies, to a hearty bouillabaisse, French bread, vegetable salad, fruit, cheese, a rich cake, and coffee, to such haute cuisine as pâté, lobster quiche, cold veal, salad, champagned fruits, and a rich torte. Packaging often sets the tone, whets the appetite. Make yours attractive.

Establish your sources Contact top-quality butchers, grocers, and gourmet-type establishments (for more exotic seasonings, ingredients). Set up some kind of a discount or special-service arrangement. If fine wholesalers or jobbers will work with you at their usual rates, so much the better. Do the same for paper goods, linens, table supplies, decorations, flowers, chairs and tables, and so forth. (Equipment supply houses often carry everything but the food.) Whether it's part of your service or not, you should be able to recommend sources for clients.

Figure costs carefully Break them down into fixed costs (rent, light, heat, gas, depreciation of equipment, insurance, and miscellany such as legal and accounting help) and variable costs (food, supplies, laundry, rental of equipment if any, and your help's time [and yours]).

Keep an accurate, running record of expenses Wise investment: an accountant can save you plenty of mistakes • Decide whether you will deliver or not. To avoid this, many food-only caterers have clients pick up, when feasible. Long hauls, a driver, and rented vehicles (or truck maintenance) may cancel out your profits or bring them mighty low. Think this one out carefully • Look into legal-eagle details—zoning rules and local tax information (town clerk); a food permit (health department); labor regulations (your state department of labor); state tax information (state: government tax bureau at your state capital; federal: [income, business and Social Security] your regional Office of Internal Revenue).

THESE CATERING SPECIALTIES MAY GIVE YOU SOME IDEAS FOR YOURSELF

Mobile Foods and the great outdoors go together naturally, particularly during warmer months, as various entrepreneurs have proven. The Better Moussetrap, a gussied-up tea cart, has taken the pushcart route to sell—you guessed it— chocolate mousse to the hungry on New York's lower Fifth Avenue. The Rolling Crêpe, a microbus, has taken the high road, the Columbia University area, to offer crêpes filled with chicken and sherry or ratatouille and spiced apple—these cooked right on the bus. Chinese dumplings and green moussaka are two other delicacies sold the vendor way in the big city. And in Los Angeles, the Moveable Feast delivers its salads, homemade sandwiches, fruits, cheeses, yogurt, cakes, and other mouth-watering fare via attractive, long-skirted, basket-toting young women. All the foods are ordered by local executives, shopkeepers, secretaries short on time and money, women in beauty salons, as well as company parties and TV and film-show workers. The Moveable Feast evolved from its founder's boredom and dissatisfaction with coffee-shop menus.

Take-out Foods Are Big Business Make the food haute cuisine instead of the usual fried chicken or Chinese dinner, and you have the answer to many a host's and hostess's prayer. In Darien, Connecticut, four women who call them-selves Phantom Cooks, Inc., make everything from hors d'oeuvres to full-course dinners, each working in her own home. It all came about when one of the women was job hunting and stumbled onto the knowledge that there's more call for people to turn out edibles than for typists. She telephoned a friend, who in turn telephoned her friend, and before long four comparative strangers with a common love for cooking launched the venture with a couple of orders. Now they're booked way ahead, with as many as seven jobs per weekend. Each assignment is given individualized attention, and the women meet once a week to review work to be done, divide cooking tasks, and appoint one of the four as coordinator for each job. Bookkeeping is rotated.

And Now a Word About Health Foods A whole new sphere of interest in eating, they offer offbeat possibilities for part-time work—from growing and selling sprouts, baking and selling stone-ground whole-wheat bread, to running a full-fledged health-food catering business like Mother Nature on the Run in Washington, D.C. This group cooks for large organizational groups and small parties, many of whom are intrigued by the idea of a health feast. Invariably, clients want to talk about the foods as well as eat them, and if the work load permits time enough, company members are willing. Mother

Nature on the Run is an offshoot of a job co-op and a food co-op, both founded by an enterprising woman named Sharon Grant. (For more on organic foods, see chapter Go Back to Nature.)

Cheesecake Lovers Love Miss Grimble The lady behind that name is, in actuality, Sylvia Hirsch, who in a few short years has become New York City's cheesecake queen— even when she's wearing slacks. Although voted least likely to become any sort of a cook by schoolmates, when her husband opened a restaurant, Mrs. H. experimented until she was able to produce a buttery-smooth, creamy-rich, sour-cream-topped cheesecake with no flour in the moist graham-cracker crust. It was part of the restaurant's menu. When the place folded, she kept selling her output to former customers and friends. Word spread. Business burgeoned. Sylvia opened a small bakery and expanded her line to include pecan pies, and the business quickly outgrew those quarters. Now with the help of Linda Cerf, she's into torten-making, as well. Miss Grimble uses thirty tons of cream cheese a year, grosses in the six-figure category, and counts many a famous name among its clientele.

How to Market Your Food Specialty There are several ways, as follows • Direct from you to consumer—local— to friends, neighbors, acquaintances, women's clubs, social groups, PTA's, private luncheons, business affairs, others • Direct from you to outlet—still local, but wider market—to your neighborhood grocers, delicatessens, small restaurants and diners, gift shops, women's exchanges, quality bakeries and food shops • Through your own salesman to independent stores and chain markets • Through a food broker to outlets—the widest possible distribution on an area basis.

IF YOU'RE A GOOD COOK, TEACH OTHERS!

Cooking lessons are very "in" these days. You'll find them given at department stores, shopping centers, colleges and universities, adult-education centers, and private homes, among other spots. What's more, cooking is me-too for men and children. Teenagers, tired of hamburgers and fudge, learn how to make beef olives, carrots Vichy, chocolate mousse, and other delectables in private lessons from pros. And being king of the barbecue pit is much too circumscribed for any man with culinary imagination, so he, too, is easily lured into lessons. Kinds of cooking taught are as varied as the food specialties listed earlier.

What You Need Materially A clean, well-equipped

kitchen. Ample seating space (or working space, if your pupils will also cook!). You may want to rent kitchen facilities in a church, women's club, or the like, if the number of pupils permits the cost.

What You Need Personally Beyond being a whiz with food, you should be able to demonstrate and communicate information clearly, precisely, interestingly.

Hours You Work You set them according to your needs and your students' schedules. Number of sessions per course varies, averaging five or six, and these run from two to three hours each.

How Much You Earn Dependent on your reputation as a cook, number of pupils, and your overhead. Some cooking instructors charge separately for the cost of ingredients, others total the estimated ingredient costs for all recipes taught in the course plus other overhead, then average it out per pupil and include it in the fee. (Remember, your students will also dine on what you cook for demonstration purposes or what they make.)

How You Get Started Sharpen your cooking skills, then decide what you'll teach, number of lessons per course, and fee. Also determine whether you'll teach by participation or demonstration. Prepare your kitchen for classes or arrange to give them under the sponsorship of a community or commercial group at their premises. (A food company's test kitchen is an ideal place to teach, pulling in their products, of course. They could foot the overhead, even pay you a fee, and use it all for publicity.) Line up your best food sources (if you're doing it on your own). Promote your course.

THERE ARE MANY OTHER WAYS TO USE YOUR FUND OF COOKING KNOWLEDGE

Write Cookbooks, for instance—under your own name or for a cooking authority who can't write. If you have a marvelous collection of old family recipes, or know someone who has, interpret them in present-day terms and put yourself in print. Or do cookbooklets for a food or food-related company as well as publicity releases, reports for chemists and test-kitchen experts and other food workers.

Work for a Food Company Doing any of the above; (or for a liquor, appliance, or equipment company) or do research, supply seasonal and special ideas for kitchen testing or photographic work. Grace M. White, FAMILY CIRCLE magazine, started her career by working for a stove manufacturer, compiling recipes for cookbooks to be distributed to buyers of new stoves. In reverse, Marjorie Deen, publicity director for General Foods Corporation for twenty-one years, started as a food editor for three Dell magazines, MODERN SCREEN, MODERN ROMANCES, and SCREEN ROMANCES.

Demonstrate Food This is a business idea you can apply from either employer or employee angle. Demonstration services hire women to talk up clients' food and food equipment at consumer outlets such as department stores' food departments, food trade shows, and supermarkets. According to David Margolis, who operates Food Store Demonstrations, Inc., in New York City, 90 percent of his demonstrators are housewives. They're paid by the hour plus transportation; the food processor or distributor pays his company. Look under "Demonstration Services—Merchandise" in your telephone book's classified pages for similar work opportunities. If there are none, call area food company executives and ask if they know of any or solicit food clients and start a service yourself.

The Birthday Cake for Far-from-Homes Making them for students away at school may not be a brand-new idea, but for a woman living in or near universities, prep schools, and colleges, it's still a dandy one. Ednearl Thomasson of Nashville, Tennessee, has found it so. With the help of directories from Vanderbilt and other local schools, she contacted parents with a letter and order blank. Only three days after mailing, the orders started pouring in, and in the three months after that, before schools let out, she grossed $600 with about $100 overhead. Since then, her project's gone ahead full steam. She also supplies home-baked cookies, brownies, and rolls on a contract basis ($12 for eight months, once-a-month delivery), which entitles the student to a free birthday cake. (This also can be done by making a special low-price arrangement with a good local bakery based on bringing them this consistent, extra-volume business. You make the extra mark-up plus additional for the service and delivery.)

Sell Your Own Recipes and Ideas If you have a reputation as a fine cook, put all your recipes together in a looseleaf notebook. Or sell them through the mail as a Menu-of-the-Month idea, using mailing lists.

Prepare a Directory for Dining Do it for your town, county, or region, listing its restaurants, describing their cuisine, decor and price ranges. Either restaurants or advertisers (often the same) will underwrite your journal. Or sell this idea to your newspaper as a column.

Do Food Editing An idea for all former college English majors, or those with some related work background, this can be done quite nicely on a freelance basis, using all the cooking know-how stored in your noggin.

Be a Food Company Representative Nancy Ann Graham of Falls Church, Virginia, has been one. Part of her colorful career has been spent as the living trademark for a New England dairy company in Boston. She did all sorts of public relations work for them, even to christening boats, marching in parades, and writing a weekly newspaper column (paid advertising for the company). She also developed new recipes, wrote cook-booklets, and did other consumer-directed chores. Nancy Ann has touched all bases, including research for documentaries, interview shows, MC-ing her own news show, and doing on-camera food demonstrations for the long-running Home Show. "I turned up in some of my jobs by sheer accident, and by the time I discovered that I really didn't know what I was doing—I did!"

Meals on Wheels A way to share your food knowledge that can be a godsend to the ill, the elderly, the indigent—to all who are housebound and/or without helping hands. Set up such a service in your community or work for one as a volunteer. For specific guidance, write to Meals on Wheels, 210 North Grove Street, East Orange, New Jersey, or write to Baltimore Meals on Wheels for their manual ($4): 5820 York Road, Baltimore, Maryland, 21212.

Home Lunches for Children In many schools across the United States, particularly in primary grades, there are no lunchroom facilities. This, coupled with the ever-growing number of working mothers and the fact that even nonworking mothers occasionally have to be away at the noon hour, makes this a useful venture. Simple, wholesome cooking planned with nutritional values in mind, plus the space and practical accessories are all you need. It won't earn you a two-week vacation in the Caribbean, but you'll see some profit, enjoy the experience (you must like kids), and feel a good deal of satisfaction.

DIETITIAN

In the past few years, the news media have been pointing up the painful nutritional lacks and outright hunger rampant throughout much of the United States, for all it's being a land of plenty. The dietitian has a golden opoortunity to help raise the standards of health care here and elsewhere in the world. The professional in the food world, "dietitian" is the generic term for both dietitians and nutritionists. As a dietitian, you specialize in any of the following jobs:

Clinical Dietitian Serves as a specialist in nutrition on the health team in a hospital, nursing home, related health facility, or with community services. You care for patients' or clients' personal food requirements by planning nutritional· menus, consulting with medical, nursing, and other concerned professionals, noting pertinent information about your clients' food habits, instructing them and their families in proper nutrition for their condition and way of life.

Public Health Nutritionist To qualify for this title, you must first serve a dietetic internship, and have some experience plus graduate education. You evaluate nutritional needs of individuals, groups, and the community and see that these are cared for properly. You're responsible for all elements of nutritional care in health services, and you're also likely to conduct or take part in dietary and nutrition studies and other related research. Most public-health nutritionists work with individuals or special groups as part of a health team in health departments, visiting-nurse associations, prenatal and well-baby clinics, day-care centers, and with elderly folks, different national groups, mass media, consumer groups, teachers and their students, other professional groups.

Teacher You're responsible for programs in food, dietetics, nutrition, and food-service management in colleges, universities, and health-care facilities. You work up the curriculum, plan educational experiences, and teach medical, dental, nursing, and dietetic students and related health people how to apply nutrition principles to individuals, both well and ill, through various stages of life—plus numerous other related responsibilities.

Researcher You're particularly interested in the scientific and technical side of dietetics and advise and help to plan, organize, and conduct programs in nutrition or food service-systems research. Other specialty areas can lead to research for improving foods, developing new ones (good example: those taken to the moon by the astronauts).

Administrator You apply your knowledge of food, nutrition, and managerial sciences to assure quality, safe food for a hospital, university, school, restaurant, nursing home, industrial commissary food service or any other type of institution. You major domo all aspects of their food service.

Dietetics work can lead to all kinds of unexpected and exciting jobs beyond the above categories. You might start working for a large food or appliance company, discover that your knack for public speaking and presenting facts to important clients fits best in the company's public relations or advertising department. Or you might use your knowledge and knack doing valuable consumer-contact work. And managing a small restaurant successfully has been known to win ownership of same, or even a whole chain of them.

Where You Might Work • Hospitals (government and private) • Other health-related facilities • Hotel or individual restaurants or cafeterias • Industrial plants • Food companies • Other large businesses • Market research companies • Major ad agencies with food or food-related clients • Consumer service departments of public-utility companies • Public health agencies • Colleges, universities, private schools • Public school systems • Magazines and newspapers • Television and radio • Armed Forces.

In any of these other than a health facility, you could run the cafeteria or restaurant, or work in the test kitchen on food-research projects—recipe testing, food photographing for packaging, ads, TV, trying out new equipment or methods. And for you who can travel, there are the World Health Organization, Peace Corps, Hope, and FAO jobs that can take you anywhere and everywhere in the world to spread the gospel of good nutrition, good food.

What You Need Educationally A bachelor's degree with a major in foods and nutrition or institution management. To qualify for professional recognition, the American Dietetic Association recommends a dietetic internship (approved by them) or, in lieu of this, two years' approved experience. An internship in a hospital, college, business or industrial organization give you on-the-job experience, classroom work punctuated by seminars, special projects, supervisory duty in food service, conferences with doctors, and visits with patients (if you're in a hospital). You've a greater chance to be accepted for an internship if you're a good student and in good health (e.g., not overweight). Tuition and other expenses vary widely among the hundreds of colleges offering dietetics. Internships usually do not charge a tuition unless university graduate credit is given, and most of them provide a stipend for living expenses. After obtaining ADA membership, you take an exam to become an RD (registered dietitian). A given number of education hours accumulated on a five-year basis maintains this RD status.

How Much You Earn Dietitian Classifications I through V have recommended annual **minimum** salaries ranging from $8,000 (nonregistered dietitian) to $18,000 (director), varying according to work category and experience. Part-time salaries are proportionate and determined by your administrator, qualifications, and salary scale of your region.

How You Get Started • Take any job under a registered dietitian that exposes you to dietetic work: storeroom assistant, head of tray service, assistant in diet kitchen, storeroom controller, supervisor of cafeteria, office assistant to head dietitian, food production assistant, assistant in staff dining room, counter girl, tray service assistant, assistant supervisor, or work as an assistant in a local nutrition program, do teaching or extension work, get an apprenticeship (offered by some states) or take a year of graduate study. With required experience, you'll be eligible for membership in both the ADA and the American Home Economics Association • Speak to working dietitians about your interest and ambitions • For additional information, write to the American Dietetic Association, 620 North Michigan Avenue, Chicago, Illinois, 60611; American Home Economics Association, 2010 Massachusetts Avenue, N.W., Washington, D.C., 20036.

RELATIVELY NEW—DIETETIC TECHNICIAN WORK

Requires a two-year prescribed course leading to an associate degree from an accredited college. Look into this. Inquire when you send for information.

FOOD SERVICE SUPERVISOR

A relatively new occupational title in the food field, this work actually has been done for many years in hospitals, restaurants, industrial food services, college dining halls, and the like, but without the name. Large hospitals and institutions with several dietetic divisions, each headed by its own dietitian, have an equal number of food service supervisors who are second in command. Working under the dietitian, you're likely to supervise employees, oversee preparation and serving of meals, order food, supplies, and equipment, and keep track of inventory, help train new workers, check sanitation and safety of work methods used. In a very small setup with no dietitian, you're head of the department, and the dietitian's work will also fall to you.

What You Need Educationally Until recently, you could only work your way up from basic food service work, on the job. Today, there's specialized training given at work, and in some parts of the country, hospitals, public vocational schools, public health departments, and state universities are beginning to work together to establish short-term training schools or courses for future food service supervisors, giving both class-room training and supervised practice. High-school home economics courses are helpful; so are courses in algebra, chemistry, biology, typing, and business arithmetic. College training is the extra push that can often send you into top jobs faster.

Hours You Work Where you work will affect this, e.g., part-time hospital fill-ins also are needed from 3 P.M. to 7 P.M., a four-hour period. (Note: In some hospitals, if you work a four-hour, five-day shift each week, you get full fringe benefits including vacation.)

How Much You Earn Your personal qualifications and where you work will determine this. Independent cafeterias and large commercial restaurants usually pay highest salaries; hospitals, schools, and colleges tend to lower rates but offer other attractions.

How You Get Started • Telephone your local school cafeterias (call the board of education for the names of your schools' food supervisors), hospital dietitians, restaurants, and cafeterias, and nearby summer camps. Tell them **any** business experience you've had to indicate business-and-people exposure, and whether or not you're a wife, mother, home-maker (these relate directly to the food field) plus any organizational work you've done, such as church suppers, club luncheons, etc. (These carry more weight than you think) • Ask about part-time or training positions • Check local vocational schools, community and junior colleges for classes in food administration, quantity food preparation, and related studies.

FOOD SERVICE CLERICAL WORKER

Someone must do the paper work for the dietitian or food supervisor. This is another relatively new position that's rapidly gaining recognition, particularly in hospitals. You do general secretarial and clerical work, type menus, purchase orders and recipes, tally food supplies against the cook's worksheets, calculate recipe and menu costs. What you need personally and educationally are typical of office work in other jobs; hours you work depend on the need for your services and what arrangements you can make. Earnings are comparable to other office jobs in your community.

How To Get Started Call food-service supervisors and dietitians at all possible job spots and inquire about work—either as a food department trainee or as a food service clerical worker.

FOOD SERVICE WORKER

This is the blanket term that covers all the jobs from chief cook to bottle washer, handling storing, preparing, cooking, dishwashing and drying, serving, kitchen cleaning, setting up trays, and counter work.

What You Need Educationally No previous training required; you're usually trained on the job. With an interest and aptitude for food work, you can learn about nutrition, preparing and cooking foods, and sanitation in classes taught by a professional dietitian.

How Much You Earn Your newspaper's help-wanted ads will clue you in on salaries for this in your neighborhood.

How You Get Started There's only one way—call all the places that might use a food worker, and inquire. For further information write to National Restaurant Association, 1530 North Lake Shore Drive, Chicago, Illinois, 60610, and Council on Hotel, Restaurant, and Institutional Education, Statler Hall, Cornell University, Ithaca, New York, 14850.

3

The Social Life:
Get It All Together

In this impersonalized world of ours, socializing plays a more important role than ever, and with a four-day work-week on the way and more leisure imminent, party-giving is bound to increase. The trend today is away from the big and grand. The hire-a-hall approach has yielded to more intime, at-home affairs with fewer people but given more often. As a party or wedding planner, you can be all things to every occasion you cover. The only element over which you have little if any control is the guest list. If you set the stage down to the last little detail, and it's attractive, the service gracious, and if the mood established is warm and alive, you'll have created great memories for the clients and the guests, and new customers for yourself.

PARTIES
What Kinds Does a Party Planner Plan? • Block parties • Cause rallies • Businessmen's gatherings • Organizational fund-raisings • Sweet-sixteeners • Children's parties • Housewarmings • Talent shows • Community sings • Theater bashes (backstage, back-at-the-house) • Bon voyages • Seasonal flings (Christmas, Chanukah, New Year, Halloween, etc.) • Graduation get-togethers • Wedding showers • Celebrity socials • Engagement and anniversary joyfuls • Product presentation affairs • Company openings • Political wingdings • Picnics • Homecomings • School reunions • Now add your own.
What You Need Personally • Creative imagination • Good taste • Enough business sense plus administrative know-how • An up-to-the-minute savvy about what's current or

coming • Since the job isn't for your ego satisfaction but to satisfy a client's needs, you must be willing to express what the latter wants (within the boundaries of reason and good taste) • For the client who's receptive, a contemporary approach and the courage to be fresh, even charmingly way-out in planning visual themes, can make the job more effective • You should be able to see the overall picture as well as oversee each part of it.

What You Need Materially • Work space for a desk, telephone, shelves for reference materials • If you plan to cut and assemble favors or decorations, a large, flat work surface and the wherewithal—crepe paper, tissue paper, wire, wood stapler, and so forth, depending on what you make • Once your party service is started, you'll need a calling card, stationery, a company name, a presentation brochure or folder about you and your work • Sources for all required items and personnel: tables, chairs, tents, linens, flatware, china, flowers, photos, food, entertainment, films and projector (and projectionist), invitations, and technical aid plus helping hands • If you're not going to do any of the creative work yourself, ferret out a talented friend or freelance designer (either split the profits or pay her a flat fee per job).

What You Need Educationally Forget formal education. It's how bright and hip and eager-beaver you are, and how much you've stashed away in your noggin about every vital subject, every trend. You get this plus great funds of material on decorating, food, and people, from reading, theater, movies, TV, radio, etc. The more you take in, the more you'll have to work with when it comes down to the wire on idea-producing.

Hours You Work Plan your time around your home schedule.

How Much You Earn As big chief of the whole show, you can work on a subcontracting basis with suppliers .and other help, including merchants, and be paid a commission of 10 to 15 percent of their fees. Or charge your client a percentage of the total amount spent, such as 15 percent. Or add up all costs, divide by number of guests and add so much per guest (your fee). If you work as a central agency for all types of services, charge a flat handling fee or a percentage for each element you supply. If your party-planning services are used consistently by certain commercial concerns, you'll probably work on a large-sum retainer basis covering a specified period of time and work. If people merely want suggestions (on invites, food, etc.), charge a brain-picking fee.

How You Get Started • Look over your market. Is there a potential for party planners? If so, decide just how large scale you want to be and whether you'll handle the works or just a specialty, one phase of it all • If there's anything in your past experience or personal background that can be adapted, use it. Example: Anita Goodman of White Plains, New York, runs a business called Fête Accompli. She had some background in commercial flower arranging (see Go Back to Nature chapter). This, and her involvement in local theatricals, add dimension and skills to her work. She's done private affairs as well as special occasions for large food and fashion industries, and is currently very busy with weddings, as well • Or if you've had any child orientation, consider children's parties. They come in all sizes, themes, and stages of growing up, and are much in demand, particularly for very small fry • Round up all your sources of supply and help, and make appropriate arrangements • You might work out an assorted group of package plans to suit various types of get-togethers, including settings, food, entertainment, and the like • It's a good idea to have your own bakery arrangement or cake baker for birthday cakes. When you have everything organized and synchronized, promote your service. (See Promotion Hints) • Do only as many parties as you can handle well. One bungled job can put the kibosh on your future. Six well-done, well-paid jobs a year are better than double—and trouble • Be selective; avoid clients known for using people. They're liable to try to learn all your ideas and sources, then abandon you by the wayside.

Party-Planning Offshoot—Bartending No longer an all-male domain, women do it, too, and with equal success. Take Ruth Steinberg of Philadelphia, Pennsylvania. Thanks to a noncredit course taken in college, this happily extroverted woman can shake a cocktail with the best shirtsleeved pros in the business, and although she hasn't worked in a bar, per se, she's mixed drinks for scores of parties, keeping her in luxury money. But women **are** tending bar at drinking spots, and you can pick up a healthy sum working just Saturdays and Sundays, if this fits your home scheme. To learn, volunteer your help to an understanding bartender or sell a catering service on the idea and ask for on-the-job training while working as a barmaid. (Liquor and package stores give all sorts of recipe booklets away free; ask for them. Or browse through the cookbooks in your public library.)

WEDDINGS

Do party planning, and it invariably leads to wedding planning. Although "to marry or not to marry" may be a big dilemma for many—others, many others, are still middle-aisle-ing it. However, how they do this varies enormously, as bridal write-ups in any city newspaper show. Today's weddings can take place in all kinds of unconventional places—open fields and meadows, barns, riverboats, and public-interest spots such as cultural centers, as well as the traditional settings. Big, pretentious affairs are giving way to small, at-home breakfast weddings. Ceremonies, too, take off on tangents from the traditional formats and, likely as not, are planned and written by the bride and groom. The wedding planner adapts. Nor is your job lopsidedly sectarian. You'll probably work with people belonging to all different religious faiths, or none at all. Add to this the differences in personalities, background, tastes, and customs, and this can't help being a colorful, fascinating business.

What You Need Personally A liking for people and ability to relate well to them (particularly women) • An open mind • Good taste • A feeling for fashion • Flair, creativity, and sense of the dramatic • Capacity to supervise with motherly authoritativeness • Some head for figures • Sense of humor

What You Need Materially • A telephone • An active list of current future-brides' names • One or more reference books on etiquette • A smart wardrobe (not necessarily extensive—just a few well-accessorized outfits per season) • An active idea and resource file

What You Need Educationally • Enough cultural background (or flexibility) to deal with the varied social, economic, and intellectual levels of your clientele • More social know-how than your clients • Knowledgeability about wedding preparation, including the attitudes and practices of different religious and ethnic groups, customs regarding remarriage and divorced couples, etc., proper allocation of wedding budget, menu planning, seating and floral arrangement, varieties and uses of flowers, basic know-how in the use of linens, glassware, china, sliver, wines and liquors, foods, fashion, music, photography and the like. Learn by reading, observing, and assisting (if you can be helper to a wedding planner—ideal!).

Hours You Work   (See Party Planning)

How Much You Earn   Earnings are determined by

all facets covered by your services, clients' budgets, etc., as with party planning and catering.

How You Get Started • Learn. By reading. Through on-the-job exposure as a salesgirl in a trousseau or bridal shop, with a florist, in a store selling linens, glassware, etc., or in the bridal registry of a store • Other job-training possibilities: Work as secretary or assistant to a banquet manager in a hotel. Get a job with a bridal publication. Be Girl Friday to a society editor. Work with anyone who deals with brides, e.g., a dressmaker or manufacturer of wedding gowns • Go to all kinds of weddings (generally, no one stops a stranger from observing a ceremony) • If the fashion aspect is what intrigues you, take a course in design or merchandising. (See Fashion Is Fun chapter). Or, on your own, research wedding styles through the ages including right now • Compile a list of brides-to-be by subscribing to newspapers or an area clipping service • Decide exactly what your services will include, all phases of the wedding, or a specialty—e.g., creating table decorations, booking music and entertainment, giving fashion guidance—purchasing gowns, etc., through your own sources or simply accompanying your client to the stores to guide her choice of gowns and accessories for members of the wedding party. (Hint: the most suitable bridesmaid's dresses are sometimes found in fashion departments other than bridal) • Line up: locations for ceremonies and receptions, transportation (limousines, etc.); buying and rental sources for men's formal wear; fashions for the mother of bride and attendants; printers and engravers (announcements, invitations) and all other needs • Announce your service and follow up with phone calls to recipients • Once you've lined up a client, establish size of wedding desired, finances available for it, and how much of this goes for each need • Draw up a written contract to protect all concerned • Subscribe to leading bridal and fashion publications, and follow weddings in newspapers • Note: A wedding planner is privy to many family secrets; these are confidential. Tales told out of school can totally squash your business. Also, according to Anita Goodman, a seasoned pro, "The choice of wedding dress is your clue to which way the party will go. If the girl starts off with a traditional number and no hassle, you've got it made. But if she wants to be married in jeans and compromises by taking a white dress that's sexy, you know it's going to be an uphill battle to please both the now generation and the usual then generation." She also points out that when the wedding is over, all that's left are memories and pictures, so "have the best photographer you can get."

TEEN CENTER
Teens need a place to go that's all their own—to talk their talk, to listen to their music, and just be sociable, and even if a town already has a teen center or coffeehouse, chances are it can use another. You can set one up with help from your friends—the teens themselves and an interested community.

What You Need Personally • A liking for kids and interest in them and their world • A desire to give them something positive • A bubbling enthusiasm that's catching • Sincerity and the ability to make guests feel welcome • Administrative ability and some business sense • Any special interest, talent, know-how that can help the project (not essential but helpful).

What You Need Materially • A place for your center (in your home, a basement, barn, made-over garage, community room, any adaptable location) • Furnishings (go as way out as you want) • Helping hands • An official okay from zoning, health and fire departments • Insurance coverage • Food (simple but good) • Extras for atmosphere and entertainment— decorative items, games, phonograph, tapes, records, films, performing platform, spotlights, etc. • Imagination and creative skills to take the place of money in setting it all up.

Hours You Work Probably after-school (with week-night curfew) and weekends. Ordering supplies, contact work, and publicity, etc., will take time, too.

How Much You Can Earn Decide whether you're in this to make a profit and work at it. (You may be happy to break even and let it all pay off in satisfaction for a job well done.) Your community's cooperation, your overhead, and how it goes over will determine earnings.

How You Get Started • Find a place • Choose a theme for decor, and a name • Get the kids charged up over fixing the place up their way, and corral volunteers for each part of the project. (There's loads of talent around. Find it.) • Arouse community interest in your project by enlisting the help of civic, congregational, service, and private groups. If you can sell them all on the need and value of a teen gathering place, this can net you a rent-free or low-rent place for your center (unless you use part of your home), furnishings, food sources, and much more • Furnishings can be found in secondhand shops, given as personal donations, or made up by your helpers • Tell local food jobbers and wholesalers about your venture; offer to share publicity with them in exchange for real help • Keep your menu prices low to fit teen allowances. A delicious specialty at a super-low price can lure kids in and keep them coming, providing you offer atmosphere and fun, too • Entertainment can be scheduled or spontaneous performances of rock, folk, dancing, guitar, and other instrumentals, poetry readings, drama sessions, jazz, rap sessions, art showings, filmings, tapes, games, dance, and various workshop activities, as well. Work it out with the kids • Publicize your center in every possible way. Again, the teens will help. It will be their place, you'll be their friend and advisor (or provide someone with the listening ear, open mind, and warm heart) and in your town, no one will ask that old movie-title question, "Where are our children?" They'll know.

4

When Persuasion
Pays Off

Like people? Stores are people, involved in the important business of buying and selling. Only have so many hours a week that you can spend away from home? Stores, large and small, need part-time and full-time help, particularly sales help. In fact, that need is steadily on the rise, thanks to population growth, upward income levels, new products and business expansion, and longer store hours in suburban and metropolitan areas. Are you untrained for any kind of a job or a bit creaky in what you can do? Stores train you for selling, telephone order taking, credit clerking, etc.—and if you take any work offered, you'll learn retailing the best way, on the job. Need a challenge? Working in a store may be hectic, even wild, at times, but it's never, never dull, and doors are open from one department to another; if you've got the pizzazz, drive, or call-it-what-you-will, you move up fast.

It's a particularly hospitable world for women. Geraldine Stutz, head of Henri Bendel in New York, summed up the reason for feminine success in store operations a few years ago when she remarked, "All those boys [other leading store presidents] are more experienced than I—but they are not women. I am. I am the customer."

Femininity is not your only asset. Maturity, too, will stand you in good stead. Thanks to it, you know more about everything, including merchandise. And if you've had specialized experience that can be applied, head for any store and lay your credentials and ambitions on the table.

Lee Berkley of Allentown, Pennsylvania, did. She'd worked her way up to national publicity director for a nonprofit organization manned by volunteers. This and some advertising experience were what she offered Hess' Department Store who promptly took her on for special executive training. After several months' indoctrination, she's writing the company's newsletter and doing other personnel and public relations jobs.

Selling is the jumping-off place for just about every spot in a department store and for dozens of different careers both inside and outside the retailing sphere. Besides department stores, there are discount, dry goods and variety stores, as well as single-line stores, featuring a broad range of related merchandise (groceries or hardware, etc.) and specialty stores (shoe shops, florists, etc.). Large stores offer a greater variety of jobs. Small store work has its own advantages. Everything is more closely knit—the premises, the people, the work—so there's greater chance for you to learn facets of retailing.

Jobs in Retailing (availability depends on size and type of store) • Stock girl • Stock-clerical • Head of stock • Assistant buyer • Buyer • Merchandise manager • Cashier • Wrapper (regular, gift) • Packer • Maintenance • Stylist • Fashion coordinator • Bridal consultant • Model • Alteration hand • Teen Board supervisor • Publicity assistant • Publicity director • Advertising production manager • Proofreader • Production people • Decorating consultant • Store detective • Advertising copywriter • Advertising manager • Art director • Layout artist • Paste-up girl • Retoucher • Illustrators (fashion, home-furnishings, etc.) • Display assistant • Display manager • Comparison shopper • Clerical • Section manager • Finance administrators (treasurer, comptroller, credit manager, department manager)

Let's say you land a job at the suburban branch of a department store as a wrapper, do a good job, and move up to a stock-clerical position. (Don't forget to let them know you want to move up; otherwise, nothing at all may happen.) As a stock-clerical, you might • Keep fitting rooms clear • Check incoming merchandise • Invoice outgoing merchandise • Keep records of all items sold • Keep a running count of money coming in • Write credits • Keep files • Phone in reorders • Call customers about merchandise • Close and check cash register at end of day • Do figure work on month's sales • Write postcards to advise customers of sale days • Keep credit lists for each salesperson in department.

Possibly, after a season of this, you're moved to the high-priced fashion department. There you're likely to run their unit control, a record of every garment coming in or going out of the department. By this time, you should know whether you want to stay with retailing and where you want to go in it. Or you might move upward via a different but parallel route—then decide.

What You Need Personally • Neat appearance • A liking for people and ability to communicate with them courteously, tactfully • An interest in some phase of retailing • Initiative and the desire to advance • Common sense • Talent and imagination for jobs such as writing, art, publicity, decorating, bridal consulting, etc.

What You Need Educationally All the book-larnin' in the world won't prepare you to deal with people or everyday merchandising problems. If you have the right combination of personal attributes, it doesn't matter how far down the job scale you start, you'll get there. Just before the winter holidays offers the best chance of training; apply before Thanksgiving. Department store flying squads give great exposure to all kinds of merchandise, since this is a group of sales people who move from department to department when and where needed. Take any starting job you can get to learn. This might be peak-hour relief work in selling, wrapping, cashiering, or stock work. Once trained, you're likely to be kept on call, to work as steadily as you can, part-time or full-time. Read up on retailing in your library. Get experience. Then, if you need additional training, take courses in facets of retailing in a technical school, a vocational high school adult-education course, a state or private college extension program, or college evening classes. Any art or fashion training can be used in advertising, buying, display, fashion shows—or simply to give a broader base to your work.

Hours You Work When a store needs you will depend on its location, size, the season, the type of customers it gets. Selling can usually be done part-time; so can other customer-service jobs, depending on the store's busy days and hours. Specialized work can be done freelance. Once you're into buying, if that's your choice, you'll be full-time—and, more than likely, six days a week.

How Much You Earn A new salesperson usually earns the current minimum hourly wage; with experience, this goes up. Ditto, other starting jobs such as wrapper, cashier, stock work, others. In retailing, even part-timers are usually given a healthy percentage off on the store's merchandise, so consider that part of your earnings.

How You Get Started Simple. Just list stores where you'd like to work in order of preference, telephone for an appointment with those in charge of hiring (personnel department, in big stores) and grab your first good opportunity. (Specify your work interest—they may have a training spot open in it.)

Opening Your Own Shop There's no doubt that one's own store is the American Dream for thousands of women but, contrary to what you may believe (and forgive us for another honest negative), it's not a big money-making business even when it's done the more economical way—in your own home. The net profit, in relation to what you must put into it, is small. Opening any kind of a shop today is a gamble; the odds that you'll survive are less than 50-50. What's behind the failures? Mainly managerial inexperience or general ineptitude. And even if these figures should take an upturn, the odds would still be against your commercial survival unless you had enough experience, competence, courage, and capital.

The bright side of the coin shows the advantages of owning your own business. You're your own boss. There's security in knowing you won't be fired. You have more outlet for your ideas and can make your own decisions. Whatever you achieve, you've done yourself.

What You Need Personally • A pleasing personality. Unless you like people and can deal with them effectively, your shop can flop • Selling experience, particularly in the merchandise you plan to carry, is a big boost toward success. It teaches merchandise sources, customers' viewpoints • A knowledge of your locale—its tastes, level of artistic awareness, receptivity to fresh ideas, shopping and spending habits, competition, and other pertinent factors • Buying and pricing know-how • A background knowledge of what you sell, particularly in specialties with a story such as antiques, fine needlework • Ability to sense and follow trends • A solid business head or help that can supply it • Promotional know-how

What You Need Materially • Room. It need not be large. (If it's in your own home, you save rent, get income-tax deductions.) In fact, a shop not much bigger than a walk-in closet can jump with activity if it's the proverbial better mousetrap. Case in point: The Ladies Hobby Shop in New York is just that size; it takes only three customers to fill it. Their lure—"East Side needlework at West Side prices"—original needlework designs painted by their own artists, evening weaving and macramé workshops one night a week, plus all the consistent help needed to do needlepoint. Its co-owners are Janice Harrison, a former textile designer, and Mary Sharmat, erstwhile TV actress, coffeehouse manager • Space for stock • Capital. Determine this by estimating costs of all your needs (display units, gift wrappings, etc.) plus initial stock. If your shop's not at home, add rent and utilities. In addition, financial advisors recommend a cash reserve to cover six months.

Hours You Work If you're at home, set these to suit yourself—you can even be open by-appointment-only. Allow time for buying and bookkeeping. Commercial items may require trips to their sources during the year, though you can order much by mail or through sales representatives who visit shops (traveling salesmen, remember?). As to paperwork, if you must, put up the "closed" sign one day a week and knuckle down. (A good accountant is indispensable.)

How You Get Started • Phone the regional office or write to main office of SBA, U.S. Department of Labor, Washington, D.C., 20416, for their CHECKLIST FOR GOING INTO BUSINESSS. Just as its name implies, it asks a hundred questions covering all phases of your potential venture and your qualifications, and can save you many a wrong decision. Ask them for any other available help, as well, and do the same with your state's department of labor • Serve a selling apprenticeship in your preferred type of merchandise beforehand, if possible • Test market your ideas. Discuss merchandise with friends, relatives, others, to learn which has most appeal and sales potential. You may unearth excellent and unexpected suggestions and sources of supply, such as local craft talents. (Selling their output can save you a large initial outlay, as you can buy a few items at a time, whereas, with manufacturers, there's often an established minimum purchase, requiring a large cash outlay. If you take items on consignment, you'll save even further on inventory costs) • Check your city clerk on zoning rules for a home shop • Find a smart, reliable lawyer and that aforementioned accountant • Establish bank credit. You can't order from any accredited business firm without it. (The bank can also help you with money matters and provide needed business loans.) • Ask your insurance agent about fire, liability, theft, and other coverage • Set up shop. Hint: Secondhand stores yield all sorts of storage-space ideas. Remember, painting and refinishing can work wonders. Standards, brackets, and wood planks are another solution for shelving • Start buying stock. Visit city and area manufacturers; take along your bank credit card. Buy sparingly on your first trip, ordering sure-sale merchandise first plus a few new and unusual things. If the latter sell, you can increase them gradually • Keep a file system on all sources and your receipts • Your grand opening date should be set only after sufficient merchandise is in the shop. Allow time for deliveries and delays • Arrange all items attractively, for easy viewing. (Observe, in advance, how other stores do this). Promotion and display techniques are vital to good marketing. See trade journals and helpful government pamphlets as well as books in your public library • Follow Promotion Hints.

SOME SHOP POSSIBILITIES

Unique Souvenir Shop A cut or so above the usual, it features fine, lasting mementos, items indigenous to your state. Find stock by locating your state's top industries making gift-type items—china, silver, fine fabrics, whatever. Also explore your region for items made by crafts people. As a guide, read up on your state's history and industry; contact its department of commerce for suggestions.

The Sick-a-Bed Shop Features gifts for convalescents and invalids. Survey gift stores to learn what they sell for this purpose. Possible offerings: crossword-puzzle books, bed caddies for facial tissues, bed socks, fold-up slippers, dry shampoo, shoulder throws, fancy sheet and pillowcase sets, nail kits, therapy kits, craft items, Auto-Bridge and other lone-player games, body lotions, a small, select book selection (mostly light reading). Add to these and give your shop a cheery name. (You might also run this as a service, selling at the hospitals and homes, etc.)

Antique Collecting It's such an absorbing hobby for so many, you might follow the example of five women in Stamford, Connecticut, who pooled their time, this interest, and the desire to earn in an Antiques Supermarket. Most of their wares are left with them on consignment, but they sometimes buy up estates. One secret of their success: They keep a request book—customers tell them specifically what they want, and they try to find the items for them.

More Nostalgia Specialize in the type of memorabilia you can sell—e.g., genuinely old and charming children's clothes, books, and toys along with more modern ones. (There are several such stores in New York—one, the Wherewithal Boutique, has a tiny restaurant in the back called Sybarites, featuring all kinds of sundaes, sodas, and shakes.)

Old Magazine Stores They let you earn as much as half the publications' original prices. Scour your neighborhood for attic discards. Buy them up from janitors, rubbish collectors, institutions, and through ecology-recycling groups who collect them. If you or someone in your family can restore antique radios and clocks, you'll have a good market with collectors and antique dealers.

Thrift Shops These have been big with city sophisticates and teenagers who love their campy old clothes—so big, in fact, that a leading New York department store opened its own, called Yesterday's News.

Nearly New Shops The Pennywise Shop or just plain Secondhand Shop works on a consignment basis, so you save cash outlay for stock. Commissions run from 20 to 40 percent of resale price, depending on type of merchandise, locality of shop, and selling price. Clothing sold must be clean, in good condition. Provide ample rack space. Find merchandise and customers through all kinds of community groups, friends, and classified ads run in the newspaper. One husband-and-wife team I know has two such shops. They accept only top-designer fashions, including Norells, Trigeres, Diors, and the like, and their source list reads like a fascinating Who's Who in TV, theater, and social circles.

Mutual Benefit Shop Works in much the same way as a Nearly New shop except that the goods sold are new and based on an unlimited variety of handiwork. Start searching, and you'll turn up all kinds of undiscovered creativity in your town, the works of artists, craftspeople, designers, etc. Write for the SBA's free bibliography, HOBBY SHOPS, NO. 5 available from any of their field offices or from Small Business Administration, United States Department of Labor, Washington, D.C., 20416. It gives basic information, lists books, and other publications of help.

Hold Everything Shop Start with the premise that there are all kinds of containers and bags used every day, then design and make some originals (or buy them commercially). Possibilities: pomanders, nightclothes bags for children, yarn and string bags, laundry bags, clothespin bags, button bags, diaper bags (plastic lined), beach bags (ditto), shopping bags and totes, book carriers, placemat holders, toy bags, bean bags, marble bags—now you add some. These should be gay, clever, good-as-gifts, and useful.

Other Specialty Shops There are countless specialties a shop can feature but your choice should hinge on how marketable it will be in your town. Jardinieres and planters, copper and brass goods, antique buttons, decorative tiles, on and on—the selection is endless. You might feature handpainting and monograms on all sorts of things. Or original designs such as custom screens, folding stools, unusual pillows, stuffed toys.

Write to the SBA outlining your plans. Ask for guidance as well as helpful printed material including SBA COUNSELING NOTES NO. 24, a bibliography listing sources of information to help you select and operate your business. To buy commercial gift-shop items, write to National Gift and Art Association, 220 Fifth Avenue, New York, New York, 10010 for (a) a calendar of the gift and art shows they sponsor in various American cities (this will tell you where and when these take place) and (b) a directory from the latest show (the New York directory is the largest; ask for this one if you plan to buy there), and (c) a directory from the latest stationery show, which will give you sources for your gift-wrap materials: boxes, ribbons, paper, decorative accessories, etc.

DIRECT SELLING

This is a major form of retail distribution and America's oldest method of merchandising. Currently, it accounts for 2 to 4 percent of all our national sales. Over 80 percent of the 2 to 3 million direct-selling people in the United States work right in their hometowns. More than half of them are women and most work part-time. Every type of woman imaginable does direct selling—all sizes, shapes, colors, ages, social and economic backgrounds and personal conditions, from the well-heeled to the disadvantaged—housewives, students, minority group members, retirees, the handicapped, and senior citizens. If the latter two can't get out to sell, they do business via telephone and customers come to their homes to pick up merchandise. Before trying direct sales, many of these women had no selling experience; others never had worked before at all.

If you want to be on your own, direct selling has some distinct advantages. You need no experience. You set your own work hours. No capital is required to start. And the sky's the limit on what you can earn, depending on how much you put into it. Maybe that's why this method of selling is as old as history. Reach way back, and you find that Roman women went from house to house selling exotic perfumes and beauty ointments to other ladies of the early Christian era. Castle-to-castle salesmen pounded on gates in King Arthur's day. The sixteenth-century London of Good Queen Bess had its door-to-door hawkers, and our own early peddlers helped to forge American frontiers. Today's direct selling is a comparatively breezy road to travel in every way. With new products being sold in this manner each year and the consumer's increasing preference for the convenience of buying at home, the field is on the upswing.

Types of Direct Selling Five different plans; companies use one or a combination of these:

•**The Party Plan** A hostess arranges for a product demonstration in her home for a group of friends, combining shopping and sociability. She's usually paid in merchandise.

•**The Route Plan** Popular for selling foods, cosmetics, brushes, and household products. Orders are usually solicited at the door and delivery is made on the next regular call.

•**The Home-Office Plan** Combines the best features of direct-mail ordering and personal direct selling. The company mails attractive catalogs of their products to the consumer, who may order for herself and also take orders from her neighbors, dealing directly with the home office of the firm.

•**Neighbor-to-Neighbor or Door-to-Door** Traditional method of salesperson calling on her neighbors in the community to take merchandise orders for future or immediate delivery.

•**Advance Appointment Plan** After making advance appointments, you call on individuals in their homes. The initial contact may be yours, or you may be referred by one of your regular customers.

What You Sell Think of some of the giants— World Book and Childcraft (Field Enterprises), Avon, Fashion Frocks, Fuller Brush, Stanley Home Products, Realsilk, Electrolux—and right there, you have a broad product range. There are between one and two thousand direct-selling companies; a hundred of the leading manufacturers belong to the Direct Selling Association (DSA) offering over sixty different kinds of products and services.

What You Need Personally • A friendly personality • Self-motivation • Empathy (being able to appreciate the way others think and feel) • Organization and planning ability • Emotional resilience (you can't discourage easily) • A sincere belief in what you sell (and the ability to communicate this enthusiastically, convincingly) • Honesty and integrity • Good grooming

What You Need Materially • A car, but not always; in party-plan work, someone else may provide transportation • A calling card and/or other credentials giving company name, products, your name, where you can be reached

What You Need Educationally It requires no special background in either schooling or selling; successful direct-selling people come from all educational levels. Most large companies train you, and in many, trainers and field supervisors subsequently earn additional commissions and advancement on the strength of your sales, which assures you as much supervisory encouragement as you may need. Incidentally, companies, recognizing that wives and mothers who've been out of the working world may need guidance on grooming—hair, makeup, even fashion—often supply this, too.

Hours You Work It's been estimated that, selling part-time (say, an hour or so a day or a couple of days a week), your earnings may be about $30 to $50 a week; working full-time, you can average $10,000 to $15,000 a year, and if you're a born saleswoman (or the field supervisor of any), you could reach $40,000 or more annually. You get 25 percent to 45 percent of the retail selling price in commissions, plus the benefit of sales contests, bonuses, promotional aids, and sales convention attendance (including gifts and social events) for you and your family. If you're an independent saleswoman working for any DSA member firms, you're eligible to join American Individual Merchants (AIM) which, for a nominal fee and your dues, permits you to buy life and hospital insurance at group rates.

How You Get Started Write to the DSA (Direct Selling Association), 1730 M Street, N.W., Suite 610, Washington, D.C., 20036. Ask for a free copy of DSA MEMBERSHIP DIRECTORY CODE OF ETHICS. This lists names, addresses, phone numbers, and persons to contact of their one hundred member manufacturers, by both name and product or service category. Decide which type of product or service appeals to you for selling and make direct contact with its company. If it involves door-to-door soliciting, check your town's city clerk about possible license requirements. Also, you'll find job opportunities in direct selling advertised in the classfied section of your newspaper and in various sales magazines (SPARE TIME, SALESMAN'S OPPORTUNITY, etc.) found at magazine stands and in the public library.

If you're not certain which direct-selling method is best for you, trial-test several. Choose—then stick to it long enough to give it a fair chance; the first year is the hardest. Keep in mind that direct selling is one of the finest training grounds in salesmanship you can get and **always** offers work.

INSURANCE

Although most of us are on a chatty basis with our insurance people, we know little about insurance as a field of work. It's a far more interesting world than you may imagine, and since it rests firmly on a math foundation, it's a natural for anyone who enjoys working with figures. Life insurance jobs for women range from beginner-clerical all the way to top-echelon administration, and take in a long roster or professional jobs, as well—lawyers, nurses, librarians, dieticians, doctors, researchers, and others. Companies give on-the-job training for a variety of insurance specialties. Income for women is comparable to that of men performing the same job, which is more than can be said for many other vocations. Selling commissions alone can go as high as a woman's ambition takes her—from a modest $4,000 or $5,000 a year on up to $50,000 plus.

What You Need Personally • Ability to verbalize (particularly for selling) • A penchant for details and statistics • Enough self-discipline to organize your time and follow a schedule • Integrity and mature judgment. (Specialized jobs have their own requirements.)

What You Need Educationally Formal education is not stressed for starting jobs. With interest and a desire to learn, you can move up through added training—e.g., a part-time clerical job augmented by a home-study course. Or attend school sponsored by a large insurance company to learn insurance selling. Insurance companies and associations of both companies and agents offer several kinds of training programs. National, state, and local associations offer home-study or evening courses in various aspects of the business. Other classes deal with the organization and operation of home and field offices and are sponsored by the Life Office Management Association, which also provides programs for developing supervisory and managerial personnel. Often tuition and materials, including books, are provided free. Companies frequently train employees in office skills, too.

In life insurance, you can't sit on your hands and are expected to keep on learning, since there are facts about the field that can only be absorbed on the job. There are women actuaries, underwriters, agents, and executives who've risen from the ranks of secretaries, clerks, typists, business-machine operators, and other white-collar jobs. The increasing use of electronic data-processing equipment to speed up services has opened more job opportunities. (Key-punch operating is the obvious and probably most frequent part-time opportunity.) In light of this, you might take a preliminary course in such work before you're interviewed.

For names and addresses of schools giving courses in insurance and related subjects, write to your state's department of education, or to Community Services, Institute of Life Insurance, 277 Park Avenue, New York, New York, 10017. For information about property-casualty insurance jobs, write to Education Department, Insurance Information Institute, 110 William Street, New York, New York, 10038. The National Association of Insurance Women can send additional help: 1847 East 15th Street, Tulsa, Oklahoma, 74104.

Hours You Work Part-time office work compares to such jobs anywhere. As a life insurance saleswoman or agent, you put in a full but flexible workday. To achieve this, you can concentrate on a particular type of clientele with hours that dovetail with your own.

How Much You Earn As office help, the prevailing local rate of pay; as an insurance or other kind of specialist, the rate paid by your company, influenced by geographical location. As an insurance saleswoman, you'll work on commission, so the more you sell, the more you make.

How You Get Started Call home-office insurance companies or their brokers and ask about any of the following starting jobs: **Underwriter clerk**—Checks policy applications. Can move up to underwriter, determining if applicants for insurance are good risks on the basis of their health, occupation, character, finances. **Accounting or payroll clerk**—Works with figures and details, and moves up to doing more of same with higher pay, status. **Library clerk**—Larger companies often have specialized libraries (see Library Work Can Be Dynamic chapter) You help to keep files, circulate books to staff. **Stenographers**—Vital to every insurance company, since correspondence and filling out forms are the life's blood of the industry. **Accounting department bookkeeper**—Can move on to home-office cashier where she's in charge of all company cash transactions—premium receipts, interest, and other income, as well as payments to company. In a local agency office, she's office manager in charge of policyholder service.

    Job Opportunities in Local Insurance Offices Liable to include a secretary, a stenographer, a clerk specialist, an agent, and a cashier or office manager. Many agencies in small communities operate as one- or two-woman offices. An insurance agent represents one large insurance company, a broker more than one. Both sell insurance, issue and collect premiums, renew policies, make out loss reports and service clients in all ways needed. Contrary to popular belief, you needn't be a minor math genius, since all it takes is accurate but simple figuring and the ability to read arithmetic tables. The company you represent will probably help you to find clients and give you leads until you're running on your own.

    Most states require an agent to be licensed. To learn what's needed for this, write to your state department of insurance at your state capital. The first few months of training for life insurance work are salaried. After that, it's earning by commission with service fees for continuing policies.

    Property liability insurance starts an agent on commission right away. To learn more about this type of work, talk to major life insurance home-office people or local brokers. The constant demand for life insurance agents should assure you a warm welcome. Be sure to ask about training programs given through parent companies.

REAL ESTATE

    Like a marriage matchmaker, the real estate agent brings together client and property in order to make a sale. If you've ever played Monopoly, you've had a tiny taste of the real estate game, and it can be just that kind of challenging fun. Women make ideal real estate salespeople, particularly for homes, since, in most cases, it's the wife who does the groundwork in hunting for a new home—and who can talk to a woman on her own terms better than another woman?

    What You Need Personally • A liking for people •

Ability to talk to them with ease • Enthusiasm and natural selling ability • Common sense • Some understanding of business

What You Need Materially • A car • A real estate sales license. (If you go on to become a broker, that takes a special license, too) • Enough cash-on-hand to cover car maintenance

What You Need Educationally Knowledge of your county or state rules and regulations in order to pass a test, get your license. Specialized schools give courses in this work (check out their qualifications with your county board of realtors, board of trade, or chamber of commerce before you sign up). Colleges and universities and some public-school adult education also teach elements of real estate. The National Association of Real Estate Boards (NAREB), through local boards, sponsors courses in both fundamentals and more advanced facets. Some of the facts you should know when selling property: floor plan (room arrangement), heating unit and fuel burned per year (cost), architectural style, year built, nearness to schools, stores, transportation, community facilities, condition of roof, cellar (wet or dry), plumbing and wiring, yearly taxes, zoning rules, income potential, plus details about loans, title searches, property transfer, and other technicalities related to the actual sale.

Hours You Work Weekends are busiest. You can set up appointments to dovetail with home needs.

How Much You Earn A broker's commission for selling a house generally runs between 5 percent and 6 percent of the sale price. The agent who makes the sale earns up to half of this commission. However, this varies from one firm to another and from state to state. Anne Meyer of New Rochelle, New York, who sold her first house after about a month on the job, figures she's earned about $7,000 each year since she started. Her husband followed her lead and is now a spare-time broker.

How You Get Started • Attend classes and/or learn on the job, working in a local real estate office as a clerical, secretary, switchboard gal, or as a renting or selling agent on the premises of a new building or development • Or simply call a real-estate office and inquire about a selling job. Most will be happy to have you, since you'll be working on a commission basis • For information on licensing requirements, get in touch with your local real estate board or write to your state real estate commission. Many states send a manual to help you prepare for the written exam required for a license. To learn which colleges and universities give real-estate courses, write to Department of Education, National Association of Real Estate Boards, 155 E. Superior Street, Chicago, Illinois, 60611.

TELEPHONE SOLICITING

To any woman unable to leave home to hold a job—because of small children, a handicap, or age—telephone soliciting is ideal work, providing the company is reliable and fair, has an authentic, saleable product or service and a good reputation. Many different kinds of firms and organizations use this type of help—e.g., building contractors, diaper services, market research companies, health groups, cemeteries, fire-alarm-systems manufacturers, magazine circulation groups, and clothing drive sponsors.

What You Need Personally • A friendly personality • Pleasant voice • Good speech • Poise and courtesy • A persuasive personality • The know-how for presenting selling facts to advantage (your employer probably will help you with this).

What You Need Materially A telephone, preferably with unlimited local service. (Once your business expands enough, you can get service for an additional geographic area for an extra monthly fee.)

Hours You Work Usually about four hours per weekday (10:30 A.M. to 12:30 P.M., 6-8 or 9 P.M.—with proper apologies for any dinner interruptions), and Saturday mornings. In bad weather, you can work more hours, since there's a better chance to catch people at home. With experience, you can average sixty calls per hour (half of them, no answers).

How Much You Earn Some jobs, like market research, pay by the hour; others (in fact, most) are strictly commission. Mrs. Hortense Samual of New Rochelle, New York, homebound with a heart condition, has earned a substantial income selling magazine subscriptions by phone. Her yearly bonuses have been equally solid—items such as a Naugahyde BarcaLounger and a TV set, among others. She's done so well, her husband plans to work with her when he retires next year.

How You Get Started • Answer your newspaper's help-wanted ads for telephone solicitors. (Mrs. Samual has done a political poll for Gallup and the READER'S DIGEST, solicited charge accounts for a department store, touted the virtues of a good nursing home to people over sixty-five, and was area coordinator of volunteer fund-raisers for several health organizations before she settled into magazine selling—and almost all of these, she found in help-wanted columns) • If you find a job possibility, be sure to check out the legitimacy and reliability of the company with your chamber of commerce or Better Business Bureau. Reason for this: There are many unscrupulous companies out to take advantage of the home-bound woman's need to do something and earn extra dollars. They pay peanuts and may just fold their tents some night and disappear, leaving you unpaid • Working hints: Don't waste even a moment on uninterested callees; don't call a no-answer number again until later in the day; don't overtalk or get too personal; don't take rejections personally, no matter how nasty. Keep dialing, keep smiling.

MAIL ORDER SELLING

According to a Small Business Administration folder, MAIL ORDER RETAILING BY SMALL ENTER-PRISES, mail-order selling is a "multi-billion-dollar segment of the nation's economy, but its mortality rate is higher than that of any other type of business enterprise." And from their booklet, SELLING BY MAIL ORDER, under "One Man Enterprises and Spare Time Homeworkers," it notes:

Selling by mail is often thought of as an easy way to make money in one's spare time. Stores and advertisements give the impression that several hundred dollars or more can be made by using little effort to sell various kinds of merchandise. The truth of the matter is that selling by mail is hazardous for the inexperienced person. So much organization is required, even for a part-time business, that the beginner finds himself spending many hours of his spare time with little or no return.

Despite what some sharp-witted operators of franchise services may claim, there is no easy road to mail-order success. You can't sit down at a kitchen table, making a mailing, count orders, and drift effortlessly into a million-dollar enterprise. It just doesn't happen. The advice of government and independent mail-order experts is unanimous in its cautioning. Andi Emerson of Emerson-Weeks, Inc. in New York, a mail-order consultant for large corporations, has learned everything she knows in fourteen years of hard, unrelenting work and maintains you need a practical mind and a creative business approach to succeed.

Given these, the people most likely to succeed are those selling special or unique merchandise. Case in point: Carol Brown of Putney, Vermont, whose consistently fine, imported Irish goods—lush tweeds by the yard, unusual items such as her now-famous knee rugs and Irish fishermen's sweaters (among the first in the United States)—have made her home-based business a means of comfortable self-support. Prompt service and a warm personal philosophy, as well as the qualities cited by Andi Emerson, have also helped. She sold largely through personal-column ads in the then SATURDAY REVIEW.

Mrs. Olivia McMillen of Grants, New Mexico, had a new idea with a waiting market when she launched Holiday Home Exchange Bureau, Inc., a pioneer in the field of exchange homes for vacations. Many factors inspired this mail-order venture—her personal yen for travel and adventure; her dislike of leaving her home empty when away on vacation, trends like the shorter work week and earlier retirement allowing for more vacations; and the fact that Grants is located on busy highway 66, which gave her a close view of thousands of cars en route. "All those vacationers were looking for accommodations as comfortable as home, and worrying about their own homes all the time they were away." For a nominal registration fee, Olivia sends out a directory plus monthly up-to-date listings of those wishing to exchange homes in all parts of the world. Most of the money she's earned above and beyond costs has gone into advertising.

What You Need Personally Those qualities already cited plus: • A positive personality • Business savvy • Emotional resiliency to roll with punches • Patience (a mail order business isn't built in a day) • Physical stamina • Basic math ability

What You Need Materially • Space to work • Equipment—typewriter, stationery, some kind of duplicating machine (either rented or purchased) • Files (use shelves and boxes to start) • Work surface for assembling materials, wrapping and labeling packages • A vehicle for transporting packages to post office • An inexpensive local printer • As for capital, the SBA booklet MAIL ORDER RETAILING FOR SMALL ENTERPRISES said, before the last rise in costs:

Initial capital requirements for mail order selling vary considerably. A few successful operations have been started with as little as $50. Others, with an initial investment of

$50,000 or more have failed. About 60% of the successful firms cooperating in the study began with more than $1,000. Enough capital is needed to cover the initial promotion and to keep the business going for 6 months to a year. [Ed. note: Some say two years.] The average beginner would be wise to start on a part-time basis with risk money, keeping an outside source of income until financially ready for full-time operation.

What You Need Educationally Formal education and a selling background are not important. If you can read and write, think clearly, have the personal attributes and capital required, and if you seek your guidance from qualified sources, you should gradually become successful.

How Much You Can Earn It bears repeating: Mail order is seldom a big money-making business. Whatever comes in is usually reinvested over the first few years. After that, you· should start showing a small but growing profit percentage. New· York State's SBA Supplement No. 19, SELLING BY MAIL, states under "Operating Statistics":

Over 60% of all year-round mail order businesses have total sales of under $50,000. Nearly 45% of the firms gross less than $20,000 and 30% have sales volumes of under $10,000. If yours is a well-run operation, you can expect to work up to a net profit of 8% to 15% a year on gross sales. Although an extremely successful product can occasionally produce a profit of as much as 50%, the duds will keep the average near 10%.

How to Get Started • Read all you can on the subject of mail order businesses and about the type of merchandise you may be selling. Send for the SBA Bibliography No. 3, SELLING BY MAIL ORDER, free from Small Business Administration, Washington, D.C., 20416 • In selecting a product or products to sell, avoid competition with other well-known mail order products, shun standard merchandise unless it has some unique, built-in advantage in style, color, price; seek products with benefits that can be photographed; stay away from items that depend on color and texture for their appeal—they are too hard to project by mail • Seasonal goods are a risk—what will you do with leftover inventory when next year brings fresh designs? • Consider ease of mailing in selecting your product. Breakage prone, too-large, or too-heavy items present postal difficulties and run up your overhead • Also, read and know your postal rules and laws as they relate to your mail-order articles • Do not accept C.O.D.'s—too costly; you pay postage both ways, which can tie up merchandise for as much as fifty days. Do publicize and practice a cheerful money-back guarantee to maximize sales response • Set your selling price to cover your carrying expenses and still give a profit—not higher than what other companies are charging for the same product; not so inexpensive that it gives the impression (especially for handcraft items) of being junk • Add up wholesale costs, other expenses, your salary (your time is valuable), rent, and a percentage of your home-office costs (light, heat, space, etc.) and refunds on lost merchandise • Above all, test, test, test before taking any big-money plunge. The following items and figuring method are basic to all mail order operations:

_____ Product cost to you (product-cost factor)
_____ Postage
_____ Carton
_____ Package insert (additional products; important even if a repeater offer). Called Bounce-Back
_____ Instruction sheet
_____ Order processing
_____ Address label
_____ Packing and shipping labor
_____ Bank charges (for handling deposits)
_____ Overhead
_____ Miscellaneous

_____ Total Costs

List _____
Postage_____
Printing_____
Insert_____
Label_____
Seal_____
Sort, Tie,_____
   Mail _____

Cost per M in the mail _____

Subtract total costs from selling price. Money remaining must cover your profit objective and your order cost (also called advertising cost per order).

Example: Your product sells best at $10. It costs you $4. All other costs total $1.45. Subtract $5.45 ($4 plus $1.45) from $10. The remaining $4.55 has to cover your profit and your order cost. If you wanted $1.50 net profit (15 percent of $10), you'd have $3.05 to pay for order cost ($4.55 minus $1.50 equals $3.05).

Now, if your ad costs $300, you'll need ninety-nine orders to pay for it (ninety-nine times $3.05 equals $301.95). Profit would be ninety-nine times $1.50, equaling $148.50. To break even, you'd need sixty-six orders. To find this point, divide $300 (cost of ad) by $4.55 (above), eliminating provision for your profit ($300 divided by $4.55 equals 65.9 or sixty-six orders). You can experiment with any number of probable results to find what will be an acceptable profit to you. Try different selling prices if there's a doubt. Then if you feel—and competent advisers agree—that it's feasible, go ahead with your mail-order offer. Example:

Tally sheet for proposed and/or actual sales
(basis: 115 orders and above data)

Sales (115 times $10)		$1,150
Cost of product (115 times $4)	$460	
Cost of fulfillment (115 times $1.45)	167	
Cost of ad or mailing	300	
	$927	927
Net profit ($1,150 minus $927)		$223

$223 equals $1.94 profit per order or 19.4 percent

The absolutely nonbreakable rule is "If it doesn't cost out profitably, forget it!" Another hint: Don't sell too-cheap items—what you sell must be worth postal rates. (A $4 ticket is too cheap today unless it costs you about $1) • Test-market your item. Advertise it in a newspaper to determine response before you go all out, spending on advertising. The best way to build a mailing list is to compile your own through responses and contacts, then swap with other mail-order people. You'll swap mutual reliability, too.

It's rarely advisable to rent a customer list when you start, but if you decide to do so, be certain to deal with a reliable list broker, a member of the Mailing List Brokers Professional Association, 541 Lexington Avenue, New York, New York, 10022. Try to keep your lists clean of "nixies" (upon your request to and your payment to the postal service, (ten cents extra) addressed packages that reach a dead end are returned to sender (you) with address correction and can be remailed). Send for NATIONAL MAILING LIST HOUSES, Small Business Administration, Washington, D.C., 20416 • Drop-ship manufacturers ship their merchandise to your customer for you on receipt of your check and a pre-addressed shipping label. If the firm you work with is reliable, this saves you a great deal of work, but you must be sure they don't include advertising of their own in your parcel or delay shipments without informing you (this upsets customers). Be sure they ship immediately • Choose a business name (avoid current slang that's soon outdated). Unless you use your own personal name, you must register your choice with the county clerk. Use an address rather than a box number if possible • Keep records on which merchandise is selling well, which is not, who ordered what and how they paid for it, what was shipped when and to whom. Have at your fingertips prices and services of possible suppliers • Establish an idea file for advertising and publicity. Keep a general correspondence file • Base your advertising methods on your products. Carol Brown and Olivia McMillen advertised and built impressive mailing lists through responses to small ads in the personal columns of SATURDAY REVIEW magazine. You might use a similar classified-ad outlet or run small block ads in national publications. However, the latter are expensive, and can either pay for themselves in both income and new mailing list names or flop terribly. (This is one reason you need a good backlog of capital.) • Get free publicity in shopping columns, newspapers, shelter (home) magazines, etc., and make certain your packaging speaks well for you (see Promotion Hints).

5

For Animal Lovers

You never feel alienated or rejected by a pet, and you may very well feel thoroughly protected having one, providing it's large enough, fierce enough, or just loud enough. These are primary reasons why the animal population census has skyrocketed to 700 million, or more than three times the human population. It's been estimated that almost three quarters of all American homes own at least one dog, cat, or other pet. All these living things create a great variety of jobs. What's more, today's all-out interest in conservation has opened still other work spheres. Animals are even being used to monitor pollution, and in Texas, there's a family that's raising frogs for major learning centers around the country. So whether it's with pets themselves, or some animal life facet of ecology, if this is your world, there's a job for you.

Where You Can Work With Some Form of Animal Life • Kennels (boarding or breeding) • Dog-walking services • Hunting clubs • Nature museums • Pet stores • Animal-grooming salons • Obedience classes • Animal preserves • Bird sanctuaries • Veterinarian offices • Pony clubs • County and country fairs • Farms • Race tracks • Riding stables • Circuses • Animal hospitals • Aviaries • Shelters • Humane societies • Summer camps • Animal shows • Ecology and conservation groups • Fish hatcheries (state, other) • Special animal-life group—e.g., bird-watchers • Government services—county, state, national, dealing with conservation or wild life • Specialists in any form of animal life—e.g., writers, breeders, etc.

Animal research is an entire field unto itself, done in hospitals, veterinary, medical and dental schools, pharmaceutical houses, colleges, commercial-feed companies, testing labs, research institutions, and federal regulatory agencies. Large hospital complexes, for example, need laboratory technicians to work with their animal labs, giving injections, taking samples of body fluids, observing animal reactions to test situations and chores similar to human lab work. A great many animal workers learn on-the-job—zoo people such as curators and keepers often get started simply by hanging around as helpers. You can start in this way, too. Visit where you'd like to work. Learn what starting jobs are available. Area conservation and 4-H groups can help you locate one. There are just as many city opportunities as suburban and rural; dig a little, and you'll find them.

Be a Pet Sitter Done all the time for neighbors and friends on a no-pay basis, this could be a paying business, since kennel and vet boarding charges are so sky-high these days, and many simply don't have the room to handle the number of pets. You look in on the animal(s), walk, feed, and/or clean cages plus other essential chores while owners are away. Combine it with plant watering and housewatching, and your fee can go up. Or run a pet-sitting service the way you'd run a baby-sitting service and use eager teenagers or other animal-loving women as your work crew.

Pet Boarding Given enough space, a bit of cash, and a handyman to help build kennels and a run, you can board dogs at your home. Fish, birds, turtles, hamsters, and similar small creatures simply need space for their cages or tanks. (Check zoning laws first.) Or you can work for an established kennel as the owner's assistant.

Assist a Veterinarian You can either work at the reception desk, handling billing, appointments, patient files, and help a bit with the animals, or just do the latter, cleaning the treatment room, sterilizing equipment, helping to feed, medicate, and give post-surgical care. Also, dogs, like people, have their hangups and are subject to ESP and depression as well as psychosomatic ailments such as asthma and paralysis, and neurotic dependence on their masters. They need help. A book, UNDERSTANDING YOUR DOG by Dr. Michael Fox (Coward-McCann Geoghegan, 1972), gives valuable insights and perhaps a working idea for you.

Work in a Pet Shop Clerk or manage the place, selling all kinds of food and equipment for pet care as well as caring for the animals on sale. You'll meet animal people this way and possibly make contact for other animal work, as well.

Be a Dog Trainer   Volunteer as an assistant to one first, to work with obedience classes and learn the whole sit-stay-heel routine with dogs of all breeds. Generally, there are ten to twelve classes given at a blanket price, with about twenty to thirty dogs and masters at each training session. These are held in a large place such as a Y, school gym, armory, or parking garage, after work hours. For lists of classes near you, write to the American Kennel Club, 51 Madison Avenue, New York, New York, 10010. **An offshoot idea:** One big-city trainer specializes in teaching difficult animals, all kinds, and is doing very well financially.

Work with Show Animals   As a **dog or cat handler,** you train the animal to show, then do the actual showing—bathing, trimming, and grooming it, then presenting it to be judged. To learn, apprentice yourself to a breeder, kennel owner, or full-fledged handler. From this work, you can move up to be **a dog show superintendent** (not many of these around or women doing the job) or **a show judge** (you get a license to judge your own breed, prove your worth, then take on other breeds to judge).

Run a Bathing, Clipping, and Grooming Service Relatively uncomplicated and requiring only a small outlay of funds for cleaning materials and tools, these can be done in the home. A brief apprenticeship and/or helpful books are adequate teachers. Dorothy Podesta of Bronx, New York, started poodle clipping and bathing at home purely as a lark, and her clientele grew so large, she had to lease extra space for her work. A friend and a good book taught her clipping techniques. With names secured from the dog license bureau, she mailed out business announcements and received about 250 answers. Gradually, she took on other breeds. Check your area pet shops for rates in order to help set your own. A good dog groomer can earn as much as $10,000 a year, depending on circumstances. A well-behaved dog averages one half hour, an obstreperous one can take an hour and a half. East Coast suburban grooming salons give toy and miniature poodles the works for $12, do standards for $15 and other dogs are comparable. Claw clipping, dogs or cats, runs $1 to $2.50. Being dogs that get lap-of-luxury treatment from owners, poodles are indulged with items like fancy jewel-studded collars, ribbons, fancy (even twenty-four-karat gold) leashes, simulated ski suits, baseball uniforms, and fancy raincoats. Poodle accessories sold along with their cosmetic services can up your income considerably.

Pet Photography Highly paid, much in demand, its commercial outlets are newspapers, magazines, books, TV, and animal lovers. If you're good at it, you can be the official photographer for animal shows and clubs. Or you can do animal portraits as Paula Wright does in New York City. She maintains that it takes infinite patience for posing them, particularly cats, independent creatures that are hard to keep still. Related thought for the artist: Animal illustrations are used for books, museums, children's publications, sports magazines, murals, and many other purposes.

Animal Writing See Writing chapter for procedures and suggestions. Also, animal-related industries present a specialized area for writing talents—foods, equipment, medicines, pet supplies, agriservices—using brochures, booklets, mailing pieces, advertising, publicity, promotions, presentations, on and on. Animal fiction writing has such universal appeal, particularly when geared to a particular breed, it's a surefire money-earner.

The Village Blacksmith Helene Coutermash, wife and mother, is also a farrier. She shoes horses for about thirty local families in the South Salem area of northern Westchester County, New York, and plans to keep at it for at least fifteen to twenty years more. She's a slightly built, middling-height "weakling" who carries her eighty-five pound anvil as easily as a box of eggs. A two-week summer farrier course at the University of Connecticut and growing up around horses during her Ohio childhood helped to set her up for the work. A do-it-yourselfer, Helene fashioned her forge from an old metal milk can. Learn this trade, and you can use it at harness and racing tracks, riding stables, working ranches, dude ranches, police stables, horse shows, and country fairs.

And at the Track Women jockettes are racing thoroughbreds at tracks all over the United States. Take Bobbe Huntress, five-feet-two, who's been at it since 1953, when she was the first woman to qualify for a license as a harness racer. She made the trotters' "world series" at Yonkers and Roosevelt raceways. When not racing, she's driving, training, and caring for a stable of eight horses. More and more stable grooms at the big tracks are women. They're paid by the horse—so much for each one they handle plus extras. (Women, because of their gentle hands, have always been better with horses.)

Other Animal-Work Jobs to Consider • Companies that manufacture or distribute products for animal care need researchers, public relations people, those lab workers mentioned earlier, and other help • Special-interest magazines involved with animal conservation or the breeding, training, and care of special breeds need staff workers. Various pet breeds have their own organizations and branch units, e.g., Junior Collie Fanciers of America • With enough experience in any phase of animal work, you can teach what you know • Related to this last thought: Form a Saturday-morning children's class and take them on field trips to explore all kinds of animal life. Monetary returns may be modest, but satisfactions can be very large indeed.

6

Health: An Expanding, Vital Field

Back in the mid-sixties, shortages in health personnel had reached alarming proportions. Some still exist, but the steps taken to help offset the situation brought about changes that are much in evidence today—e.g., the paramedic field, a whole new breed of worker created to relieve the overwhelming work load of the overworked professional.

The nursing field is another good example of these changes. Government and other funds have since been offered for nursing education. Colleges and hospitals give refresher courses to nurses who want to return to practice but feel they're no longer competent in the highly technical hospital environment of today without needed updating. (These sometimes require a fee or an employment commitment to the sponsoring hospital.) There's a trend, related in part to the government's sponsoring of health maintenance, toward nurses working in community-health organizations to prevent illness and maintain health.

Still another trend is that of the nurse doing jobs previously assumed by physicians. Nurses are delivering babies (midwifery), giving **family** health care, screening patients to determine their needs prior to the doctor's exam, and, in some cases, setting up their own offices as private practitioners to help patients with problems which may not require a doctor's care. Their emphasis, through care and teaching, is on helping patients to stay healthy. Consider, too, the fact that the invention and use of new diagnostic and treatment devices have created a need for special skilled operators—and that new fields have been opening up (nuclear medicine, environmental health, pediatric homemaking, nurse anesthetists, and many others) all requiring specialized workers.

Shortages still exist in many of the health disciplines, depending on geographic location, population density, and other factors. It's best to check out the situation in hospitals and health services where you live, if this is where you plan to work after training (or retraining). With the help of scholarships, loans, grants, and government funding, tuition costs for education in many health jobs can run as low as zero. Another plus—part-time work is usually easy to find. If you have a predisposition to any of the biological sciences and a real concern for your fellow humans, one of the jobs in this chapter could be for you.

VOLUNTEER HEALTH WORK

If it's easy to picture yourself scooting around gleaming white hospital halls, but you're not certain whether this interest is the real thing, or just what type of work you want in the health field, do volunteer work. Any hospital (and, no doubt, other health facilities) will welcome you with open arms and put you to work in one of a number of areas—the admitting office, helping nurse aides, in escort service (taking patients to and from departments) or in the medical record office or school of nursing library. In fact, there are all kinds of volunteer jobs (see below).

Where You Can Work (Volunteer or Paid) • General hospital • Public or private clinic • City, state, or county hospital • Rehabilitation center • Maternity center • Home for the elderly • Camp • Mental health clinic or office • Citizens' health group • Visiting-nurse group • Research lab • Veterinary hospital, clinic, or office • Institutions for all types of handicaps • Veteran's hospital • Any group giving health care

What You Might Do as a Volunteer • Deliver lab reports • Assist wherever there are help shortages in a department • Man the information desk • Be a blood donor • Help to feed patients unable to feed themselves • Carry food trays • Refill water pitchers, change flowers, water plants • Read and talk to patients, write letters for them • Assist recreational, occupational, or physical therapists • Type reports, make stencils, run mimeo machine, file reports, etc. • Wrap surgical sponges • Work on the mobile x-ray unit • Work with library or toy cart • Take coffeeshop orders from patients • Sort and collate medical literature in the hospital's medical library • Work in the gift or coffee shop • Help the chief housekeeper and central supply to maintain linen closets and utility rooms • Take and deliver phone messages • Work in the hospital pharmacy or in supply rooms • Care for any indoor gardens or lab animals • Work with children in the pediatric ward—feeding, reading, entertaining, crafts, etc. • Use talents and skills as therapy for patients • Plan and run special events for patients • Do fundraising—planning methods, making phone calls, helping with solicitations.

Handicapped Volunteers There are 30 million people in the United States with some kind of a physical handicap, yet many of them also serve others. Here are two good examples: Nancy Kreisler of White Plains, New York, a former Powers model, has been in a wheelchair for going on seventeen years since a polio attack. Almost immediately after, she began to collect and dispense information on gadgets available to make life easier and more enjoyable for the disabled. Now a veteran of many TV talk shows, she calls herself "the Ann Landers of the handicapped." Her husband acts as her booking agent, and the family (three children) travel from show to show all over the country in a twenty-four foot motor home especially designed for Nancy.

Pearl Nudelman's life began when most people would have felt theirs were over—when she entered a hospital for the chronically ill. Despite a back damaged by spinal surgery, Pearl, who lives at Beth Abraham Hospital in New York City, is involved in speechmaking, demonstrating, visiting the governor on issues, and working as president of Community Voice, a patient organization that strives to make life as normal, active and involved in outside community affairs as possible. The group has innovated all kinds of helpful changes in the hospital. Pearl also finds the time to "mother" patients more ill than she is.

SALARIED HEALTH JOBS

Nursing With all the changes in recent years, this work has become varied and specialized, and even when performed in the conventional image, it's not all blood and guts. There are many joyous moments: the pleasure of seeing a close-to-death patient respond and recover; the shared delights new babies bring; the many positive, hopeful moments that happen because you have helped to give patients good care.

Types of Nursing Jobs (a sampling) • Staff Hospital work • Private duty (hospital or home) • Public health or community work (visiting nurse, rehabilitation work, mental health, care of chronically ill, handicapped, aged, teaching baby care to new mothers at home, work with citizens' groups on community health, teaching classes for parents-to-be, speaking at PTA meetings on various aspects of children's health) • Overseas nursing (American embassies, Peace Corps, etc.) • International transportation or industrial nursing • Military (armed-service nurse with any chosen branch of the service) • Teaching (instructing or directing junior college or hospital school of nursing; be a professor or dean of nursing on college faculty, university-graduate program teaching, preparing nurses for clinical specialization) • Clinical specialties (maternal and health-care nursing, geriatrics, mental-health and psychiatry, medical-surgical nursing, public health) • Research • Industrial (occupational health, concern with safety and health of employees) • Doctor's office • Nursing home • Camp • School infirmary

Many of these are particularly, and obviously, adaptable for part-time work, such as camp and school jobs, or working in a doctor's office. And if you're a "returnee," get ye to a refresher course!

Note: Some hospitals care for small children of student nurses, aides, and other workers on a daily basis. This may apply to returnee learners, too. Ask.

What You Need Personally • Concern for others • Physical and emotional good health • Intelligence (academic ability) • Ability to assume responsibility • Good judgment and accuracy • Awareness and perceptivity (you should be constantly alert to changes in a patient's condition and be able to allay often unspoken worries and fears as well as meet any emergencies) • Patience and understanding • Initiative (be self-motivating when the need arises) • Ability to keep medical and personal secrets • Courage (old-fashioned guts) • A sense of humor (this can cushion many a tight moment, lift many a low point in your patient's day or your own).

What You Need Educationally to Be an RN (Registered Nurse) In order to study, you need a high-school diploma. You earn your state license by graduating from an accredited nurses' education program. You have a choice of four programs: (a) A three-year course at a hospital school of nursing, leading to a diploma; (b) a two-year program at a junior or community college, leading to an associate degree; (c) a four-year college or university program where you major in nursing, take courses in science, the arts and humanities, as well, and earn a bachelor's degree (This is the quickest route to top administrative and teaching jobs in the field; nearly 287 colleges offer baccalaureate nursing programs, and the trend today in nursing is toward preparation for either an associate or baccalaureate degree; over two thirds of these schools are accredited by the National League for Nursing, which guarantees you the best possible education for professional nursing); (d) a two-year postcollege course for the college grad with no nurse's training, a unique graduate school for nursing is part of the New York Medical College, but in time, there may be others like it around the country; entrance requirements: either a B.A. or B.S. degree, no age limit; graduates earn a master of science degree—write to Graduate School of Nursing, New York Medical College, Valhalla, New York, 10595.

For each of these programs, there are scholarships, loans and traineeships that cover tuition and provide a living stipend per month, tax-free for both half-time and full-time students.

What You Need Educationally to Be a Licensed Practical Nurse (LPN) A one-year course in a public vocational educational system, hospital, community agency, junior or senior college. You'll learn nursing theory and practice with selected background information in behavioral and biological sciences. Schools prefer high school graduates, but some take candidates with one or two years of high school, and a few will take those with eighth-grade educations. Most schools require entrance tests.

A Unique School For you who can arrange to live in and learn in a home-and-school environment, the Hannah Harrison School of the YWCA of Washington, D.C., provides scholarships covering room, board, and tuition for practical-nurse training to women eighteen to fifty years of age. The school gives a twelve-month course—more than half spent in laboratory and clinical experience, the rest in concentrated study. Your training will qualify you for your state's licensure exam. (The school is accredited by the National League for Nursing.) Write to the Hannah Harrison School (see Index).

For lists of state-approved schools, coded to snow NLN accreditation admission policies for RN's or LPN's, write to ANA-NLN Nursing Careers Program, National League for Nursing, 10 Columbus Circle, New York, New York, 10019. Note: Age limits for professional nursing schools are usually set at seventeen to thirty-five, but the figure is frequently stretched. Age range for practical-nurse training is from seventeen to fifty, which makes it exceptionally advantageous for the mature women wishing to start out on a career.

Financial Help This can come from numerous sources—federal and state government, service clubs, foundations and college-alumni funds. National and state careers committees can send you lists of scholarship sources. Also, there are loan funds, part-time jobs, and other aids available. (Ask the head of your chosen school about these.) And in all schools, a student nurse can pay for part of her expenses by the care she gives patients while learning. Write to the NLN (address above) for their SCHOLARSHIPS AND LOANS FOR PROFESSIONAL AND PRACTICAL NURSING to help you to choose your nursing category and find financial help, books, and other pamphlets about scholarships and college costs. Also the Nurse Training Act provides loans to student nurses in accredited associate degree, baccalaureate, and diploma programs. Funds are administered by the individual schools.

Hours You Work Full-time shifts or possibly a minimum of four consecutive hours as a part-timer. The latter varies around the country, depending on the need for nurses and number available. Most hospitals will adjust working hours.

How Much You Earn To learn current local rates, speak to the superintendent or director of nursing in hospitals near you. Or for RN salaries, write to American Nurses Association, 2420 Pershing Road, Kansas City, Missouri, 64108. For LPN salaries, to National Federation of Licensed Practical Nurses, Inc., 250 West 57th Street, New York, New York, 10019. Part-time RN salaries are either proportionate to full-time or higher, to compensate for lack of benefits, depending on the institution's policy. Practical nurses usually earn approximately three quarters the amount of registered nurses' salaries.

How You Get Started • Read up on the subject • Do volunteer work • Talk with working nurses and others in the field • Visit health agencies, and observe, including enough of the grubby side of the job to judge whether or not it's your cup of tea • Then—write to the ANA-NLN Committee on Careers, American Nurses' Association, and ask for helpful information plus lists of state-approved and NLN-accredited schools • If you take a refresher course, at its completion, register with the professional counseling and placement service of your state's nurse association, or the similar service of the ANA.

Midwifery It has returned, but in a different form—practiced by highly-trained professional nurses who relieve overworked doctors by handling normal deliveries. Endorsed in 1970 by the American College of Obstetrics and Gynecology, this new breed of midwife sees the patient from the time she thinks she's pregnant until postpartum care in the tenth month. There are currently twelve hundred American-trained midwives practicing in the United States, supplying the kind of attention most doctors no longer have the time to give. Ten medical colleges or nursing schools offer this training, which ranges from eight to twenty-four months, depending on whether you have your RN, bachelor's, or master's degree. There are no age limitations for training, and salary begins about $2,000 higher than that of the starting registered nurse. Write to American College of Nurse-Midwives, 50 East 92nd Street, New York, New York, 10028.

Nurse Aide This work can give you almost instant employment and lead you up the career ladder, if you decide to go.

General Nurse Aide Feeds and bathes patients, answers their calls for bedside attention, tidies up their rooms, adjusts bed angles, escorts them to and from other departments, distributes diet trays, counts and stacks linens, and delivers messages.

What You Need Personally (for all aide work) • Patience • Understanding • Desire to help and serve • Manual dexterity • Attention to detail • Cheerful personality • A sense of responsibility • A gentle way with people, both socially and physically

What You Need Educationally • High school background preferred but not a must. Paid on-the-job training is given in a hospital, clinic, nursing home, or other health facility—usually up to two months of lecture-demonstrations and supervised practice.

Hours You Work Varies. You work on call, on a consistent basis (so many hours per day, so many days per week), nights, or weekends.

How Much You Earn Varies. The tri-state (Maryland-Delaware-Pennsylvania) Delaware Valley area monthly salary is given at $492 plus fringe benefits (vacation and sick pay, etc.)*

Psychiatric Aide Works closely with patients in the psychiatric department of a general hospital, mental hospital, mental clinic, or specialized nursing home under the supervision of a professional nurse.

*1973 SURVEY OF SALARIES, FRINGE BENEFITS AND RELATED SUBJECTS, Delaware Valley Hospital Council.

What You Need Educationally High-school education is desirable but not essential. On-the-job training takes up to three months, includes formal classes, staff demonstrations, specific work assignments.

Surgical-Technical Aide Works under a professional nurse, caring for patients in hospital operating and delivery rooms. Helps with care, preparation, maintenance, and use of supplies and equipment, and is a member of the surgical team during surgery.

What You Need Educationally High-school education or its equivalent. Paid training consists of four to six months of classroom instruction and supervised practice. General aide work can qualify you for this training.

How You Get Started as an Aide (any kind) Call local hospitals, clinics, public-health agencies, nursing homes, and other health facilities to inquire about job openings, salaries, and training available. For further information, write to American Hospital Association, 840 North Lake Shore Drive, Chicago, Illinois, 60611. Note newer aide categories: pediatric (children) and geriatric (elderly).

Ward Clerk (Sometimes called floor or station clerk) Relieves nurses of much paper work, distributes records needed by doctors as they visit their patients, does general record keeping, and deals with certain aspects of the patients' charts. Also acts as receptionist in the patient-care unit, directing visitors.

What You Need Educationally Usually trained on-the-job, averaging about five weeks. May be promoted to this from nurse aide work. Must be high-school graduate, preferably with some clerical training, and should be accurate in spelling and arithmetic—and able to type.

What You Earn Tri-state monthly salary plus fringes, $475.* Check your own area.

Central Service Technician (Also called central supply worker, hospital aide, and materials handler) Cleans and sterilizes instruments, equipment, and supplies. Collects or receives used materials from all over the hospital to reprocess for reuse. (Must also know how to operate and maintain much of this equipment.) Once these are reprocessed, you either store

*1973 SURVEY OF SALARIES, FRINGE BENEFITS AND RELATED SUBJECTS, Delaware Valley Hospital Council.

them or distribute them to designated areas in the hospital. Also responsible for assembling and reprocessing sterile and non-sterile treatment and procedure trays or packs used by the medical personnel. Depending on the size of the department, you may also store new supplies, fill requisitions, and take inventory.

What You Need Personally • Ability to work on your own or with minimum supervision • Must accept the routine of repetitious, organized work • Be manually dexterous • Handle instruments well

What You Need Educationally High School diploma with courses in science. You can take central service technology courses in a trade or vocational school, or learn on-the-job for a period of three to six months. With experience, you can move up to senior or chief technician and eventually to assistant supervisor or supervisor of the department.

What You Earn Varies according to size and locale of hospital. To learn salaries, call your local hospital or write to American Hospital Association, 840 North Lake Shore Drive, Chicago, Illinois, 60611.

Electroencephalograph Technician Plays a vital role in the diagnosis of brain disease, injury, and tumor by using a special device that records brain waves. Works with a neurologist or neuropsychiatrist, supplying the electroencephalogram from which they diagnose brain disorders.

What You Need Personally • Maturity and emotional stability plus a sunny outlook on life • Ability to control patients and allay their fears about the examination • Good visual-motor coordination to work with complicated electrical equipment

What You Need Educationally Minimal requirement: high school diploma with emphasis on social and physical sciences. Majority of EEG technicians learn on-the-job. Some hospitals, colleges, and universities have formal programs of from three to twelve months. A growing field, in which opportunities are excellent.

Hours You Work Usually a forty-hour week with all the fringe benefits of the institution.

How Much You Earn Some senior technicians earn twelve thousand dollars and up. Varies according to size and location of hospital as well as your training and experience. Tri-state* monthly salary plus fringes—$594. The 1972

*1973 SURVEY OF SALARIES, FRINGE BENEFITS AND RELATED SUBJECTS, Delaware Valley Hospital Council.

HEALTH CAREERS GUIDEBOOK of the U.S. Department of Labor gives the annual range as $5664 to $7080.* To learn about EEG technology training, contact your hospital, state or city hospital association, or American Hospital Association (address, see above).

Admitting Officer Works in the nerve center of the hospital—the admitting office • Arranges for admission of patients • Interviews patient or relative for necessary information • Assigns rooms • Notifies appropriate hospital departments of the admission • Prepares and maintains records of admission, transfer, and discharge

What You Need Personally • Supervisory ability • Emotional stability and maturity • Tact and poise, even under pressure • Ability to judge people accurately and quickly

What You Need Educationally You're trained on the job (usually) as a lay person, or you come to work via a background in nursing or medical social work (less usual). College degree is desirable but not usually required. Any knowledge of psychology, sociology, personnel practices, and business administration can be helpful.

What You Earn Depends on institution's size and its admitting office staff. The figures for 1971-1972 were given at $7,000 to $11,000.** Ask your hospital for current salaries or write to the American Hospital Association (address, see above).

Medical Technologist A registered medical technologist runs complicated laboratory procedures with a minimum of supervision and helps pathologists to detect and diagnose disease and analyze symptoms and reactions. Don't confuse this work with that of the medical laboratory technician or lab assistant; they do more routine tests under relatively close supervision (covered later in this chapter).

About 85 percent of the fifty to sixty thousand medical technologists working in the United States are women, and mature women are frequently preferred by lab directors for their dependability and longer work tenure. Part-time work is available, especially for weekends and evenings, and more and more hospitals are assigning women to part-time day shifts. This is also ideal work for the disabled, since little physical activity is needed. Medical technologists who left to have families are taking refresher courses to learn up-to-date techniques before returning to part-time or full-time jobs.

What You Need Personally • A strong interest in

*1971 figures.
**Hospital Financial Management Association.

science and scientific fact-finding • The ability to evaluate results of your tests intelligently • Patience and accuracy • Dependability to do top-level work on schedule • Ability to work under pressure (work loads and time limits can't throw you) • Manual dexterity and good vision (with or without glasses)

What You Need Educationally Minimum of three years of college to enter a twelve-month accredited hospital program. College credits must include sixteen hours each of chemistry and biology, and a math course. Some programs require a degree to enter. To become an MT(ASCP) you take the national certification exam of the Registry of Medical Technologists of the American Society of Clinical Pathologists. Look into scholarships and loans for the college part of your education. Many medical technology schools are tuition-free. A number offer scholarships, loans, and stipends.

Where You Work In hospitals (mostly), and private labs, clinics, physicians' offices, health agencies, industry, government agencies, the armed services, research and educational institutions.

How Much You Earn In 1969-1970, the median annual salary was $8,576. By 1972, it had risen to about $9,690. Those with graduate degrees earned more. Part-time salaries were, on the whole, proportionately lower.

What You Do • Perform a wide variety of laboratory procedures in chemistry, hematology, urinalysis, blood banking, serology, microbiology, virology, enzymology, and other areas of lab work • Microscopic examination of body fluids and tissue samples • Analysis of materials for bacteria content • Preparation and examination of slides with sample tissues and body cells • Typing and cross matching blood samples • Antibiotic susceptibility testing • Develop and evaluate new procedures • Troubleshoot any problems or breakdowns of equipment • Interpret reactions • Initiate and evaluate quality-control procedures. In a small lab, you'd probably do many types of tests. In a large laboratory, you're more likely to specialize, using automated electronic equipment that performs blood chemistries, cell counts, and other procedures in a matter of minutes. You might specialize in research on new drugs or new procedures, develop and improve lab techniques, teach, supervise, or administrate.

How You Get Started • Speak to your hospital's chief medical technologist or the pathologist who directs the laboratory. Ask to watch members of the lab team at work •

Learn all you can from firsthand observation. (Nothing beats audiovisual lessons.) • Don't be timid; ask questions • Write to American Society of Medical Technologists, Suite 1600, Hermann Professional Building, Houston, Texas, 77025; Registry of Medical Technologists, ASCP, Box 4872, Chicago, Illinois, 60680 • For information about job opportunities in Veterans Administration hospitals, write to Department of Medicine and Surgery, Veterans Administration, Washington, D.C., 20420.

Medical Laboratory Technician Performs lab tests under supervision but does not interpret the results or methods for developing quality-control procedures. Work is more complex than that of a lab assistant, but excludes the supervisory or teaching responsibilities of the full-fledged medical technologist.

What You Need Educationally • Either a junior- or community-college associate degree or equivalent, including chemistry and biology, with a medical-laboratory technician curriculum • Or a structured curriculum in medical-laboratory techniques • Or a military-training program in medical lab work • Or five years of acceptable lab experience. With any of these behind you, you're eligible to take the national certification exam of the Registry of Medical Technologists to become MLT(ASCP). Many community colleges charge no tuition.

What You Earn Pay compares favorably with other technical-level jobs in the medical field. Inquire about current rates. Write to the Registry of Medical Technologists, see address above.

Certified Laboratory Assistant Performs the simpler, more routine lab procedures under supervision of a medical technologist.

What You Need Educationally A high-school diploma, preferably with shown ability and interest in science and math, plus twelve months of training in an AMA-accredited certified laboratory assistant school. Graduates take the Registry of Medical Technologists' national certification exam to become CLA (ASCP). No tuition is charged in many CLA schools, some of which are supported by United States Manpower or Vocational Education Funds. A number offer scholarships and/or loans.

How Much You Earn National median salary for full-time CLA (ASCP) in 1972 was estimated at $6,720. Write to Registry of Medical Technologists, see address above.

Cytotechnologist A skilled scientific assistant in pathology labs who examines slides of human cells for abnormalities that could be early warning signs of cancer.

Cytotechnologists are needed in most parts of the country to screen cervical smears taken from the growing number of women over age twenty-one who recognize the value of regular examinations for early detection and prevention of cervical cancer. In addition, this type of study is uncovering early cancer signs in other parts of the body, such as esophagus, lungs, mouth, etc. National estimated need: one thousand cytotechnologists.

What You Need Educationally Two years of college with twelve semester hours of science (at least eight in biology), plus twelve months of cytotechnology training, six months in a hospital school accredited by the AMA and six months of supervised experience in an acceptable cytology lab. Passing the Registry exam qualifies you as CT (ASCP). Many schools are tuition-free, some grant scholarships. For information and a list of AMA approved schools, write to the Registry (see address earlier).

Histologic Technician Cuts and stains body tissues for microscopic examination by the pathologist for questionable or malignant cells.

What You Need Educationally A high-school diploma plus a year of training in an AMA-accredited program, or a two-year junior-college program. For certification as HT(ASCP), take exam given by the Registry.

Other Types of Special Work Certified by the Board of Registry of Medical Technologists
•Specialist in blood-bank technology: a medical technologist with one year of training approved by the American Association of Blood Banks and the AMA, who passes the registry exam. Alternate route: B.S. degree in biological or physical sciences plus one year's experience in a clinical lab, and the one-year training program plus the exam for MT(ASCP)BB or BB(ASCP).

•**Chemistry or Microbiology Technologist** C(ASCP) or M(ASCP)—B.S. degree with major in chemistry or bacteriology plus one year's experience in the subject in an acceptable laboratory plus Registry exam.

•**Nuclear Medical Technologist** NM(ASCP) or MT(ASCP) MT training plus one year's experience in an acceptable clinical radioisotope lab, or baccalaureate degree in biological or physical science or chemistry, plus two years' experience or two years of college with specified science courses plus four years' experience or high-school diploma plus six years experience—all plus Registry exam.

•**Specialist Certification** Specialist in hematology, microbiology, chemistry, or cytotechnology available by examination for those with a master's or doctorate in the specialty plus three years' experience in an acceptable lab plus Registry exam.

LABORATORY WORKER JOBS

If you enjoyed chemistry or biology in school and any time spent in the lab, you'll find this work fascinating, since you have a nice broad choice of things to do, and none requires advanced education—you learn on the job. If your interest and ability grow, there's a good chance you can go on in your education under the aegis of the hospital or organization that employs you. (Today, with the new career categories and entry-level jobs in health for the disadvantaged, there are more starting opportunities and growing chances to move up through experience, proficiency, and equivalency exams.)

Laboratory Aide (assistant, helper) • Checks supplies • Labels materials • Helps with basic tests • Sterilizes lab utensils • Makes simple solutions • Weighs, measures, and mixes substances according to instructions • **Supply Room Worker** Responsible for lab materials that require special handling, either because they're scarce or expensive, or because they're dangerous and need proper care. You also keep inventory and inform the chief medical technologist when supplies start running low • **Caretaker for Experimental Plants and Lab Animals** A great job for the green-thumb brigade and pet lovers (including fish and insects). Note: The types of institutions using these workers are usually in large cities or university communities. Your state employment office and the personnel officer of local laboratories can cue you in on possibilities in your area. Also, call commercial research labs, hospital research labs, industrial firms that make cosmetics, food products, drugs and chemicals, and inquire. Part-time hours are adaptable. Salaries run much like those of nursing aides and other helpers, depending on the need and your locality.

Radiologic Technologist (X-ray Technologist) To give you an idea of the enormous scope of this work today, here's a quote from CAREERS IN RADIOLOGY, published by the American College of Radiology:

As a new and rapidly developing science, radiology has also assumed responsibilities beyond immediate health problems. With widespread use of radiation in medicine, industry, research and elsewhere in atomic-age technology, radiation scientists have become responsible for proper use of radiation and for protection from radiation hazards. Protection from fallout, disaster planning and radiation's influence on space travel are some of the expanding areas which require the skills and knowledge of the radiology team.

What You Do   Operate X-ray equipment under the direction of radiologists (doctors who are X-ray specialists) • Take pictures of internal parts of the body for diagnostic work • Use special equipment for treating specific diseases • Assist radiologists working with radioactive materials • Keep equipment in good working order • Keep records of services performed for patients • Process film • Operate other types of equipment (such as those used to diagnose heart disease, brain damage) • Administer chemical mixtures to highlight body organs for a clear picture • Use mobile X-ray equipment at bedside or in surgery

What You Need Personally   • Good vision (with or without glasses) • Intelligence • Precision and accuracy (though safety measures help to avert exposure, carelessness in handling X-ray equipment can be hazardous to the technologist and patient) • Willingness to keep up with rapid advances in the field

What You Need Educationally   A high-school education or its equivalent to enter any AMA approved X-ray training programs—usually twenty-four months in any of the thirteen hundred approved schools; a few offer three- and four-year programs, and thirty-two award a bachelor's degree. Also, approximately two hundred junior colleges coordinate academic training with work experience in hospitals in two- or three-year programs, and offer an associate of arts degree. A background of high-school courses in math, physics, chemistry, biology, and typing is desirable. A few schools require one or two years of college or graduation from a nursing school, for entrance. Those thirteen hundred aforementioned schools are conducted by hospitals or medical schools connected with hospitals. Vocational and technical schools also offer x-ray technology courses.

Where You Work   • Hospitals • Research labs • Air-space fields • Veterinary offices • X-ray equipment and film manufacturers • Public-health services • Clinics • Art museums (authenticating works of art with X-ray) • Hospital schools and universities

How Much You Earn To start, technologists (not administrators) average between $6,500 and $8,000 a year.* Part-time salaries are generally proportionate to full-time.

How You Get Started For advice and information, talk to the chief radiologic technologist at your hospital, call your local X-ray society (your hospital will steer you to it) and write to the American Society of Radiologic Technologists, 645 North Michigan Avenue, Chicago, Illinois, 60611. (For Canada, Canadian Association of Radiologists, 1555 Summerhill Avenue, Montreal, Quebec.)

OCCUPATIONAL THERAPIST

You use educational, recreational, and creative activities to rehabilitate people physically and also work with the psychosocially disabled in activities that contribute to their emotional health and independence.

What You Do Help patients to regain or maintain physical, mental, and emotional stability. Combat boredom and depression during a long-term illness. Develop maximum self-sufficiency in daily activities (eating, dressing, writing, etc.). Perform in a work situation. You work in manual arts (crafts), creative arts (music, painting, etc.), writing and reading, homemaking for daily living, recreational activities (individual and group) and prevocational guidance and training (business and industrial skills). You may supervise volunteer workers, occupational therapy assistants, and nurse aides. And on an administrative level, you're likely to orient medical and related health personnel, direct occupational therapy programs, coordinate patient activities, and act as a consultant to health departments and mental health authorities.

You Work With • Psychiatric patients (largest group) • Physically disabled • Children (including those with cerebral palsy) • Mentally retarded • Geriatric (elderly) patients

What You Need Personally • Intelligence • A sincere desire to help people • Emotional stability (the nature of your contacts can be upsetting; it takes a well-balanced personality to cope) • Physical stamina • A sympathetic but objective approach to illness and disability • Manual dexterity (a must) • Imagination and ingenuity (these oil the wheels of your work, smooth the course of a patient's progress)

What You Need Educationally A college education with a major in occupational therapy taken in one of the

*1972 figures.

forty colleges and universities approved by the AMA and the American Occupational Therapy Association, plus six to nine months' clinical experience. Educational requirements vary. Some of these colleges offer an accelerated program to holders of B.A's (usually eighteen to twenty-two months) leading to a certificate or diploma of proficiency. If you've completed about two years of college and want to enroll in an occupational-therapy course, the occupational therapy director at the school you wish to attend can evaluate your transcript or college credits. Tuition in private institutions ranges from $600 to $2,500. Scholarships and grants are available.

Hours You Work Part-time opportunities are excellent; hours can be flexible.

How Much You Earn According to the AOTA, suggested starting salary for a full-time therapist is $10,500*; part-time earnings are proportionate.

Occupational Therapy Assistant A high-school grad can become an assistant by successfully completing an approved program leading to an associate degree or certificate. These programs vary from full-time, intensive twenty weeks to two academic years, and are given in junior/community colleges, technical institutions, or hospitals.

How You Get Started Make an appointment with a working occupational therapist at your hospital, a rehabilitation center, or community health center to talk about the work and see how it's done. Then talk with a guidance counselor or faculty advisor at your local high school, or write to the American Occupational Therapy Association, Inc., Suite 200, 6000 Executive Boulevard, Rockville, Maryland, 20852, for a list of schools that can send you specific information.

MEDICAL RECORD ADMINISTRATOR

If you lean toward the medical world, and have an orderly mind (or work at it), and if facts and figures fascinate you, then this may be just the work for you. Mary-j Waterstraat, executive director of the American Medical Record Association, says that the national shortage of medical-record administrators and technicians is so acute that, many medical-record departments are without any trained help whatsoever, and part-time job opportunities are excellent.

The AMRA states that, as a medical record administrator, you have four major responsibilities • "To obtain complete

*1972.

records on individual patients from each member of the professional staff (surgeons, pathologists, nurses, others). The job often involves planning medical-records systems and designing new forms to provide all necessary information • To design and maintain a filing system capable of making each record available on a moment's notice • To release information from the record files to authorized persons. Medical records of former patients often are needed for emergency treatment. Doctors, health officials, insurance companies, and others must have accurate information found only in medical records • To analyze the records that pour into the department and prepare them for future use. The medical-record administrator compiles statistics which serve hospital directors, doctors, and public health officials, and others."

You might also direct activities in the department, supervise medical record technicians under you, if any, and assist the medical staff with any research programs.

Where You Work • Hospitals • Nursing homes • Insurance companies • Clinics • Medical-research organizations • Government agencies e.g., local and state health departments

What You Need Personally • Interest in details • Meticulousness (to be of any value, your work must be orderly, accurate, legible) • Willingness to pursue data • Discretion (most of the material will be confidential)

What You Need Educationally You must successfully complete a program in medical-record administration in an AMA-approved school, pass a professional examination. There are thirty AMRA-approved courses offered in American colleges and universities. These fall into two main groups: For the high school graduate—twelve-month college or university undergraduate programs leading to a bachelor's degree with a major in medical-record science or administration; For the college graduate with a bachelor's degree—twelve-month postgraduate programs offering a certificate in medical-record science or administration.

What You Study Theory and practice in • Anatomy and physiology • Organization and administration • Fundamentals of medical science • History of medicine • Medical-record science • Legal aspects of medical records (medical law) • Hospital admitting and discharging procedures • Standard indexing and coding practices • Compiling statistical reports • Analysis of medical data from clinical records • Knowledge of medical-record systems for various hospital departments such as X-ray, pathology, outpatient

Cost of Training   Anywhere from no charge at all to $650 tuition per year. Loan funds are available from the AMRA and state medical-record associations.

How Much You Earn   Salaries for medical-record administrators range from $9,000 to $25,000 a year.

MEDICAL RECORD TECHNICIAN

Let's say you'd like to be a medical-record administrator but can't spare the four-years' training time and/or the money needed for training (if any). No need to throw in the towel. Plan for a technician's job instead. Less training, less cost, and generally speaking, less administrative in nature when you start, the technician's job gives most of the satisfactions of a medical-record administrator without the professional standing. That can always be acquired later on. Responsibilities and amount of work you do depend on the type and size of the place where you work.

What You Do • Review medical records for completeness, accuracy • Translate diseases and operations in proper coding symbols • File medical records (or supervise file clerks) or prepare records for microfilming • Type medical reports of operations, X-ray or lab exams, or special treatments given to patients • Compile statistics of many kinds, including hospital's daily census, information on reportable diseases for public-health authorities and others • Assist medical staff by preparing special studies, tabulating data from records for research • Supervise day-to-day operation of medical-record department, take records to court, and maintain flow of health information to all departments of the hospital

What You Need Educationally   A high-school diploma plus one or two years (depending on the school) training in any of the approved thirty-seven schools, or on-the-job hospital training. Accreditation by the AMRA and the privilege of adding "ART" after your name come with successfully completing a special exam.

How Much You Earn   The range is from $7,000 to $12,000 a year.

Correspondence Courses   To provide on-the-job training and relieve the shortage of qualified medical-record administrators, the American Medical Record Association developed a correspondence course to help further the technical education of persons already employed in medical-record departments. Complete this course successfully, and you can take the accreditation exam.

A second correspondence course to train medical transcriptionists is also available through AMRA. Students learn by studying and transcribing many types of medical reports, using nine cassettes of taped material, a manual, and a tape recorder. This can be done at home or as part of an on-the-job training program. No credit is given, but you get a certificate of completion. Medical transcriptionists are usually paid higher salaries than general typists because of their knowledge of medical terms.

How You Get Started Write to the American Medical Record Association , Suite 1850, 875 North Michigan Avenue, Chicago, Illinois, 60611, for a school list—names of schools, locations, program directors, entrance requirements, length of course and tuition charge (if any), your premedical-record administrative curriculum, and loan information. Also inquire about their correspondence courses.

PHYSICAL THERAPIST
As a physical therapist, you work with patients who are disabled by illness or accident, or were born with a handicap. You evaluate neuromuscular, musculoskeletal, or sensorimotor and related cardiovascular and respiratory functions of the patient; plan and implement treatment programs on the basis of test findings working with the patient's doctor or dentist; instruct the patient, his/her family, and anyone else involved in the treatment or convalescent period.

Where You Work • Departments of physical therapy in general or specialized hospitals • Schools for crippled children • Physicians' or physical therapists' offices or clinics • Hospitals and nursing homes for the elderly or chronically ill • Rehabilitation centers • Armed forces • Home health agencies • Public-health departments • Research centers • Universities and colleges offering physical therapy programs

What You Need Personally • Patience and resourcefulness • A sympathetic attitude • Good verbal expression to communicate and establish rapport • Manual dexterity (you'll use your hands for guiding and supporting patients, working with braces, crutches, artificial limbs) • Physical stamina (others will lean on you, literally and figuratively)

What You Need Educationally The equivalent of two or three years of college plus one or two years of professional training including basic health science, clinical sciences, and supervised administration of work with patients in a hospital or treatment center.

There are fifty-three physical-therapy programs accredited by the AMA and the American Physical Therapy Association. Of these forty-seven are in four-year colleges, fifteen at the certificate level. The latter require a bachelor's degree in a major other than physical therapy and specified science requirements for admission, and twelve to sixteen months of concentration in basic and clinical sciences. If your goal is a teaching or supervisory job, you go on to two years in a master's-degree program.

How Much You Earn The average beginning salary for recent graduates of four-year or certificate programs is $9,000 to $11,000 per year, depending on geographic location and local policies.

Physical Therapist Assistant (relatively new job category) A skilled technical assistant to the therapist.

What You Need Educationally Two-year community or junior-college accredited course to earn an associate degree in physical therapy. You study biology, physical and social science, humanities, physical therapy technical courses, and get clinical experience. If you decide to become a full-fledged physical therapist, you can complete your requirements for a degree in a college or university.

Write to American Physical Therapy Association, 1156 15th Street, N.W., Washington, D.C., 20005, attention: Department of Educational Affairs.

PHARMACIST

The demand for pharmaceutical services in community and hospital settings has been increasing steadily, and federal, state, and local government agencies and teaching and research positions are open and waiting for those with pharmacy degrees. What's more, if you only have limited hours to give, part-time work is plentiful.

What You Need Personally Since in dispensing prescription orders and providing other services, you assume responsibility for human life, you need • High ethical standards • Accuracy • Orderliness • Cleanliness • Ability with details • Good judgment • Tact

What You Need Educationally A good high-school background in math and science and a minimum of five years in college. You can take the first one or two years in any accredited junior college or university, the remaining in a college pharmacy. Costs vary from $600 a year for a state university day student to $2,000 a year or more in a private college. Scholarships, loans, and grants are available. Write to the American Association of Colleges of Pharmacy, 8121 Georgia Avenue, Silver Spring, Maryland, 20910.

Hours You Work Find relief or part-time work in local community or hospital pharmacies. Work as little as one evening a week, every day during school hours—or name your free time. (Check your state rules; some limit times women can work.)

How Much You Earn Part-time salaries range from a low of $3 an hour to a high of $10. There's no age limitation. No formal retraining programs are available. It's assumed pharmacist housewives have kept up with the field and can recall skills with additional experience. (Check your state board of pharmacy about continuing education and reciprocal licensing requirements.)

How You Get Started • Take a part-time or seasonal job in a community or hospital pharmacy doing routine chores in order to confirm your interest in the field • Write to American Association of Colleges of Pharmacy, (see address, above); American Pharmaceutical Association, 2215 Constitution Avenue, N.W., Washington, D.C., 20037; American Council on Pharmaceutical Education, 77 West Washington Street, Chicago, Illinois, 60602; National Association of Retail Druggists, 1 East Wacker Drive, Chicago, Illinois, 60601 • For information on college entrance requirements, curricula, and scholarships, contact the dean of any college of pharmacy.

DENTAL HYGIENIST
For those who can't brush after every meal (and even for those who can), the dental hygienist provides a vital part of tooth and gum care. Basic responsibility is the scaling and polishing of teeth and teaching patients how to care for these at home. Depending on the size and type of dental office that employs you, you also: • Take and develop X-rays • Apply fluoride solutions to teeth • Record medical and dental histories • Mix fillings, prepare solutions, and sterilize instruments • Chart tooth and gum conditions • Massage gums (oral prophylaxis) • Provide dental-health education (mouth care and diet) • Make appointments and keep records • Help develop classroom projects and assembly programs on oral health • Assist in research projects • Teach in a school of dental hygiene

Where You Work • Private offices • Hospitals and institutions for the handicapped • Industrial or union clinics •

Public and private health-care programs • Military installations • Schools (public, college, dental) • Volunteer programs such as hospital ship **Hope** or **Medico**

What You Need Personally • A liking for people • Above average intelligence • Interest in and aptitude for science • Manual dexterity

What You Need Educationally Training in this work can be acquired in several ways, each leading to possibly different goals. All require a college-preparatory course and high-school diploma for acceptance • Two years in an accredited dental-hygiene program in a junior or community college, technical institute, four-year college or university to earn a certificate or associate degree • Post certificate/bachelor's degree—additional two years of academic work offered by some four-year colleges and universities (usually in preparation for teaching career) • Bachelor-of-science degree earned through four years of college work. Prepares graduate for supervisory and administrative jobs as well as office practice • Also, continuing education courses or refresher programs may be found in local schools or sponsored by professional associations. Tuition costs range from less than $100 (residents at state-supported junior colleges) to over $2,500 in a private university. Scholarships and loans are available

Hours You Work Flexible, and varied according to local needs. Part-time hours are usually easy to come by.

How Much You Earn National average monthly salary, $702.*

How You Get Started • Watch a dental hygienist in action, possibly in your own dentist's office • Write to the American Dental Hygienists' Association at 211 East Chicago Avenue, Chicago, Illinois, 60611, for their career booklets, list of accredited dental-hygiene programs all over the country, and information about their dental-hygiene testing program schedules and financial aid • Contact your state's board of dental examiners to learn about licensing requirements.

DENTAL ASSISTANT

Work is varied and interesting. Due to the constant shortage of dental assistants, part-time work is usually easy to find.

*June, 1972 issue of the JOURNAL OF THE AMERICAN DENTAL ASSOCIATION.

Where You Work • Private offices • Hospitals • Government agencies • Clinics • Public health agencies • Institutions for the chronically ill, handicapped, aged, etc.

What You Do   Depends on size, type, and location of office. For the sake of clarity, possible responsibilities are listed under two categories:

•**Office Work** • Answer telephones • Greet patients • Prepare monthly statements • Collect fees • Make bank deposits • Keep expense and tax records • Keep waiting and operating rooms in order • Order supplies • Keep patients' records • Take dictation (speedwriting or shorthand helpful) • Type and file

•**Dental Work** • Prepare patients for examination, treatment, or surgery • Assist dentist while patient is in dental chair • Mix cement, amalgums, and silicates for fillings • Prepare dental solutions • Sterilize and lay out instruments • Assist dentist when taking and processing X-rays

What You Need Personally • A sympathetic attitude • Ability to get along with patients • Accuracy • Discretion • Good health and stamina (you're on your feet a lot)

What You Need Educationally   Dental-assistant training. Given in specialized schools and junior (community) colleges, it covers all phases of the work. Time: one- or two-year courses. Junior colleges award an associate-of-arts degree for the longer program.

Hours You Work   There are many part-time opportunities for after school, evenings, and Saturdays.

How Much You Earn   Variable, depending on size of the dentist's practice, locality, and other factors. See local help-wanted ads to get an idea of the range for your town. National average monthly earnings, $397.*

How You Get Started • Talk to your own dentist and to practicing dental assistants to learn more about the work and job possibilities. Clinics, hospitals, and community public-health agencies can also guide you • For all pertinent facts, write to the American Dental Assistants Association, 211 East Chicago Avenue, Chicago, Illinois, 60611. Also ask for their handbook on certification • Once trained, you'll find job-placement help through your school's placement office, through your state's dental-assistants association, and through the placement service of the ADAA.

*June, 1972 issue of the JOURNAL OF THE AMERICAN DENTAL ASSOCIATION.

WORKING FOR THE BLIND

Close to a thousand American G.I.'s have returned home from Vietnam blinded from combat, and there are hundreds of thousands of others in the United States who are sightless from earlier wars, birth, accident, or disease. You can help them by making tape recordings of books or by transcribing them into Braille and large type. This is being done by volunteers all over the country. Either you work in a recording studio (Recording for the Blind, Inc. 215 East 58th Street, New York, New York, 10022, has twenty-five studios in various spots around the map) or you work on your own with cassette recorders (preferred), in which tape costs may be paid for by sponsoring organizations like the Xavier Society for the Blind, headquartered at 154 East 23rd Street, New York, New York, 10010. For further information, contact either of these organizations or write to Division for the Blind, Library of Congress, Washington, D.C., 20405.

MENTAL HEALTH

Yes, there are jobs in this field that don't require intensive medical and psychiatric training. Psychiatric aide is one of them. You can either work with the mentally healthy to help keep them that way, or aid in the care and recovery of the mentally ill. Statistics on children alone are appalling. It's been estimated that over 500,000 American school-age children are emotionally unable to adjust to the usual public-school classroom.

Some Mental Health Worker Training Programs
The Department of Psychiatry of the Albert Einstein College of Medicine, Bronx, New York, trains women to be psychiatric rehabilitation workers. Graduates of this program, originally designed to help psychiatric patients handle daily living problems, work in mental health centers, family agencies, general and psychiatric hospitals, nursing homes, and a variety of other settings where they deal with patients with a wide range of physical, emotional, and social difficulties and diagnostic categories.

Training, set up by Dr. Ida Davidoff and Ida C. Lauga, takes four and one half days a week for twelve months. Trainees must have raised their own children, be between thirty-five and sixty-five, and have a high-school diploma. Tuition is $1,500 a year. Many of the program's graduates have gone on to get their bachelor's or master's degrees after receiving academic credit for their training.

For information on the current program, write to Mrs. C. Fosco, secretary for the Psychiatric Rehabilitation Workers Training Program, Department of Psychiatry, Bronx Municipal Hospital Center (Room 1023), Pelham Parkway South and Eastchester Road, Bronx, New York, 10461.

Women in Elmont, New York, help on a volunteer basis as teacher-moms in a program initiated to solve the problem of teaching disturbed children. Although their educational backgrounds range from incomplete high school to postgraduate college, their common attribute is emotional stability and love of children. They teach basic subject matter and establish strong, healthy relationships to help the children overcome anxiety. After an average of two years in this program, most pupils have been able to return to normal school activities. You can help to launch or work for a similar program in your town. For other suggestions and information, address inquiries to National Institute of Mental Health, 5600 Fishers Lane, Rockville, Maryland, 20852, and to Department of Health, Education and Welfare, Washington, D.C., 20201.

7

Fashion Is Fun

Dynamic, exciting, highly competitive, and tough—and often kooky (that's a large part of its charm)—fashion runs a frenetic pace from season to season and always at least six months ahead of the times. Yet most of those involved in this somewhat zany business love it.

The fashion world takes in business and activities concerned with the creation, manufacture, distribution, advertising, promotion, selling, and consumption of apparel and accessories, and frequently spills over into home decor, as well. Areas of work take in designing and actual making of styles, retailing, display, art, advertising and publicity, and editorial work, as well as many important fringe jobs.

The Following Offer a Wide Variety of Fashion-Related Jobs (Also, see index, Sewing) • Clothing and accessory manufacturers • Department stores • Fashion specialty stores • Mail-order and catalog houses • Boutiques • Radio and TV stations • Cosmetic and perfume manufacturers • Textile fiber manufacturers • Advertising agencies with fashion accounts • Fabric stores and departments • Publishing companies • Fashion-design studios • Fashion photographers • Magazines (women's, fashion, travel, others with fashion section) • Museums • Package TV show producers • Bridal consultants • Commercial art studios • Fashion-show producers • Pattern companies • Public-relations concerns with fashion clients • Educational institutions (vocational, college level, others)

Some Possible Starting Jobs, Depending on Your Interests
• Manufacturers' showroom saleswomen sell seasonal fashions to store buyers who come there from all over the

country (a great way to get in on public tastes) • Sketchers either put the designers' ideas on paper or sketch high-priced garments in stores and their windows to be copied down for lower-priced merchandise. Designers' assistants (trainees) learn every step of creating new garments or accessories • Retail stores with fashion merchandise are great proving grounds. Almost any phase of their work gives you the inside view. Department stores, thanks to their size, offer advertising, publicity, display, fashion coordinating, styling, teen-board work, and the stock-to-sales-to-buyer route—all involved with fashion • Fashion-show producing or coordinating can be adopted to a modest-sized town. To put shows over you need a sponsor, a store to provide the fashions and publicity, a theme and commentary, music, display backgrounds (can be simple) and models. Businesses and nonprofit organizations, such as causes and charities, use shows for fund raising and promotion purposes. You make the contacts, find sponsors, arrange with stores to show their latest styles, and take care of all other details, for which you earn a fee. Figure all costs involved in your service plus value of your time when determining your earnings • Your local daily or weekly newspaper as well as house organs and organizational bulletins may welcome a what's-new-in-fashion column. Suggest it, with sample columns in hand. If you can cull samples of these styles from local stores, it will be a shopper's column and earn advertising revenue for the paper; you'll earn a fee plus commission based on number of advertisers • Be a fashion shopping service for women (or men) who have the money but neither the time nor inclination to shop, or who are geographically removed from fashion sources. You get it all together for them—clothing, accessories, beauty makers. But first, you visit the person, learn her/his needs, size, coloring, personality type, likes and dislikes, clothes and budget, and life style. You go over her/his current wardrobe and make suggestions for improving and/or adding to it. For this, you charge a consultation fee, and either the person shops alone, following your suggestions, or for an additional fee, you may go along to help. You'll need a solid grounding and/or built-in antennae in fashion. You should know all the best sources for a wide variety of clothes and accessories.

A FASHION RELATED BUSINESS (Look around for one for yourself)

JHB Imports is the button-importing company of Jean Howard Barr of Denver, Colorado—"the largest wholesaler of novelty buttons in the United States." It started some years back with a $15 investment and a request by a small shop for some interesting buttons when Mrs. Barr went to Europe. Those she brought back earned her a small commission, and mention of the exchange to other store buyers set the business in motion. Working from the basement of her home, she sent a button brochure to two hundred yarn shops around the country. Today, that brochure is a sixty-eight-page catalog mailed to four thousand accounts, including fabric and department stores, and Jean Barr has an office, twenty-four full-time employees, and a solid five-figure profit annually.

    Still Other Fashion-World Jobs (Most of these are advanced positions in that world, but they all have starting points. Decide which interests you, then head for it via the work-to-learn route) • Sales director • Fashion coordinator • Alteration supervisor • Fashion instructor • TV hostess • Stylist • Woman's representative for a fashion-related company or organization • Fashion reporter • Beauty reporter or editor • Editorial assistant • Creative consultant on women's accounts (can be for a variety of places) • Style consultant • Copy director • Writer • Advertiser representative • Merchandise manager • Personal shopper (in store) • Textile designer • Fashion editor • Fashion researcher • Account executive on a fashion account • Fashion illustrator • Textile artist

FASHION AND ACCESSORY DESIGNING

    To design clothes successfully, you need not be boxed in to an eight-hour schedule working for a manufacturer. Instead, work at home and market your creative output in any number of ways—e.g., custom designing for a private clientele, selling through boutiques and specialty shops, or designing free-lance for manufacturers, pattern houses, or textile companies. (Because of high production costs, manufacturers are more open to freelance buying than ever; it saves them designer overhead.)

    Let's say you get an idea for a fashion item—flash! You want to turn it into reality fast. You can either make up a sample yourself, get a handy friend to do it, or find a professional sample maker. (If you turn it out yourself, you save on costs, of course.) Armed with samples, you can storm fashion stores and boutiques to solicit orders. If your quest is successful and you come home with a sheaf of orders, you'll either need extra hands or a qualified contractor to fill them. Examples of those who've done designing at home successfully are legion. Here are a few to chomp on—and they barely nick the surface.

While planning the menu for a dinner party, Felice Mortner of West Caldwell, New Jersey, decided she needed a gorgeous apron to protect her expensive new hostess outfit while she served. She never gave the party, for the very next day, she and a friend, Rolene Schliff of Woodmere, Long Island, went into the long, dressy apron business. They sketched their designs, found a patternmaker to interpret them, had samples made up, then took them around to better New York specialty stores. They clicked on their first visits.

Marion Moore's New York company, Pampered Pinafores, followed the same road except that she sewed up her own samples. Audrey Gluckin had a penchant for picking up unusual stones and pieces of jewelry for herself and friends when roaming Europe on business trips with her husband. Among those friends was a gentleman in the jewelry business who suggested she try her hand as a designer. Four weeks in Europe on her own, making up samples, plus her fresh approach launched her career. ("Jewelry is a fashion accessory. One should not have a 'forever' attitude about it. Old pieces need reinterpreting in the light of current fashions.") Audrey now designs unique, one-of-a-kind jewels for the finest specialty shops in America.

After a period of making and selling her own children's wear designs freelance, Liliane Emanuel of Cherry Hill, New Jersey, made a deal with a Southern children's dress manufacturer to produce her designs under a boutique label, Cari Couture by Liliane. She and a helper made the samples for this at home, and she also did all the selling and publicity.

Liliane earned a base fee plus sales commission on each style and bonuses for whatever magazine publicity she arranged—all very lucrative. She points out that working on a small-volume basis with one contractor can be very profitable, since keeping quantities small saves the use of high-priced cutters who reduce your profit margin. Such an enterprise can be kept to designing and sample-making only.

Prerequisites for Fashion Designing

•**What You Need Materially** (depending on how you approach your work) • Sketch pad and pencils and/or sewing needs • Fashion publications (consumer and trade) to keep you up-to-the-minute

•**What You Need Personally** • Creative imagination • A sense of style and proportion • A feeling for fabric and an eye for color • The ability to adapt ideas in different ways • A knowledge of how clothes should fit and how to achieve this

•**What You Need Educationally** (Commercial design kits for accessories like tote bags, belts, and precut fashions are a good way to get yourself moving creatively.) Any courses related to clothes-making will boost your overall facility: sewing, cutting, draping, pattern making, finishing, sketching, etc. These are found in public-school adult-education classes, college and university home-economics courses, county extension classes, and other community sources. Bona-fide training for a fashion career runs one or three years in a fashion design school (diploma) or four years in colleges offering a major in fashion design (degree). A job with a working designer or a fine seamstress is a worthy apprenticeship; you can augment it with outside classes. Whatever school you investigate, be sure to check out exactly what facets of fashion it offers. (See Sewing for other suggestions.)

There are always exceptions to the education rules, women who make it without the usual training, thanks to talent, drive, or tricks of fate. Elaine Rosenthal of Scarsdale, New York, came to designing circuitously and unexpectedly. With no art or design background whatsoever, she found herself doing fashion coordination in the sales-promotion department of Associated Merchandising Corporation, an association of large retail stores. Through this, she met the heads of Girltown, Inc., a large children's-wear manufacturer. The styling suggestions she gave them led to an offer of a designing post, which she held for six years on a full-time basis.

After having three children, she returned to Girltown on a three-day-a-week tandem arrangement with another designer. Now, recently widowed, she's returned to full-time work as a design director for one of the largest children's-wear companies in the United States. Her job involves choosing fabrics and colors, teaching and supervising a staff of six young designers and doing some designing herself. This time, she picked her company by what she'd read and heard of them, sent a letter and resumé to the president, and received a call to start work.

Liliane Emanual is another exception to the schooling rules. She made her own clothes from age twelve on up, and a conglomeration of jobs contributed to her home-based design career—selling, modeling for manufacturers, ad-agency work, working as an editorial assistant at GOOD HOUSEKEEPING magazine, as executive secretary to a fashion designer, in public relations, and doing styling for a fashion photographer.

•**How You Get Started** • Learn all you can about the rudiments of dressmaking, sewing, or whichever fashion area interests you via practice and study. Subscribe to fashion publications, watch store merchandise, learn terms for latest and standard fabrics, for styles, cuts, etc. • Carry a pencil and sketch pad at all times; when an idea hits you, put it down fast • Find wholesale or discount sources for quantity purchases of fabrics. Unless you order five hundred yards or more per pattern or color, your best bet is a fabric jobber, since textile giants won't bother with smaller orders • To market your designs you can either (a) make them up yourself, for yourself or others, and build a custom business or (b) sell your ideas on paper to dressmaking establishments, fashion design studios, custom salons in department or specialty shops, pattern companies, and fashion manufacturers. Make colored croquis, simplified fashion-figure drawings that are easy to do (see fashion books in your public library for examples) and attach fabric and trimming swatches to the sketch sheet.

You must use the newest, freshest materials from the stores and the fabric sources in New York City. If you live outside of New York, check sources near you • Visits to your manufacturer-client are essential, because one vis-á-vis conversation can clarify what letters and phone calls often cannot. (Do **not** send your sketches through the mail when soliciting orders; they can be lost, misplaced, or copied, and you'll never realize an ounce of credit or profit for them.) Don't forget to include round-trip transportation costs for work trips when you figure overhead.

Advice • Administrative heads of companies do not necessarily have visual imagination. This is why color and detail of each design must be spelled out in your sketch and/or by you verbally • Avoid having to make garment samples from your sketches as these are expensive—unless, of course, you have the money and the skill to do it yourself • Whomever you work for, do it on a contract basis. That is, whatever terms you agree upon should be written in a letter to the company and sent with a carbon for their signatures • Human nature being funny-odd, often the more money you ask for your work, the more people think you're worth, so don't sell yourself short.

The Mountain Goes to Mohammed Carol Sherman, a New York designer, runs a shop-in-your-own-office service, taking her portfolio of fashion designs, mostly classic separates, and swatch samples to be selected and fitted in the customer's work quarters. A boon to harried career women, the service takes three visits—(a) choosing styles, fabrics, taking figure measurements; (b) trying on; (c) completed garment delivery. A nifty idea, this also can be done with ready-to-wear—a one-visit, show-and-buy basis.

SEWING

Needles and pins, needles and pins, they're how many a career begins. With all kinds of new gadgets and sewing aids constantly cropping up and fabrics becoming more beautiful and practical every year, sewing is more of a creative challenge than ever. What's more, it's kind to the budget, and what you might have spent for nice moderate-priced fashion off a store rack can go into a far lovelier fabric, more expensive details. Being hard-to-fit is another incentive. Is it any wonder that 46 million American women are currently stitching away at home? If you're one of them, why not make it pay off—in profits as well as savings—by sewing for others? And if you can't sew, well, learn now.

What You Need Personally • Good eyesight, with or without glasses • An amiable disposition • Tact and diplomacy (remember, clothing involves a woman's figure, often the core of her sensitivity) • A sense of style and design

What You Need Materially • Work space—cheerful, light, airy, large enough to house your equipment, a try-on area, and working room • Tools—sewing machine to notions. (Suggestions: A good secondhand factory-type machine sews faster, lasts longer.)

What You Need Educationally • Sewing know-how and experience with needle and machine • Ability to work with patterns and a dress form • Ability to drape, cut, figure measurements, alter patterns for individual figures

How You Get Started • Take orders on fashions or home decor items you've made for yourself or others • To improve your technique and learn shortcuts, enroll in classes given by your public-school adult-education program, local "Y", Singer Sewing Machine Company store, county extension home-demonstration department, department store—or take private lessons. Sometimes tailors with large enough shops conduct evening classes on the fine points of tailoring and suit making (you can initiate this by planting the idea). Also a six-month-to-a-year apprenticeship as an alteration or factory hand will give you solid grounding for your future at-home business • Find your best sources for equipment, notions, fabrics • Set up work space with the best lighting possible • Set up a bookkeeping system • Establish your prices, basing them on current ready-to-wear prices and those of your competition (if any). (Word of advice: you can't set prices low and expect to raise them quickly without losing your clientele. Nor can you afford one price for friends and relatives, another for unknowns. Know your worth. Be consistent) • Specialize, e.g., if you live in a young and expanding community where maternity clothes are constantly in demand, fill the demand. Or you could develop a knack for hiding figure flaws with clever sewing—and what an appreciated knack that could be! Some other specialties: • Baby layettes and christening clothes • Tall-girl and small-girl fashions • Using old or unusual fabrics for new high fashions • Children's wear (hand smocking is back and a big custom-work idea) • Remodeling heirloom wedding gowns for today's brides • Making costumes for local theater productions and costume parties • Clothes made to customer specifications or from sketches • Turning last year's style into the smartest thing going • Repair work (for local cleaning, tailoring shops) • Resewing seams, reweaving, darning, hand-hemming, replacing old linings, and replacing zippers and decorative accessories • Tell the world you're in business (see Promotion Hints)

Some Commercial Sewing Jobs How many times have you tried on a dress, suit, slacks, any fashion—and found it wanting in some way? Even if you're a flawless size twelve, most store-bought clothes need a stitch here or there. The fitter, alteration hand, and hand-finisher make perfect fit possible. So important is their work, they often outnumber sales help in a store. One swank emporium we know of has thirty—count 'em—thirty alteration hands and only eight salespeople. **Fitter** She determines alterations needed, fits and pins garments. **Alteration hand** She resews garments by hand or machine according to fitter's markings, then presses each garment. **Hand-finisher** She sews on labels, buttons, decorations, and stitches hems by hand. The least difficult job, this lets you learn the first two by watching the work as it's being done. **Note:** Soft-goods manufacturers use part-time or seasonal help in working and learning jobs: cutter, marker, inspector, sewing-machine operator, hand sewer, finisher, packer, floor woman, etc. If there are any factories near you, inquire.

Other Ways to Earn with Your Sewing Skills

•**Busy Woman's Mending Service** A tiny mound of sewing-to-be-done can become a small mountain before a busy woman finds time to tackle it. If, for a reasonable fee, you offer practical abracadabra to make it disappear, you could be deluged with takers. Figure your charges based on time, overhead, and what the traffic will bear.

•**Sewing Lessons** For all age groups and either gender. If you know knitting and crocheting, teach these, too.

Base your fees on the same factors as the mending service's. And if earning money isn't as vital as earning satisfaction, show less advantaged boys, girls, and their mothers how to make their own clothes so that they can dress better and pay less—on your own or as part of a community project.

•**Table Coverings** The fact that so many people have tables that aren't standard sizes or shapes, plus the need for linens to go with today's casual china, prompted Mary Ann Zimmerman to run up cloths in everything from an unbleached muslin trimmed in lovely old lace to rustic checked ginghams with deep hem ruffles. She's also made up a wildly good-looking variety of place mats. All are part of her custom linen service housed in Bonwit Teller (New York) stores. Incidentally, magazines like WOMAN'S DAY and FAMILY CIRCLE frequently feature ideas such as unusual tablecloths, offering directions for making right there or by mail. These could be the basis for a similar business.

MODELING

You need only follow fashion photography in a moderate way to see that beauty standards are constantly changing. The one requirement that has remained fixed through this continuing evolution is the ability to wear clothes well.

Where the Jobs Are Models are employed in publishing, fashion, advertising, TV, and art in all the major American cities. Not-so-large cities have their share of modeling needs on a proportionately smaller scale.

Kinds of Modeling • Photographic—illustrates fashion to promote the sale of merchandise through magazines, newspapers, catalogs, bill enclosures and other printed materials. Requisites: It's more important to be photogenic than beautiful; for high fashion, you should wear a size eight dress or, at the most, size ten, and stand five feet seven to five feet nine and one half tall in your stocking feet, have long legs and long torso. (More mature figures and good looks play a role in photo modeling, too.) You must be adaptable, responsive to direction, endowed with grace of motion and spirit. Assignments are erratic • **Fashion Show Work** Probably offers the greatest opportunity to the most women, especially on the local scene, doing civic and organizational fashion shows. Good way to get experience, develop poise—enough to move on to paid work for fine stores • **Showroom Modeling** Done for fashion manufacturers. Requirements are more flexible for this and fashion show work than for photographic modeling • A flair for wearing clothes • A well-proportioned, slim figure • Good legs and carriage • Poise • A sense of showmanship • You should also know how to sell, which is not difficult and can be learned on the job. For high-fashion work, models are usually size eight; specialized shows—e.g., junior sizes, less high-style—use other sizes (ten and twelve get the most call). During market showings (at least four times a year, several weeks at a time) manufacturers use freelance models, pay by the hour • **Television Modeling** Many who model for this are also radio or TV actresses. It's done live (on camera), on tape, or on film. If you feel qualified for any of these, apply at your nearest TV stations, contacting their casting directors, or reach them through modeling or TV casting agencies. For further information, get in touch with Screen Actor's Guild, Inc., 551 Fifth Avenue, New York, New York, 10017, and American Federation of Television and Radio Artists (AFTRA), 1350 Avenue of the Americas, New York, New York, 10019.

Other Places Where You Might Model • Conventions • Fund-raising shows • All kinds of special events (show openings, resort events, other) • Fashion clinics in fine stores or fashion-related shows sponsored by cosmetic companies, fabric manufacturers, etc. • Promotional events for local companies and businesses

What You Need Educationally The tricks of the modeling trade are how to dress, wear your hair, and makeup for various types of lighting, how to stand, walk, and pose, and—in the case of spokeswoman-modeling—how to speak well. Many model agencies help with informal training, and many of today's top models learned by doing. You can also learn the how-to's by watching models work or taking a charm school or modeling course. This can teach you the whole works or just the segment you may need (such as a course in eye makeup).

Hours You Work Type of modeling you tackle and number of calls for your services will determine this. So will your clients' needs.

How Much You Earn Photographic models in metropolitan areas make from $25 to $75 an hour; professional show modeling pays from $25 to over $40 an hour. Nonprofessional modeling, such as for church and civic groups, may pay just a few dollars an hour and if the show runs one and a half to two and a half hours (with or without rehearsal) you make make $5 or $10. They might even pay you in merchandise—or not at all if you're new at the game. Chief virtue of this work is the training it gives. Modeling for filmed commercials is paid by the day and no less than union-scale minimum for each commercial. For a network show, video-taped, models are given the prevailing union rate plus residuals on some reruns. Fees for live TV modeling vary according to length of appearance and other factors.

How You Get Started • You do **not** need photos of yourself to do fashion show or store modeling. Such photos are expensive • A fashion coordinator or publicity gal working in your town could judge your modeling potential. So could the heads of model agencies or fashion editors • Read fashion periodicals and columns to keep up with trends in styles, beauty • Watch your newspapers for ads for models or fashion show assistants • Follow social and woman's pages for articles about near-future fashion events; call up those involved and ask about their modeling needs, make an appointment to see them • To learn the ropes, work gratis for local organizations' fashion affairs. For a list of photographers, TV producers, ad agencies, illustrators, and fashion manufacturers using models in New York, Chicago, Detroit, Miami, Los Angeles, and San Francisco, write for the MADISON AVENUE HANDBOOK, c/o Peter Glenn, 17 East 48th Street, New York, New York, 10017 ($7.95). To locate qualified modeling schools, workshops, or courses in your locality, write to Model's Mart, same address.

Beauty Therapy You teach others—disadvantaged teenagers and women, the handicapped, women prisoners, and down-in-the-dumps housewives—how to apply makeup, and all other modeling techniques related to grooming in order to help build self-confidence. Usually volunteered, the experience can lead to consultant work at a salary.

HERE'S A BIG IDEA

Sybil Weinman of Brooklyn, New York, produces fashion shows for women who are too short, too tall, or overweight. (Hooray for Sybil!) As a tall, skinny adolescent, she offset her own gawkiness by developing skill with makeup for herself and becoming a model. She discovered she also had a feeling for color and design. Years later, married and a mother, she met a woman with a handicapped child and decided to give a fashion show for the organization representing that handicap. Now her clients include health and community organizations, foundations and charity groups, as well as commercial firms. A store that caters to large-size women pays a major part of her show expenses along with the client. It's a business idea that adapts nicely to other cities and towns. How about yours?

GROOMING FOR GOOD LOOKS

Lately, some dynamic things have been going on in this world. For one thing, men have moved into the women's sphere. Motivated by the changes in their fashions and hair styles, they're sharing our beauty salons and consultants for care of their skin and locks. For another, the increased interest in health—how to acquire it, enjoy it, keep it—has sprouted some intriguing offshoots. A wide range of cosmetic surgery—face, nose, and eye lifts, breast lifts, and hair transplants—have become almost commonplace. So have hairpieces and wigs for both sexes. Related to most of these changes is the study of at least one facet of cosmetology.

The Licensed Cosmetologist She has a nice choice of skills to pursue and can become any of the following: • Manicurist • Hair stylist • Haircutting expert • Permanent wave technician • Demonstrator • General beauty operator • Hair colorist • Hair and scalp specialist • Wig worker (making, cutting, setting, fitting, cleaning) • Institutional beautician (hospitals, homes, other) • Beauty school owner, director, supervisor, registrar or instructor • Personal hairdresser • Makeup technician (private, television, drama and other performing arts, models, stores, group sessions) • Cruise ship cosmetologist • Hair straightener • **Note:** An easy one to learn for picking up part-time earnings is manicuring. Many schools give separate courses in this.

Where You Work • Private beauty shop • Department store salon • Ocean liner or cruise ship • Hotel • Broadcasting studio • Filming studio • Hospitals and other health facilities

Also, people in the performing arts, and others who appear publicly, use many of these services on a freelance consultation basis—particularly hair styling, makeup, and skin care. (For an interesting inside view of this, read the book OVER 50—SO WHAT! by Hildegarde, the supper-club chanteuse.)

What You Need Personally • Manual dexterity • Ability to get along with customers • A good eye and a sense of form and artistry • Physical stamina • Specifics for your specialty (good color vision for hair colorists; eye-hand coordination and touch discrimination for hair stylists, etc.)

What You Need Materially A license, uniforms, and small equipment—e.g., brushes, combs, etc. (Many states issue special licenses for manicurists who require fewer training hours than general operators.)

What You Need Educationally Anywhere from an eighth to twelfth grade education, depending on your state's requirements, plus the successful completion of a state-approved cosmetology course (to take state exam). In some states, apprenticeship training is accepted in lieu of formal schooling; check yours. Basic courses given in private beauty schools (six months to one year) and run anywhere from $300 to $1,200, depending on length of course—the longer the course, the smaller the cost. Public vocational-school courses (free) run one to three years. Schools must be state-approved and state-licensed. To learn about schools and licensing requirements where you live, contact your state cosmetology board or write to Mr. N.F. Cimaglia, director, National Beauty Career Center, 3839 White Plains Road, Bronx, New York, 10467.

Hours You Work Part-time opportunities are unlimited, especially for peak work hours—Fridays, Saturdays, late afternoons. As a specialist, set your own hours.

How Much You Earn Earnings are based on experience, skill, speed, location of shop, and your ability to build a clientele of your own. You may be paid a salary plus commission, straight salary, or commission plus tips. Working full-time, a beginner can make between $65 and $90 a week, the first-rate hairdresser in a better salon $200 to $250 or more a week. Gauge part-time pay accordingly. Also, look into any possible state rules controlling part-time salaries.

How You Get Started • Find out if your board of education gives adult-education cosmetology courses. If not, send for a list of state-licensed schools (see above) and choose one nearest you • Adjust training time to your home schedule • When it's completed, answer help-wanted ads, and apply to local beauty salons on your own or through your state employment service. (If your school has a placement service, they'll help you, too)

OTHER JOBS IN THE BEAUTY WORLD

Saleswoman Cosmetic companies will train you as a demonstrator-salesperson and pay half your working salary (the store where you work pays the other half). Frequently done part-time, this can lead to other retailing jobs (see Persuasion Pays Off chapter). Even if you live in a small town, if you're an outstandingly good salesperson, cosmetic salesmen will bring your skills to the attention of the home office through their written reports. These are read in depth and can lead to training as a consultant or training supervisor for the cosmetic company.

Writers, Publicity and Promotion Women They tell the world about beauty products and techniques through communications media and special events. **The artist** designs and illustrates package, display, advertising, and other graphic needs for product promotion. **The fashion coordinator** ties current styles and beauty together in one dramatically effective package. **Direct selling** takes you house-to-house selling beauty products not sold in stores (see Persuasion Pays Off chapter).

Make and/or Sell Natural Cosmetics Both Cheryl Lipkins of Jenny's Garden in New York City and Wayne Linney of Nature's Beauty Spot in Wilton, Connecticut, roam the vegetable kingdom with their creams, lotions, and cosmetics. Cheryl, who had a skin problem, has been making up her own products from her grandmother's natural-cosmetics recipes and from others found at the library. Now, no more skin problem, and she's been helping others to beauty the same way. Wayne, who also runs a health-food store with her husband, specializes in chemical-free cosmetics from England and the United States. For some solid help in making cosmetics, Marcia Donnan's book, COSMETICS FROM THE KITCHEN, (Holt, Rinehart and Winston, Inc., 1972).

Teach Makeup Application With an artist's eye, a steady hand, and enough know-how through practice and/or training, you can do this commercially by appointment at home (theirs or yours) or in a department store or community group with their sponsorship. Giving customers guidance has helped Adrien Arpel and Amy Green to build their own cosmetic businesses; it's part of their package. Adrien established hers on this basis when still a teenager. Amy gave lessons ($10 a session) using the customer's own cosmetics in her tiny Beauty Checkers "makeover" department at Henri Bendel in New York, until she was given her own Beauty Checkers line of beauty makers.

Conduct Exercise Classes—for Everyone The public is already so diet, health, and figure conscious, you have a waiting clientele. Lots of help for this in women's magazines, books. An offshoot idea: facial exercises, using Marjorie Craig's book FACE SAVING EXERCISES (Random House, 1970) as your guide.

Do Hair Cutting for Both Sexes Pick up the technique by watching a pro, taking a fast course, and/or practicing on all who dare—neighborhood kids, teenagers, your family. If you're good at it, follow the lead of Jackie Rogers. She may have started it all, by trimming men's locks at the back of her posh Madison Avenue men's boutique in New York.

Make and Sell Your Own Perfumes Essential oils, fixatives, diluents (special perfume solvents) can be found in apothecary shops, large department stores, health stores, and in candle, potpourri, spice and herb shops, and boutiques. Any prescription drugstore carries some essential oils. Beauty-industry trade magazines carry ads for fragrance-oil manufacturers (write to them), and CHEMICAL FORMULARY, a library reference book, lists perfume parts and tells how to put them together. Ask the reference librarian to find other books on this, including a recent one called POT POURRI, INCENSE AND OTHER FRAGRANT CONCOCTIONS, a spiral paperback by Ann Tucker (Workman Publishing Company, 231 East 51st Street, New York, 1972). Kathryn Degraff, who began perfumery for fun, has turned it into a lively and profitable part-time career as a fragrance consultant and lecturer. She offers a pamphlet called MAKE YOUR OWN COLOGNE AND PERFUME which gives formulas and variations of them. Send 50¢ to cover costs to Kathryn Degraff, 117 Waverly Place, New York, New York, 10011. (Coins or bills; no stamps, please.)

ELECTROLYSIS

Looking for a business that's not overcrowded? One that offers a solid opportunity to make good profit? Electrolysis, or the permanent removal of superfluous hair for cosmetic purposes, is a wide-open field. There is a shortage of electrologists almost everywhere except New York City. The work may have particular appeal if you or a family member has had treatments or if you're unable to stand for long periods of time, since this is a sit-down job. Work in your home, for a beauty salon, dermatologist, or electrolysis salon—all by appointment.

What You Need Personally • Good eyes (Threading a needle, with or without glasses, should not be a major challenge) • A steady hand (You need the precision of an Annie Oakley. Put yourself in the client's seat and imagine a wobbly needle heading your way) • Patience and fortitude • The ability to instill confidence (Let's face it, a woman usually approaches this kind of treatment with mixed emotions—anxiety, hope, and perhaps a measure of embarrassment) • Neatness (both you and your surroundings must have a scrubbed, professional look)

What You Need Materially • In many cases, a license. (Currently, seventeen states require formal training and state certification to practice. Check with yours) • A market for your work (even though the field's wide open, there must be enough people in your locality who want and can afford treatment if you're to make a go of it. Although large cities provide a greater market, living in a small town doesn't rule you out. A woman electrologist living in a tiny Virginia town does a land-office business, drawing her clientele from a large surrounding area with small but frequent newspaper ads and mailing pieces) • Personal contacts • For a private, at-home practice, you need a room to convert into an office, a short-wave machine, chair and footstool or a professional table, stool, and a lamp (total cost: between $750 and $1,000). To work for a salon or doctor, you should have a private corner to practice. You'll probably supply your own equipment.

What You Need Educationally Training in an accredited electrolysis school—anywhere from ninety to two thousand hours of instruction and study, depending on state regulations. Major schools charge about three hundred dollars, which can be paid in small weekly installments. There's no extra charge for prolonged learning time, since most schools want you to be as proficient as possible before you go out on your own. These schools are in New York, Chicago, and Detroit, so an out-of-town student will need travel and living expenses. Your school may be able to save you money on hotel reservations. (The Hoffman Electrolysis Institute in New York, for example, has a hard-to-beat, $7-a-day arrangement with a nearby hotel.)

How Much You Earn Work for a beauty or electrolysis salon, and they receive a percentage or commission from your earnings, but many department stores pay a salary plus eventual commission. Dermatologists may use either of these systems. Your home-office earnings will vary daily and weekly and, depending on your skills and number of clients, profits can reach $300 a week or slide along at $30. Client fees avarage $5 for fifteen minutes, $10 for one half hour, and $20 per hour.

How You Get Started • Learn how many electrologists are already operating in your community by calling the chamber of commerce • Find out if local zoning laws permit a home office where you live (city clerk) • For schools, see your classified pages in the telephone book or write to Electrolysis Society of America, Inc., 701 Seventh Avenue, New York, New York, 10036, and ask specifically about those near you • Once trained, make appointments with beauty and electrolysis salons in your area. Ask if they can use your services. Or look into buying an established practice before attempting to start your own. This way, you take over an existing clientele and equipment, saving money on the latter • Check your insurance company to learn about coverage for fire, theft, liability, and professional insurance for a home office • Install a business telephone, if needed. Like your other expenses, it will be income-tax deductible • Join the Electrolysis Society of America, Inc. You'll receive its newsletter, which includes valuable reports on the field and acts as an idea clearing house. Once established, promote your business. Your school will probably supply free counseling on business locations, equipment, advertising and free placement and referral services (many prospective clients and doctors contact schools for recommendations).

8

There's Always Plenty to Do with Kids Around

The problems of childhood in the United States surround us. As a volunteer or paid worker, you can help to unravel (or prevent) such depressing snarls. There's scarcely a city, town, or village in America that doesn't offer opportunities to serve in at least one of the following group situations.

WHERE YOU CAN WORK WITH CHILDREN— PRESCHOOL THROUGH TEEN YEARS

• Head Start • Community-action groups • Foster grandparents (see Let's Get Down to Basics chapter) • Homes for children with handicaps (all kinds) • Family service agencies • Day camps (community, private) • Juvenile shelters for homeless and abandoned children • Drug rehabilitation centers • Hot-line offices of community groups • Havens for runaways • Adoption and foster-care agencies • Hospital pediatric wards • PAL (Police Athletic League) • Job Corps • Y groups • County youth commission groups • Public and private schools • Volunteer service bureaus • City playgrounds and other recreational groups • Service clubs • Community youth councils • Children's Aid branches • Any major youth organization chapters: Scouts, Explorers, Camp Fire Girls, 4-H, Junior Red Cross, Girls Clubs, and Boys Clubs, etc. Or work in a field that brings you into frequent contact with children; e.g., children's parties, art tours, nature classes, crafts and many others covered in this book (see Index).

Youth Service Bureaus It is estimated that one out of every six boys will be referred to juvenile court for delinquency before he's eighteen; in some areas, one out of every four. Many need personal help now, before their behavior grows to serious proportions. Work as a volunteer with the youth service bureau in your town. To locate it, call city hall or write to National Council on Crime and Delinquency, 411 Hackensack Avenue, Hackensack, New Jersey, 07601.

Foster Grandparents Program   If you're over sixty, are physically able to serve, and have a low income, you can work with children in a broad variety of situations for about twenty hours a week and be paid for it. You'll be given orientation and in-service training. (More on F.G.P. in Let's Get Down to Basics chapter.) Or work as part of the School Volunteer Program in your community; write to director, Volunteers in Education, NCIES, U.S. Office of Education, Washington, D.C., 20202.

HOME-BASED NURSERY SCHOOL

It follows that you can't work directly with small children unless—most of the time, anyway—you find them fascinating and not a little enchanting. Add to this an interest in sharing some talent or skill such as working with your hands, and you have two good reasons for opening a nursery school. With more and more mothers holding jobs, and national child-care solutions still far off, a good nursery school usually helps to fill a community need.

What You Need Personally   Besides love for children, a desire to contribute positively to their growth • Patience • Emotional stability • A sense of humor • Perception and awareness • Good health • Any form of creativity

What You Need Materially   • Enough dry, clean space indoors and out • Toilet and washing facilities (at least one set for every fifteen children) • Child-size tables, benches, or chairs • Adequate lighting (your local power company can guide you) • A health-department certificate for your facilities, including kitchen if hot lunches are served • Fire department approval • State and/or city license, if mandatory • Ample insurance coverage, all kinds • If you provide transportation, vehicle must be in excellent running condition, have inspection okay, special car registration of your area, and safety features • Qualified assistants who know how to deal intelligently with small fry • At least one other besides yourself to cover emergencies • Enough capital to start your school (ingenuity can save you much cash outlay) • Enough equipment for indoor/outdoor play, quiet/active periods • Record-keeping materials (file box, cards, ledgers, etc.)

There are numerous ways to cut cost corners. Margaret Rusch of Mount Vernon, New York, runs her home-based nursery school with great ingenuity and imagination. The following suggestions are hers, tried and true: • A good handyman (your husband?) can make up tables, benches, easels, outdoor play pieces, etc. • Secondhand sources yield rich and needed treasures for a song • Natural and obvious things are often as good as, if not better than, something new and expensive. Give a child the average bought toy, and it's liable to be broken or discarded in no time flat. Give an everyday object, and his/her hands and imagination will keep busy for a long time. This is called the "clothespin theory," and it's been proven over and over again • Nail kegs are great for sitting or rolling on outdoors. Tree stumps are useful as a flat surface or for climbing. Shirt cardboards have myriad uses. Bird feathers, leaves, and wood shavings are great for collage. So are all kinds of samples. Ask local upholstery, wallpaper, and fabric stores to save you their old swatch books, and printers their colored paper. Corrugated paper can be used to build, paint, cut, you name it. Your local newspaper office has large scraps of blank paper ideal for finger and brush painting. Small tree branches and twigs make fine mobiles. These can be hung with pine cones, chestnuts, colored cotton balls, colored foil wrapping discards, painted thread spools, just about anything hangable. Try wallpaper paste; it's far cheaper than the regular. But make sure it's nontoxic.

What You Need Educationally Varies from state to state, city to city. You, or at least one of your helpers, should have training in early childhood education. Even if you've had it, it's wise to take some courses in child development.

Hours You Work Your available time and the needs of your clientele will set them. You may start with a morning group and eventually have an afternoon class, as well.

How Much You Earn Government booklets on setting up a nursery school caution against going into this work **purely** for profit. Don't expect to come out ahead the first year or two, anyway; you'll probably put your earnings into improvements. Your actual profit will depend on the number of children and assistants, and the amount you charge and what you pay your help, as well as other overhead.

How You Get Started • Inquire about the need for a nursery school in your area by asking your health and welfare departments, church groups, superintendent of public schools, county superintendent of education, PTA, and cham-

ber of commerce • Decide how many children you'll enroll •
Check local and state authorities on regulations • Apply for a
state license through your state department of education • For
equipment that can't be improvised, must be commercial, ask
your board of education about sources • Take out needed
insurance • Arrange for transportation. If you're going to supply
this, follow rules on registry, inspection, and insurance • Hire
good help (figure one teacher per eight 3-year-olds or one
teacher per ten 4-year-olds) • Read up on nursery-school work
and early childhood in your public library. And if you've had
no preliminary-education courses, take some.

BABY SITTING (also, sitting for the elderly, ill, and handicapped; for pets, houseplants, etc.)

This is such a vital business these days, courses are
given in many communities, and booklets are published as
guides. Even a veteran mother can learn, so if these are
accessible to you, take advantage of them. They usually teach
safety measures, emergency treatments for all kinds of crises,
from croup to electric shock, mouth-to-mouth resuscitation,
and how to plan a fast escape in case of fire. What you learn can
be used for people and pet sitting, as well.

Advantages of Sitting Work • You decide when
you can work • You're paid after each sitting • If you work for
a registry, it makes your business arrangements—fees, transportation, hours—and defines your status • You can be selective,
and are not compelled to return to any place • Transportation
and meals are usually provided and/or paid for • If you work for
a registry, you can work up Social Security benefits •
Sociability—you meet new people

What You Need Personally • A liking for people •
Good character and a sense of responsibility • Mental and
physical health • Alertness • Cleanliness • Ability and willingness
to perform simple chores—e.g., preparing easy meals, bathing
children

What You Need Materially • A telephone, if
possible • At least three personal references

How Much You Earn There are geographical
variations (Currently,* East Coast suburban sitters are earning
$1.25-$1.50 an hour.) Learn the going rate in your town from
other sitters and from sitter services.

*1973

How You Get Started • Learn—via a course, booklets, if you can • Arrange for your references • Call local registries for interviews, answer want ads for sitters or run an ad of your own. Tell everyone you're available for sitting. Your state employment office also may handle sitting jobs—check.

On-the-Job Pointers • Wear simple, appropriate clothing • Understand what's expected of you, including hours likely on the job, whether you'll be driven home or cabbed • Get the telephone number of the parents' whereabouts, or that of a substitute family authority for emergency use. (This applies to adult charges, as well.) Local police and fire-department phone numbers also should be handy • Find out how much and which TV programs children can watch, when to bed them down, and any other expectations • For the ailing or elderly, get exact written instructions on medication, activities, meals, etc. Metropolitan Life Insurance Company puts out guidelines for the new sitter—a booklet called SITTING SAFELY. Ask for a copy at any of their offices or write to Metropolitan Life Insurance Company, Publications Department, 1 Madison Avenue, New York, New York, 10010.

RUNNING A SITTING SERVICE

Although babysitting is the blanket term and basic business of most registries, they often supply sitters for invalids, convalescents, elderly folks, blind people, houses, and animals (including feeding and walking). They may also supply chaperones, part-time mothers, companions, women who sit with hospital patients not ill enough to require a nurse (check your hospital on this—some cities don't permit it), and perhaps one or two practical nurses for emergency calls. In cities with a population of 30,000 or over, there's a definite need for a sitter service and plenty of room for expansion of its functions in new and imaginative ways.

What You Need Personally • A liking for and ability to get along with people • A reputation as a responsible person • Patience (an incessantly ringing telephone and the demands of clients can bring you joy or jangled nerves) • A sense of humor and pleasant telephone personality • A level head to cope with emergencies and demands • Sound judgment in evaluating people (your repeat business will depend on the caliber of women working for you)

What You Need Materially • A private phone, a package of file cards, and a few printed brochures to start you off • Also, depending on your city and state rules, money to pay for a license, registration, and bonding, and classified ads for sitters. You also should line up the services of a lawyer, a printer, and an accountant.

Hours You Work You can dovetail home chores and job. Ceil Grodner of Mount Vernon, New York, is the mother of five children, four born after she started her service. Each time she went to the hospital on maternity "leave," she took her work along. Home again, she expertly juggled feeding bottles and telephone. Babies and business both thrived.

How You Get Started • Find out whether or not your town has a registry, if there's room for yours and enough women are available to be sitters • See your town clerk about licensing • Check with your insurance company about liability coverage • Line up a lawyer to help you establish your business as a corporation, individual owner, partnership, or whichever, and clarify other legal aspects of your business • Choose a short, simple name for your business or use your own. (Check with your county clerk to make certain your choice is not already registered by someone else) • Make up a brochure listing rules and regulations for parents and sitters, and rates • Buy your office needs • Tack up a map of your city near the phone for giving travel directions (usually one's available from the local newspaper or your chamber of commerce) • Set your fees. Decide whether you'll charge sitter or client or both. Some agencies charge clients a flat monthly rate, others so much for so many sittings, taking nothing from sitters. Or the sitter pays the registry a small amount monthly. Methods vary; decide what's best for you. Like everything else, sitter fees keep going up. Best to learn current rates from mothers and other services before you start • Decide how much more to charge for extra chores perfomed by sitters over and above the call of duty • Interview and screen sitter applicants for health (mental and physical—they should have had recent exams including lung X-rays), attitudes toward people and children, and other attributes listed under Baby Sitting • Solicit the help of everyone you know in finding sitters and subscribers. Word of mouth may be all you need as a starting shove toward success. (See Promotion Hints)

VARIATION ON THE BABY REGISTRY THEME

Dating services match up men and women—why not match up mothers of young children so they can exchange babysitting chores and save high city sitter rates, reasoned

Bernice Lask of New York. So she placed a small ad in THE VILLAGE VOICE newspaper with her telephone number. Response proved she had a good idea. Today, she has a file large enough to match mothers in all five boroughs. Bernice interviews each mother at length on the phone, then sends out a questionnaire and application. Registration fee is $8, and each mother is given several names to call. Thus, these women have made new friends and are able to work out their own arrangements, even to overnight care.

YOUTH ON THE MOVE

What's there to see? And where? Those questions have launched any number of fascinating enterprises dealing with children and a world to explore. Getting out and rubbernecking (tours, hikes, picnics, field trips) come in all subjects—art, ecology, history, crafts, jobs, on and on—so light on one, or make a potpourri of many.

Big City Sightseeing Seena Hamilton's experience in travel editing led to her sightseeing service for children visiting New York with their families. From June to September, her Gulliver's Trails takes children aged six to seventeen to the city's points of interest. (If your hometown is in a recreational or special-interest area, you can do this on a smaller basis.) As an offshoot of this, Seena is called on to help community and school groups all around the United States to organize educational and recreational tours. Along with this service, she is a tour consultant for corporations in the travel industry. (Seena also founded and runs the largest indoor junior tennis tournament in the country, with kids from every state participating.)

Weekend Ski Trips These can corral a dozen young people per trip and net you some nice profit each week while the snow lasts. Suggestion: Charge so much per child over your costs, or figure the overhead (transportation, room, board, necessary extras), then allow as much for your profit.

Industrial Tours In all fifty states, manufacturers offer tours of their plants that are fun, educational, and usually free. Write to your state's department of commerce for guidance on these.

Farm/City Trips Children from farm areas lap up the mind-boggling activities in the big city, and the kid from the metropolis delights in the natural wonders of the farm world. Many of the latter have never seen real farm animals. This last explains the success of commercial farm ventures that open their gates to visiting youngsters for a day, or board children (and sometimes parents) for a weekend or longer. If you live on a farm, this is an idea for you. It's an educational service with earning potential, teaching children how animals are born, fed, and cared for, and how farms produce the food we eat. Visit one already operating commercially before you set up your own. FARM AND RANCH VACATION GUIDE, a publication (36 East 57th Street, New York, New York, 10022), lists farms and ranches by state, what they offer, and personal data about the owners.

Know-Your-Town Tours Science centers, historical landmarks, museums, factories, police and fire stations, city court, unusual stores, and countless other spots fascinate and teach kids. Ray Shaw, a sculptress, took her daughters to off-beat spots like fortune-cookie and ballet-slipper factories, a Japanese temple stone garden, a clown school, an ice factory, the Staten Island ferry engine room, and other fun-to-see spots. Now she's put it all in a paperback book for other parents, NEW YORK FOR CHILDREN, (Outerbridge & Lazard, 1972). Dig up your own intriguing spots, set up appointments with each, and glean as much information as you can beforehand so you can tell kids about them. Charge enough over your costs (food, transportation, extras) to give you a pat little profit.

Mobile Classrooms See-the-world situations need not follow conventional patterns. Stephanie and Charles Gallagher run a successful floating high school aboard a Norwegian square rigger. The coed students, anywhere from fifty-five to seventy of them, are the ship's crew. Math courses are geared to navigation while language, history, and social studies are tied to ports of call and field trips ashore. Called Oceanics, the idea came out of their observation that their own children's attitudes toward study improved markedly when taken on long trips.

Now the Gallaghers are planning a train school to travel all over Europe.

The Trailside Country School based in Killington, Vermont, and run by Mike and Diana Cohen, is an eleven-month school that travels some seven thousand miles in one year to observe and study at points such as the Virgin Islands, Canadian Rockies, Maine, the Smokey, Green, and White Mountains, California, and various New England spots. As with Oceanics, each locale is a classroom for history and life sciences. Snorkeling, back-packing, and skiing may be part of it all, but the students also study hard. To date twenty-nine colleges have been happy to accept Trailside training as background for further education.

SCHOOL CROSSING GUARD

If you're a hardy soul undaunted by wind and weather, this is pleasant part-time work—usually under the aegis of the police department. Inquire.

SCHOOL WORK

Although the teaching field has become crowded and general teaching jobs scarce in the past few years (general elementary education, language arts, English, social studies, fine arts) the following are among those categories offering good and/or growing opportunities:

Public School Work

•**Special Education** Projected need: 245,000 additional teachers, elementary and secondary levels, 60,000 at pre-school level. Write to NCICE (National Center for Information on Careers in Education), 1607 New Hampshire Avenue, N.W., Washington, D.C., 20009, and State-Federal Information Clearinghouse for Exceptional Children (CEC), 1411 South Jefferson Davis Highway, Arlington, Virginia, 22202.

•**Vocational-Technical Education** Thirty-one states report needs. Write to NCICE (address above) for pamphlet, CAREERS IN VOCATIONAL-TECHNICAL EDUCATION.

•**Reading specialist** Many more openings expected in next two or three years. Write to National Reading Council, 1776 Massachusetts Avenue, N.W., Washington, D.C., 20036, and to NCICE.

•**Counselor** Eighteen states indicated staffing needs at elementary level in spring 1972. Write to NCICE for pamphlet, CAREERS IN PUPIL PERSONNEL SERVICES.

•**Environmental Education** Growing field. For training information, write to Office of Environmental Education, U.S. Office of Education, Washington, D.C., 20202. Environmental Protection Agency, 401 M Street, S.W., Washington, D.C., 20024, and School of Natural Resources, University of Michigan, Ann Arbor, Michigan, 48106. Attention, William Stapp.

Outside Education

•**Bilingual education.** Eighteen states reported needs, particularly Spanish; big cities. Write to NCICE (address above) and teacher-corps recruitment and referral centers at your nearest universities.

Nonpublic School Jobs

•**Early Childhood Education** Needs in twenty-eight states. Under the Child Development Associate Consortium system, credentials will be based upon an individual's demonstrated ability to assume primary responsibility for the education and development of a group of young children rather than on acquiring professional standing through the usual formal educational process. This is a pilot program being offered at ten to fifteen colleges, length of training based on varying factors. Write for information to the Child Development Associate Consortium, Inc., 7315 Wisconsin Avenue, Bethesda, Md., 20014.

•**Adult Education** Expanding field (69 million Americans, age sixteen and over, have less than a high-school education). Many part-time jobs. Write Adult Education Association of the U.S.A., 810 18th Street, N.W., Washington, D.C., 20006, and the American Society for Training and Development, 6414 Odana Road, Madison, Wisconsin, 53719 (information on teaching jobs in business, industry).

Community colleges (two-year). New job-finding service offered by the AAJC (American Association of Community & Junior Colleges). Most require master's degree. Contact their Career Staffing Center, 621 Duke Street, Box 298, Alexandria, Virginia, 22314.

•**Correctional Institutions** Write Anthony Del Popolo, director, Correction Education Association, 1611 8th Place, McLean, Virginia, 22101.

Free Schools (alternative to public schools). Write for information: Teacher Drop-Out Center, Box 521, Amherst, Massachusetts, 01002.

•**Work-Study Teacher Training Programs** In ghetto and poor rural districts. Designed to reach and help youngsters in trouble with the law. Contact Fordham University, Bronx, New York, and ask about their program and others like it.

•**School Administration** Preschool through college.

Educational Research Development

•**Teaching** in "shortage" (few teachers available) **subjects** (math, physical sciences, consumer education, and as mentioned, environmental science).

If you have a college education behind you, want to teach, need information on full-or part-time teaching, additional training needed, financial aid available for this, certification, job placement, and salaries, write to your state education department and inquire about approved training programs in your locality. Also, write to the NCICE (National Center for Information on Careers in Education, part of the American Personnel and Guidance Association), at the address given under Public School Work.

To learn whether teaching is for you, work as an aide or assistant in a teaching situation or as a volunteer in any set-up with children. (See beginning of this chapter.)

DAY CARE

As a subject, it's the federal football of education, considered by some to be the nation's number one domestic problem. Day care takes three forms: traditional nursery schools, community child- or day-care centers, and individual homes. Add to this the large franchise child-care operations springing up around the country designed to meet the middle-class working mother's needs, since they charge anywhere from $17 to $50 a week. They offer teaching jobs to women trained in education and paraprofessional or aide work to those who are not.

To take children into your home on a day-care basis and receive reimbursement for this, apply to your city or county welfare department to learn requirements, rate of pay, and license needed. For insight into the day-care problem in the United States, read WINDOWS ON DAY CARE, by Mary Dublin Keyserling, a report on the findings of members of the National Council of Jewish Women (1 West 47th Street, New York, New York, 10036) on day-care needs and services in their communities.

If you're interested in helping to set up a day-care center in your community, write to Joseph H. Reid, Child Welfare League of America, Inc., 67 Irving Place, New York, New York, 10003, Day Care and Child Development Council of America, Inc., 1401 K Street, N.W., Washington, D.C., 20005, National Association for the Education of Young Children, 1834 Connecticut Ave., N.W., Washington, D.C., 20009, and to the Office of Child Development, Children's Bureau and the Bureaus of Headstart and Early Childhood, both under the aegis of the U.S. Department of Health, Education and Welfare, Washington, D.C., 20201.

9

Library Work
Can Be Dynamic

If you think of a library as invariably hush-hush—and librarians as society's plain-Janes hiding behind the book stacks—think again. Today's library can be a really swinging place with a setting as informal as a storefront gathering place, and its keepers (or librarians) a jumping crew who are often as not deeply involved in community activities through their work.

Until recently, there was an acute shortage of librarians. This has leveled off considerably, particularly in the big cities and in college and university libraries. There, competition is keen, and it's easier to find jobs in public and school libraries, easiest if you're willing to work in a suburban system, a small town, or in the rural South, where the starting salary is lower but the opportunity to accomplish something is big. And there are other kinds of libraries to consider, as well.

Types of libraries You know about public, school, college and university libraries. Add these: hospital, prison, geriatric center, Vista and Peace Corps, government-agency libraries, commerce, and industry, plus all the special-interest libraries covered in this chapter.

What A Librarian Does You might do any, many, or all of these, depending on the size and location of the library, and size of staff: • Plan and set up exhibits • Conduct story hours and book talks • Set up adult-education programs • Arrange interesting discussion groups and film series • Speak at meetings, library and to community groups • Write for publications • You may also be responsible for many kinds of graphic records—documents, manuscripts, phonograph records, pictures, films, film strips, tapes, teaching machines, etc. And if you're a minor travel fiend, you might work on a suburban or rural bookmobile.

That's not all. Today's librarian works with community organizations like Head Start, drug rehabilitation centers, day-care groups, and talks to teenagers in the public schools to stimulate interest in reading. So you're liable to stage an outdoor puppet show, run a knitting program, teach origami and mobile making, pass out paperbacks at public pools, set up musicales and poetry readings, rock concerts, and reading therapy workshops. You may also choose to concentrate on work such as cataloging, ordering books and records, etc., reference, bibliography, administration, budget and planning, bindery and printing for preservation of old books and manuscripts, and microfilming, or act as a media specialist or special consultant.

What You Need Personally • A liking for people and desire to be involved with them (a good librarian is a fellow human being, friend, teacher, fellow student, and co-worker) • Brains and an insatiable curiosity. (You should find knowledge and the printed word irresistible lures—even the smell of books should appeal to you.)

What You Need Educationally A college degree plus the equivalent of a year of graduate library school (usually two semesters plus a summer session). Admission requirements vary slightly, so check school catalogs. Also, look into library-school training at nearby continuing-education centers. Or become a library trainee, working and taking courses simultaneously under a civil-service arrangement. And if your home responsibilities won't permit these, go to library school at night (a longer training period).

Tuition fees for the full course in graduate library education range from about $1,000 to $3,000, depending on whether the school is a state or private institution. Financial aid for full-time and work-study students covers all or most of tuition costs for qualified candidates. Sources for help are listed in a special free booklet. FINANCIAL ASSISTANCE FOR LIBRARY EDUCATION, available from the American Library Association, 50 Huron Street, Chicago, Illinois, 60611.

How Much You Earn Starting full-time annual salary averages about $8,850 with a range of $7,365 to $10,585, depending on variables (library location, size, etc.). With any kind of previous working experience, you're likely to earn considerably more.

How You Get Started • Talk to librarians about the field • Evaluate your abilities in relation to it; determine the advantages of any previous work experience to library work and decide what type of librarian you wish to become • Write to the

American Library Association for information and their financial-help booklet (address above). Then, to test out your interest before you dive into training, you might take a job as a library clerk or assistant or work as a volunteer there. (Reference: AMERICAN LIBRARY DIRECTORY published by R.R. Bowker. It lists federal, state, education, and special-collection libraries, with names of librarians and other data.)

SPECIAL LIBRARIANS

Combines education in a specific field with education in librarianship. Instead of working in a public or school library on a general basis, you work in your specialized area of interest, wherever this unique information is needed. Some special-interest categories having their own libraries and librarians: • Advertising and marketing • Astronomy • Accounting • Agriculture • Aerospace • Art and architecture • Botany • Biological sciences • Building and housing • Business and finance • Chemistry • Communications • Cosmetics • Drugs • Documentation • Engineering • Foods • Geography and maps • Government services • Health sciences • Hospitals • Humanities • Forestry • Insurance • Industrial relations • International relations • Languages • Mathematics • Metals/Materials • Military • Museums • Music • National resources • Newspapers • Nuclear science • Paper and textiles • Petroleum • Philanthropy • Pharmaceuticals • Physical sciences • Pictures • Public relations • Public utilities • Publishing • Recreation • Science information • Social sciences • Statistics • Theatrical arts • Theology and religion • Transportation • Urban problems

Although your work is of the same professional caliber as all competent librarians, there are these significant differences:

1. Because of subject training in the field of your work, you're likely to be much closer to the needs and problems of the people you serve. Since you're liable to work with a small clientele whom you know well, you'll feel free to volunteer information and not wait to be asked—that is, your role will be more active than passive.

2. Because you'll most likely work in a small library not hemmed in by traditions and external regulations, you'll be able to try new ideas. (Much of the work with electronic equipment and computers in the field of information storage and retrieval is being done in special libraries.)

3. Because special libraries in industry and government are open during the same hours as the parent organization, you'll most likely work a regular thirty-five to forty-hour work

week and receive the same fringe benefits as other employees.

4. And because, as a specialist, you're liable to work where salary policies are liberal, you can expect to earn more than a public or school librarian.

What You Need Educationally Same training and costs as regular librarianship. Be sure the library school you choose offers the courses you need to become a special librarian. For information about financial aid, write to Special Libraries Association, 235 Park Avenue South, New York, New York, 10003.

How Much You Earn Initially, same as a top-of-the-range beginning salary for regular librarians. Graduates with science technology backgrounds can command higher salaries. Many special librarians are paid comparably with other professional employees in their organizations. Starting salaries (master of library science) with no experience, have been at $9,000 and above in recent years, and directors of major library and information systems can, and do, earn $18,000 to $20,000 and above.

How You Get Started In much the same way as a regular librarian. Decide on your special interest. If you already have a B.A. but need further training in your chosen field as well as library school, be certain that the school you choose gives the essential courses. If possible, discuss this with a special librarian who works in your subject interest. For more information, write to Special Libraries Association (address above). Your library school will help to place you in a job.

LIBRARY TECHNICIAN

This is a relatively new library post, created to offset the shortage of library help and free the professional librarian for work that uses her more intensive training. The technician's job concentrates more on doing than conceptualizing—ordering, preparing, maintaining (cataloging, giving information, making up lists, making and keeping files, etc.). You need a high-school diploma and two additional years of training in one of about sixty library technician schools that are part of two-year community colleges and four-year colleges and universities around the United States. To learn what starting salaries are in your locality, call your own public library or your county library association, or write to either of the major library associations (addresses in this chapter or Index).

10

Go Back to Nature

Green thumb or no green thumb, there is something eminently soul-satisfying about nurturing growing things, whether your garden is a flower pot on an apartment-house fire escape or the lush expanse of a country estate. And today, the intense interest in our total environment has inspired fresh ways to work with them.

PLANT SIT
This can go considerably beyond watering-sunning-feeding into plant doctoring and nurturing. To become more savvy about your subject, read; get a job (paid or volunteer) to learn—with a greenhouse, florist, or in any related situation. The New York Botanical Garden has a hot-line telephone set up to provide answers to all kinds of plant problems. They'll do the same for you by letter or in person. The botanical garden, county agricultural agent, or state horticultural society in your area may offer similar help; check it out. Many such organizations offer classes in facets of horticulture. Sign up.

RENT AND SERVICE PLANTS
It's a thriving business in various parts of the country. In fact, a pre-teenager in Dallas, Texas, is doing a land-office business raising and renting plants for homes and offices. You can do the same, and include public-building foyers, waiting rooms, working quarters on your client list. You can do this on a modest house-to-house and office-to-office basis, and if feasible, provide care and maintenance, as well (watering, fertilizing, debugging, pruning, keeping the soil chemically balanced, etc.).

One big-city greenery service bills clients $3 a month for any plant costing them from $5 to $30, $10 a month for those bought for $75 to $135. Your costs and your fees may be more modest, but be sure to cover all your overhead plus value of your time.

You'll need space, basic equipment, and, of course, enough plants to start. Space might be a sunroom, pantry, any sunny place, or a greenhouse. Today, the latter come in all sizes and shapes—indoor plantariums resembling large fish tanks, window greenhouses holding several dozen small plants, larger lean-tos that attach to a house, on up in size. Write for catalogs to Lord & Burnham Division, Burnham Corporation, Irvington, New York, 10533. Aluminum Greenhouses, Inc., 14615 Lorain Avenue, Cleveland, Ohio, 44111, J. A. Nearing Co., Inc., 10788 Tucker Street, Beltsville, Maryland, 10705. UNDER GLASS is a bi-monthly magazine for greenhouse growers published by Under Glass, Box 114, Irvington, New York, 10533 (subscription, $2 a year).

CREATE FLORAL ARRANGEMENTS

Work as a freelance floral designer making centerpieces and decorations for all types of social affairs, holidays, business shows, and the like. (See The Social Life: Get It All Together chapter.) This takes an eye for color and design, sources for flowers (wholesalers), ribbon, wire, wrapping materials, and interesting containers and accessories (attics, thrift shops, white elephant sales and other secondhand outlets yield treasures—so does the local 5 & 10).

Or try Anita Goodman's idea. She cased her town, singled out an attractive flower shop in need of an inventive touch, and offered her service at no charge to make appealing, unusual floral arrangements for Mother's Day business. Each new arrangement she made was snapped up by waiting customers, and at the close of a busy holiday, the store insisted on paying her and made a standing arrangement for her help on all other special occasions. This training, plus learning all about customers' needs and tastes, has stood her in good stead in her present business (see Index).

PLANT BOUTIQUES—A NEW KIND OF SHOP

A fresh way to market plants, these are flourishing on the West Coast, with twenty of them cropping up around Los Angeles in one eighteen-month period, raking in a total of $1.3 million. They have catchy names, and tricky environmental settings, and one (here's another workable idea) offers classes in plant care and plant psychology (yes, you read that correctly) at $25 for five 1½-hour classes, and also publishes a weekly newsletter for and about customers and their plants.

RAISE AND SELL HERBS

According to Virginia Colby of Amityville, New York, this is "the easiest kind of outdoor garden to grow because it's almost pest-free, repels most animals, doesn't get many weeds and doesn't need much watering. It does need a lot of sun, though." Mrs. Colby started in a very modest way with some cuttings of mint and a few culinary herbs. Now, sixteen years later, she's crammed seventy different herbs into her small garden.

A good way to try your hand at herb growing: buy an indoor herb kit or two (posts and seeds). These are sold in many stores today. Or plant in a window box or a tiny patch of garden. Raise enough to sell fresh to gourmet cooks, through grocery stores, women's clubs, bazaars, other outlets. Also, you can dry them and package to sell under your own label. (See food chapter for marketing suggestions.) Another thought, done successfully for generations: make and sell potpourris—dried flowers, spices, and herbs in sachets, and dry perfumes. Help awaits in library books. And Jean Hersey's article in WOMAN'S DAY magazine (January, 1973) "Herbs in the House," will inspire and help you. Ask for it in your public library's magazine or reference room.

TEACH AND LECTURE

Pick your subject from the whole range of greenery and growing techniques. Or you might try informal backyard teaching sessions on basic gardening. The lecture platform is another way to share knowledge. (See Communication via Media and Muse chapter.) Virginia Colby lectures on her herbs to garden and women's clubs, historical societies, department-store groups. Do the same on flower arranging, organic farming, and foods—you choose.

ORGANIC FOODS

More and more Americans are into this. You might raise all kinds of edible sprouts in your home to sell to natural-foods enthusiasts. Or organic vegetables, if you have hand space. On a farm you can do this in earnest, with eggs, fruits, dairy products, by-products such as homemade jams, preserves, honey. Health-food counters have even hit the supermarkets, and outlet possibilities are good. For help, write to Robert A. Crompton, ORGANIC FAMILY FARMING (newsletter), 33 East Minor Street, Emmaus, Pennsylvania, 18049, and to ORGANIC GARDENING CLUB NEWSLETTER (monthly), same address. The NEWSLETTER lists names and addresses of organic-gardening groups around the United States and will send a free community-garden kit to organic-garden clubs who send in a self-addressed, stamped envelope.

RENT-A-GARDEN

Have any land you can spare? Rent it. A Washington, D.C., landlord and his tenant discovered a mutual interest in organic gardening and wanted to help those with a like interest but no growing plot. Result, this ad: "Loudoun County cattle farm has organic gardening plots for rent; 50 x 50 plot, $15/season." It listed a phone number. Place **your** ad in early spring.

RAISE AND SELL A SPECIALTY

Orchids, mushrooms, African violets, or whatever appeals to you can be sold directly to individuals or through appropriate outlets. Every specialty has a national or state organization of its own. Learn about them at greenhouses, botanical gardens, and flower shops, then write for help. (For example, the American Orchid Society based at the Botanical Museum of Harvard University, Cambridge, Massachusetts, 02138, supplies all the education and training needed for their subject.)

WORK IN ECOLOGY AND CONSERVATION

There's barely a nook or cranny in America today that doesn't have some kind of a community organization working on some aspect of our environment. Air, water or noise pollution, litter, soil erosion, destruction of natural resources—these and others need your help. Volunteer it now. Or write to any of these: Audubon Society, 950 Third Avenue, New York, New York, 10022; Friends of the Earth, 529 Commercial Street, San Francisco, California, 94111; Consumer Action Now (CAN), 30 East 68th Street, New York, New York, 10021; Planned Parenthood—World Population, 810 7th Avenue, New York, New York, 10019, and others. Your library's reference room can help.

DO PLANT DECOR

Bone up on your botany, then apply your sense of design to greenery for all kinds of settings—homes, offices, waiting rooms, community buildings, foyers, and other areas that are the domain of interior designers. You need not grow them yourself; just find the best sources for a wide variety and plan their use, selling them as part of the package.

DESIGN GARDENS

Mrs. Leonore Baronio of Rye, New York, is living proof that creativity in one field can be switched to another with equal success. Once a successful professional dress designer, she felt this was too time-consuming after she became a mother, so she apprenticed herself to a well-known landscape architect and worked for virtually no salary for a year or two in order to learn. She also took courses at the New York Horticulture Society, read avidly on all subjects related to gardening. Thoroughly saturated in the subject, she struck out on her own and became a landscape consultant. As such, Leonore designs gardens. This encompasses all phases of garden planning and, if the client wishes, overseeing the installation.

What You Need Personally • A sense of design • Eye for color • Simple sketching ability

What You Need Materially • Sketch pad and pencils • Garden supplies • A pickup truck arrangement and male muscle power for heavy work (or subcontract the work) • Sources of garden supplies • Modest sums to pay for any courses you take

What You Need Educationally An apprenticeship like Leonore's if you can arrange one. If not, read up in depth, take courses, and possibly work for a greenhouse or nursery to learn more. Any school courses in biology, chemistry, math, physics, art and design, business administration will stand you in good stead.

Hours You Work You arrange them. Winter months are quiet.

How Much You Earn Once trained, your consultation fee can range from $50 to $75 an hour. If you take over responsibility for work involved, you'll make a profit on the trees, shrubs, etc., that you provide. Then add 10 percent to 15 percent to the total for your personal fee on good-sized jobs, over 15 percent for smaller jobs, in order to make them worth your while. (The initial consultation fee should be deducted from the total cost to the client.) If you offer only consultations and let the nursery you recommend supply materials and labor, you no doubt can make a commission arrangement with the nursery.

How You Get Started • Learn—through an apprenticeship, reading, special courses, and a job with a greenhouse, flower shop, botanical garden, nursery, flower wholesaler, or with a home-furnishings or garden trade magazine, or flower-seed company • Join a local flower club; learn the lingo, problems, preferences, people. (At this stage, keep your plans to yourself) • Join the horticulture society of your state to keep yourself informed, also the nearest botanical garden to learn about their courses • Subscribe to horticultural magazines • Learn to do simple pencil plans of gardens (or, if this is your special talent, be a sketcher for a landscape architect or consultant) • Line up all your sources and help • Learn to take color photos of your finished work to show prospective clients (You need not be a great photographer) • Promote your service

11

Communication via Media and Muse

Performing Arts What's your on-stage fantasy? To plié like Plisetskaya, flip a high C toward the upper balcony, play a plaudit-winning piece on the instrument of your choice, or outdo Duse? Whichever, if you're a late bloomer, you most certainly can enjoy a modified role, and if you've had previous training or experience, well, on with the show!

Your best entree to these performing arts is via volunteer or amateur work for churches, temples, schools, clubs, business and children's groups. Contacts made this way can lead up the ladder and to performance assignments in any or many of the following: • Company-product shows put on by large manufacturers to present a new idea or line to store buyers and dealers. (Check with large corporations near you or write to Leo Shull Publications, 136 West 44th Street, New York, New York, 10036, for information about industrial-show productions) • Fund-raising and public relations shows sponsored by large organizations and groups (health, civic, other) • Community and little-theater workshops, summer stock, repertory, opera, semi-professional and nonprofessional productions performed in schools, parks, other stage settings • Fashion shows; as a model—if your figure rates it—or as a commentator or doing theme-related skits • Public-relations functions—goodwill shows for manufacturers, large businesses and organizations, as well as cause and charity groups • Product promotion—conventions, exhibits, agency-client presentations, fashion shows, store demonstrations (often available through temporary help services) • Bistro, supper-club, coffeehouse entertaining (singing waitress, anyone?) • Children's theater (lots of room here for superior material, performances—most is pretty bad).

Two who've capitalized on their local needs are Dixi Patterson and Marge Erbe of Phoenix, Arizona. Inspired by their children's reactions to Disneyland's animal-costumed performers, they made themselves teddy-bear jumpsuits for entertaining at children's parties. An ordinary birthday affair nets them $20 an hour for ten children, 75¢ for each additional child. If they provide refreshments, their fees go up. Large commercial parties earn them as much as $80, and busy seasons bring in a minimum of $200 a week. Expenses are minimal. Chief investment: a winter and summer jumpsuit for each at $60. • Local radio and television performing. If you have a background of some experience in at least one facet of performing arts, screw your courage to the sticking point and schedule an audition for announcer, weather girl, newscaster, MC for home and interview shows, disc jockey, educational assignments or your own program (based on your abilities or an acceptable idea), any performing art in which you're proficient, announcing or demonstrating for packaged films and tapes of commercials or programs, actress-spokeswoman (seen) or spokeswoman (unseen, voice over) • Fairs, festivals, talent shows, carnivals, plus civic, religious, fraternal and social groups need performers periodically. Leave a resumé or brochure on your talents with each • Church soloists, choir members, and organists are needed.

Teach Your Talent in Private Classes This can apply to any of the performing arts or nonperforming aspects of each, and can be done in schools, summer camps, resorts, outdoor malls, and parks in the warm weather, in community centers, Y's, and similar groups, and of course, in your own home. Examples of this abound in every community.

Volunteer Entertainment You do this in hospitals, homes, schools, and other special institutions. Simple props, good scripts, entertaining dialogue, and high-quality performances are the key to success—choose which of these appeals to you and work at it. The Paper Bag Players, an extraordinarily comic and imaginative children's-theater group, uses props and costumes of cartons, boxes, sacks, and strips of newspaper plus scripts with universal appeal. Apply the same formula to adult and community projects—a theater group, drama workshop, public-school participation show, or therapy experience.

NONPERFORMING JOBS—IN THEATER

"Not all satisfaction comes from applause" is the unwritten code of backstage people. These positions, paid and volunteer, can be found in almost every community at some time in the year, often quite consistently • Producer • Director • Stage manager • Wardrobe mistress • Set artists • Designers—sets, costume, lighting • Casting director • Property manager (in charge of props) • Production assistants • Business manager • Carpenters • Special-effects staff • Publicity person • Dresser • Apprentices for all of these. And fringing these, larger productions have agents, play readers, lawyers, ad people. illustrators, musicians, secretaries, box-office personnel, subscription managers, usherettes.

Administrators Needed All of the arts, including theater, are in real need of capable people who plan the programs, deal with personnel details, supply companies and all other matters that require time, attention, and pulling together.

Costume Design: the Big Choice • According to "Theatre Jobs (Non-Acting)" one of MADEMOISELLE magazine's College and Careers series, "Second to acting, designing is the theatrical career that attracts the most women." There are thirty-seven repertory companies in various American cities; each maintains its own studio and workroom for designers. If you're near one of these, investigate. If they're fully staffed, leave your resumé, then scout around for any other theatrical situation where you can get experience until there's an opening with them.

Nonperforming Jobs—in Music • Promoting talent—press agent or representative for a performing musician • Music teacher • Choir master (usually in demand) • Record company copywriter, layout artist, or director of information services. (Also applicable to radio and television stations, broadcast groups) • Museum assistant in the musical-instrument department • Concert manager for a musical artist • Composer and lyricist for theater revues, TV, radio, or local performing companies • Music editor and arranger for music publisher, musical groups, broadcasting media • Music librarian for museums, libraries, broadcast stations, any company or organization with a music library. (See chapter Library Work Can Be Dynamic) • Selling in a retail music store or music department • Artists and repertoire woman (A & R), finding and auditioning talent, sitting in on recording sessions • Music instructor in a nonprofit community organization • Music-appreciation instructor (books, records, and tapes can be borrowed from the public library and other sources, reducing overhead costs to virtually nil) • Music therapist, helping adults and children with emotional, behavioral, learning, or physical disabilities. Pupils referred by psychiatrists, other health professionals. Can be done in a hospital, school, or camp for special children, clinics, day care and community mental-health centers, homes for the aged, settlement houses, special services, and rehabilitation agencies. To do this as a professional, you need four years of college plus six months' internship. Beginners' salaries average about $8,000 and move up about $1,000 with each added year of experience, but earnings vary in different parts of the country. With college already behind you, inquire about additional needed courses and the internship. Or, with a musical background, you can assist a professional music therapist in any of the places named above.

Music Sleuth (historian) Vera Brodsky Lawrence of New York City, a former concert pianist, turned her love of music into a brand-new job—digging into America's musical past, turning up long-lost works of both classical and ragtime composers for republication. She also writes articles on this work, and program notes for concerts, and is doing a bicentennial book project, a volume impressively titled MUSIC FOR PATRIOTS, POLITICIANS AND PRESIDENTS, 1776-1976.

Music Oral Historian (taping interviews with still-living musicians and related persons). When Vivian Perlis' children were old enough, she tucked her master's degree in music history under her arm and landed a job as part-time secretary at the Yale University Music Library in New Haven, Connecticut—not a status-y job, but an ideal place to learn. There she made herself indispensable, absorbed all she could, and in time came to realize that unless tapes were made of interviews with still-living members of the near-past music world (composers, their associates, relatives, and friends), this part of history would be lost. Funded by the National Endowment for the Humanities and with an award from the National Institute of Arts and Letters, she was able to preserve part of the late composer Charles Ives' world by taping conversations with those who'd known and worked with him. Now a Rockefeller Fund grant is enabling her to do likewise for other earlier twentieth-century composers and musicians. Vivian also teaches a course in American music at Yale and performs as a harpist—when she has the time.

Teach Music to Disadvantaged Children Many poor and/or minority children have tremendous musical talents. With help, these can be evoked and brought to a high level of achievement, working in community and private groups, and organizational programs. Spark the interest of your local citizenry, and they'll help with instruments and other materials.

Be a Piano Tuner You need a good ear, a feeling for the mechanical, some ability to play a bit yourself. Piano manufacturers train you for this work. For information, write to Piano Technicians Guild, 1417 Belmont, Seattle, Washington, 98122.

Nonperforming Jobs—in Dance • Choreography (creating dance) can be done for local theatricals • Teaching. No longer just an appendage of physical-education classes, dance is moving into its own in educational circles. Teach children or contemporaries. Keep up with trends; e.g., in London, England, tap dancing is back with all its verve. It's fun for everyone, it's cheap (tap shoes are modestly priced), it can be learned fast (with two classes a week and some home practice, you can look like a pro in six months). So former tappers, take the cue. Brush up on your buck-and-wing, off-to-Buffalo, etc., and set up classes in your home town • Dance exercise classes take many forms, going off on surprise tangents—modified ballet, modern, yoga, interpretive, and the newly popular belly dancing. Combine with traditional exercise movements. You'll need space, music and, if it helps, sponsorship • Theatrical dresser; anyone who lives in or near a town where road companies perform or on the summer-theater circuit, can enjoy the excitement of the stage as a dresser; you literally dress the performers. You'll need some theatrical background (amateur okay) some sewing and ironing ability (costume repairs, alterations) know-how for getting around backstage, dexterity (you may do as many as eight to twelve changes of costume per hour), a good memory for what you're supposed to do and when. Dressers are also used for moviemaking, television, commercial filming, and fashion shows. Rates of pay vary; you're paid by the performance plus so much per hour for handwork and repairs. Work period is a four-hour minimum. For further information, write to International Alliance of Theatrical Stage Employees and Motion Picture Machine Operators of the United States and Canada (whew!), 1270 Avenue of the Americas, New York, New York, 10020.

ADVERTISING

Glamorous, creative, dynamic—advertising can be all these, but keep in mind that its primary function is to sell the products of industry. It can be as entertaining as all get-out, win art director awards, and set a viewing public to using its deathless prose in everyday parlance, but if it doesn't move merchandise, it's off the track.

What the Jobs Are   The three basic divisions of advertising are art (layout/story boards), copy (theme and words), and production (all printing or filming details). They form the core of most ad departments or companies. Ad agencies have many other work categories, taking in the basic three plus research, radio and TV personnel, media (often absorbed by production department in print-only setups, it also buys air time for broadcasting), account work (account executives and assistants who do contact work—liason between client and agency), and fashion (for fashion accounts).

Where the Jobs Are   • Department stores • Mail order houses • Catalog houses • Direct mail firms • Buying offices • Advertisers (manufacturers, retailers, financial institutions, public utilities, distributors, miscellaneous national and local advertisers) • Advertising media (newspapers, magazines, business [trade] and consumer and farm publications, radio, outdoor advertising concerns, direct mail companies, TV stations, company bulletins and house organs). Most of these have their own ad departments as well as contact with other advertising situations • Advertising agencies (listed in McKITTRICK'S AGENCY LIST in your public library) • Advertising service and supply houses (printers, letter shops, engraver's equipment people, and miscellaneous services such as animated cartoon and jingle studios) • Art, design, and photography studios

Fields Related to Advertising That Offer an In   • Publishing • Modeling • Entertainment • Market-research companies • Fashion • Library work (ad agencies and related businesses frequently have book and/or film libraries on premises) • Home economics (ad agencies with food clients and food companies themselves, need home economists as advisers, as supervisors for test kitchens (they're involved with products to be advertised), and to prepare and present food on TV, film or "live." Similarly, consultants are needed in advertising many other kinds of nonfood products, as well • Department stores and catalog companies are ideal training grounds, and many a topflight ad writer, artist, or production person has started in a Macy's or a Sears Roebuck pasting up yesterday's ads or counting characters (number of letters and spaces per line) to make sure a copy description fits the given space or proofreading for typo errors, among other starting jobs. Any store or mail-order company can serve much the same purpose for you. Take any starting job in any of the places listed on the preceding pages to learn. You might land a launching-pad job in an agency film library or do leg work for the fashion department. In the first, you're liable to keep a film inventory, answer phones, set up screening appointments; it could land you in a production or film research job, among others. The second could move you up to assistant fashion coordinator— planning client-made wardrobes for ads, commercials. You just never know where, with some effort on your part, a starting job might lead you.

Hours You Work Advertising uses many free-lancers—artists, copywriters, models, performing artists, photographers and filmmakers, stylists, consultants in specialized fields of work, publicity and public-relations people, and others. This arrangement involves meeting deadlines and intensive work while the assignment lasts. If you have any kind of skill or talent needed by ad people, you also can try to sell them on part-time work on premises. Or, with no background, take a starting staff job and steer for your special interest to learn.

What You Need Educationally There are no entrance requirements, but creativity, inventiveness, intuition, and diligence mean a great deal in this field. Whatever education you've had, whether formal or catch-as-catch-can, use it. Take advantage of every learning situation you can find—seminars, meetings, discussions, crash creative sessions, or just eavesdropping on shop talk. Ask questions (but time them well). Your interest, imagination, drive, and personal flair will carry you through.

How You Get Started • Pinpoint your job possibilities by company and location • Get in touch with the advertising association or group nearest your home for information about courses, job opportunities, placement help. Make up your resumé, playing up related or helpful experience; slant it to the work you want. Any on-the-ball housewife must use most ad traits in her own home—research, traffic, follow-through, production, creativity, etc. Office skills can get you in, too.

PUBLICITY, PUBLIC RELATIONS

This field covers the world of written, spoken, and personal contacts between an organization, institution (public or private), or company and the general public. Its aim is to create and maintain a favorable public image for its clients.

Public relations involves eight major work categories • **Writing** (reports, news releases, booklets, radio and TV copy, speeches, film sequences, etc.) • **Editing** (employee publications, newsletters, other management communications) • **Placement of information** (press, radio, TV, magazine, trade, other) • **Promotion** (special events, time observances, programs, guest relations, visual aids, other) • **Speaking** (appearances, preparation of speeches for others, related responsibilities) • **Production** (some know-how on art/layout as they relate to PR materials • **Programming** (planning from start to finish for projects) • **Institutional advertising** (promotion of the company as opposed to its products; work closely with ad people)

Women have been highly successful in public relations work for entertainment arts, restaurant, hotel and transportation industries, food, fashion, cosmetics, home furnishings, retail merchandising, and nonprofit organizations (causes, charities, health groups, and the like).

What You Need Personally • Imagination • Verbalizing skills • Good relating-to-people skills • Sensitivity to others • Ability to plan and organize

What You Need Educationally Work experience in journalism is particularly valuable to anyone with an eye on PR work, and any specialized training is also a big boost. If you've done freelance writing, community organization work, electioneering, fund-raising, or public speaking, or have helped to promote any pet projects by working with newspapers, civic groups, and others, you're part-way there.

How You Get Started • Read up on the field • Talk to people about it—those who work in it, at it, or around it—such as media folks • Get a job in, or related to, newspaper, magazine or other publishing work as it's considered the best proving ground for public relations • Without professional experience or journalism experience, you could tackle small local or regional organizations for a public contact job. This may be public-relations work—or it might be part of sales promotion. Either way, it should be a challenge—and fun.

BE AN AGENT

Representing writers, artists, or performing talent is closely allied to public-relations work; you might call it a specialized form of it, since you project your clients' favorable images in order to gain assignments or bookings or sales. Then, too, there is the public-relations work done for show cases of these talents by agents—the art shows, museums, galleries, theater groups, coffeehouses, radio stations. And don't forget, doing publicity for fund-raising events is big business these days. Look around you. There may be talent and special events right under your nose, needing your best-foot-forward presentation to the public.

PUBLISHING

Flex your fingers and buckle down to typing practice, because it's your best way to batter down doors to publishing jobs, short of miscellaneous chores such as snip-snipping news articles, phone answering, reception work, running office machines, filing, researching, reading mail, and doing copyreading (for which they usually ask a college background and you ask for good eyes).

Childraising a fait accompli, Eunice Beckerman of Valley Stream, New York, returned to work via the temporary-help services route—a secretarial fill-in at Doubleday & Company, book publishers, for a few weeks. The company liked her, Eunice liked Doubleday. So the attachment became permanent. After just a few months as secretary to a harried young editor, she was promoted to administrative assistant, with an office and several assistants of her own.

Small or medium newspapers, magazines, or publishing companies are a good bet for starting jobs, since most beginners make a beeline for the big ones and competition is heavy. With newspapers, try the weeklies, the shopper papers, and area publications (big apartment developments frequently have their own, too). With magazines, try those catering to specialized interests (there are slews of these to choose from, nationally; pin down those near you, unless you're planning to write for them—then they're all yours to try). Current events, animals, youth interests, crafts, ecology, music—any field you can name has its own publication—pick some. Don't overlook house organs and consumer-oriented, company-sponsored magazines such as those published by auto and utility giants.

Some Freelance or Part-time Newspaper Work • Write up publicity for any local organization—church, community, PTA, art or music group—then make contact with your town's newspaper staff and learn how to turn it out their way, the professional way. Once you know how (and they know you) ask for assignments from the paper's editor • Work for a local shopper newspaper. These come out daily, weekly, or once a month • Send in fillers. Suburban newspapers and rural dailies, with circulations that cover a large geographical section, offer you a chance to be a reporter, sending in news items of interest from your area, paying so much per item • Or if you've a special interest, write about if for a newspaper or magazine. This has been an entree to publishing work for many • Do book reviews or write any other special column—religion, consumerism (a growing field), community improvements, etc.—for a newspaper, company paper, bulletin or magazine, or trade publication. Or write on minority-culture interests and progress. (To quote a "with it" editor: "If you're black and can write, you have it made.") • Make up shopping or advice column samples and submit to newspaper editors as a weekly or biweekly feature possibility. (You buy the newspaper space, figure cost plus profit in fees charged to businesses you plug in column) • Photographic skills are an open-sesame to newspaper work, since some of the best news shots are made by amateurs who just happened to be there, camera in hand. So sling it over your shoulder and get out where it's happening • Start a merchandise exchange paper. Because one man's discard is frequently another's desired object, these are invariably successful. Too, there's a great fascination in reading interesting want ads. Swap-and-sell publications can feature anything, but anything, that can be sold, as well as personals, and much that is bizarre, humorous, and colorful. THE CUSTOMART PRESS of Mamaroneck, New York, has offered such diverse and unexpected items as a printing plant (only $2,150), tugboats from $6,500, an entire town complete with water works, and such gems as a Brooks Brothers' suit (scarcely worn) $20 and fifty thousand pounds of frozen horsemeat. (You can see the potential, can't you?) People pay nothing to place the ads, but they pay the paper a percentage of the profit made on general merchandise, cars, boats, real estate. The only exceptions: matrimonials and some personals are a straight, moderate fee for use of a box number. Start your exchange paper with mimeographed editions—it's cheapest.

LECTURE
There's an old, obviously male-inspired saying that "women generally speaking are generally speaking." Since we certainly have great communications skills, why not use them to the hilt to tell others about our interests—and for money? There's much more of the ham in each of us than we realize. Once you warm to your subject, you forget all about the mike, camera, or audience—you lose your self-consciousness, **pfft!** Gone! Choose your audiences from among women's groups,

colleges, school assemblies, business meetings and conventions, service organizations, as well as all those who would naturally respond to your subject. Throughout this book, there are women who share their knowledge and experiences via public speaking. Herb-raising Virginia Colby does. Music oral historian Vivian Perlis does. Sydney Taylor, children's book writer and camp dramatics instructor, talks to schools, libraries, book fairs, among others. And antique doll collector Mimi Franke of Plainfield, New Jersey, talks to women's clubs, scout groups, schools, senior citizens, historical clubs, museums, and others about the more tnan four hundred dolls she's culled from all over the world—one, two hundred years old.

For many, platform work earns a good part of their living. For others, it's a stimulating part-time activity. The field is large enough to warrant its own organization (International Platform Association, 2564 Berkshire Road, Cleveland Heights, Ohio, 44106), and its own publication, TALENT. There is also a magazine called PROGRAM covering activities in the lecture world—its the program chairman's handbook. $1 a copy from PROGRAM Magazine, Box 629, Flushing, New York, 11352.

To locate a lecture bureau or agent for your own appearances, see the program chairman of any active organization in your town and ask who supplies its speakers. One such contact may do it—or lead you to other agents until you find the one best for you. Agent fees are usually flexible and negotiable, and are considerate of factors such as your travel costs, costumes, and other props.

Or Be a Lecturer's Agent Rather than speak yourself, perhaps you'd find representing speakers more appealing. Follow the lead of Alice Black of South Orange, New Jersey, who runs her own small, select, and buzzingly busy program service. Her specialty: supplying the speaking talent for women's groups. She herself has been a member of numerous women's clubs. As program chairman for several, she had contact with lecture bureaus, and when one of them asked her to be their representative for a tristate area, she accepted. Subsequently, Alice established her own successful bureau.

TELEVISION AND RADIO

This is a tight little island in the crazy world of communications, but given the talent and/or the determination and a willingness to start at the bottom, you can move in. You'll be bucking the tide of kids just out of college communications-arts training who'll take peanuts or nothing for pay; you must be willing to do the same until you get experience.

Almost every community with population over ten thousand has at least one radio station to cover them and some of the big cities have over ten. There are over a thousand TV stations. National Educational Television (public television) has over 225 of these and educational radio (noncommercial, usually based at colleges or universities) more than four hundred. Educational stations may be more open to hiring women—some of the men who run them are of a more enlightened breed than the commercial bunch.

What the Jobs Are • Office workers • Technical crews (engineers, sound effects, lighting staff, camera people, tape experts, etc.) • Traffic (interdepartmental communications) • Creative (writing, music, art, stagecraft, sets, other) • Administration • Selling (air time to ad agencies and clients) • Performing (the whole range) • Casting • Programming (making up annual to daily schedules) • Promotion • Others (film and tape editor, researcher, film and tape librarian, fashion and makeup, more)

Where the Jobs Are • Educational TV and radio stations • Commercial TV and radio stations • Independent film companies • Broadcasting trade publications • Film libraries • Advertising agencies • Station representatives • Network headquarters • Public relations concerns with broadcast clients • Modeling and talent agencies • Large companies and organizations with film and/or radio departments • Fashion organizations • Packaged program producers • Commercial-filming studios

How To Get Started Get in with an office skill. Or be happy to print cue cards, help to issue scripts, be a receptionist or an apprentice or helper to anyone who can use you. If you have any special skills, knowledge, or talent at all, play it up—before you land a job and after. And if a special interest or organization work has given you an earlier entree to radio or TV people, use that as a base for a job with them.

Some Jobs That Can Be Done Freelance • Film editing (learn it as an apprentice in a film-studio cutting room) • Producing (small to medium-sized ad agencies will freelance assignments; you'll need experience for this one, of course) • Makeup and hair styling (two separate jobs). You learn your skills through cosmetology training and experience. "Cricket" Garafalo, once head of makeup at CBS in New York, has freelanced since her child was born and works on call • Script clerk (follows script action, makes notes on wardrobe, times scenes being shot) • Film researcher works in film libraries digging out needed film clips for commercials, features • Stylist—selects wardrobes, accessories for performers, either privately or in a studio. Etheleen Lichtenstein, New York, works with both fashion and decorating props, collects background materials for photographers, film studios. Worked first at a public-relations company writing publicity, visiting magazine editors with clients' wares to solicit editorial mentions. Claims her job's "all instinct." Now married and mother of a small boy, just a few assignments and a few hours' work a week bring in $100 a day (she won't work less than half a day). Etheleen says that working in film is very tough today, requiring union membership which is almost impossible to get. She advises the starting stylist to tackle print media instead • Voice over—the one belonging to Rhoda Mann Winkler of Scarsdale, New York, is one you've heard as a child or adult on many TV commercials and also as the voice of many beautiful-girl announcers. It all began with puppetry as a child, led to doing all the Howdy Doody voices except Howdy himself. Ad people she met through this called her to do commercials. She's on call, with average recording sessions running one to one and a half hours. Earnings include pay for time plus residuals and additional revenue from each city showing the commercial.

For further information, write to the National Association of Educational Broadcasters, 1346 Connecticut Avenue, N.W., Washington, D.C., 20036, for listings of their stations, addresses, other material; to Television Information Office, 745 Fifth Avenue, New York, New York, 10022, for TELEVISION CAREERS, which lists and describes 182 publications and organizations (a guide for those interested in entering creative, technical and business areas of TV), and to American Women in Radio and Television, 1321 Connecticut Avenue, N.W., Washington, D.C., 20036. Also go through BROADCASTING YEAR BOOK to learn locations of broadcasting corporations, independent producers, individual stations, commercial TV production companies, etc.) and STANDARD RATE & DATA SERVICE, radio and TV reference listing every broadcast facility in the United States—addresses, personnel, etc.

Broadcast Advertisers Reports, Inc. (BAR) This company covers seventy-five major TV markets in the United States to determine who is advertising what and where and how, then sells this information as a service to TV stations, major ad agencies, and large corporations. They get this coverage with the help of housewives in these seventy-five markets, each of whom maintains, at company expense, several tape recorders in her home and records a given station's activity during any predetermined monitoring period. Her job includes receiving the tape from BAR, operating the recorders, checking periodically to make certain they're working properly. As the tapes run out, she changes reels and mails the recorded tape to BAR's play-back plant in Pennsylvania. Salary for any working week can run from $35 to $125 and depends on many factors. Although well-staffed, BAR's turnover around the country is significant enough to warrant keeping a list of women interested in doing this work when an opening does come up. Any company in your area selling, renting, or servicing tape recorders is liable to be approached by BAR for recommendations for women monitors, so it would be wise to contact them and tell the you're interested. Or write directly to Broadcast Advertisers Reports, Inc., 5th and Chestnut Streets, Darby, Pennsylvania, 19023.

MARKET RESEARCH

To learn how the public feels, thinks, and reacts to specific products, trends, people, and programs, administrators of businesses, government, and other organizations must have a line of communication that reaches individuals and groups. Market or consumer research provides this. Through surveying and interviewing, big company executives arrive at vital decisions concerning the manufacture, pricing, packaging, advertising, and presentation of their products.

Although an immense field with many job categories, this section will deal only with its most accessible facets. The   rk has many personal positives—it's often healthy, fresh-air work (unless you do it via mail or phone), it helps develop poise, it's educational and interesting (every job you take on is likely to be totally different from the last) and it's convenient—you can accept assignments at will, adjust hours to yours.

Where the Jobs Are Government agencies (federal, state, city), research and survey companies, colleges and universities, independent research (interviewing services), advertising agencies.

Kinds of Surveys • Consumer market surveys • Attitude surveys • Motivational studies • Product and package tests • Focused group studies • Media surveys • Readership surveys • Copy tests • Audience measurement studies • Audits and dealer surveys (in stores, counting number of products, etc.)

Types of Interviews • Personal • Telephone • Group • Panel • Self-administered questionnaires • Mail surveys • Diaries

What You Need Personally • An outgoing personality • Alert mind • Poise • Patience • Ability to write legibly, neatly • Accuracy • Honesty • Natural curiosity

What You Need Materially • Pencils (mechanical ones are more dependable) • Leather or plastic folio or envelope • Telephone or car, depending on type of interview you do

What You Need Educationally High-school education is adequate to do basic market interviewing. Companies train you in person or by mailed instructions. You can climb from simple to more complicated and lucrative interviewing by proving your abilities on the job.

Hours You Work Part-time or flexible. (If you work for a number of companies, you can keep consistently busy.) Given a certain number of interviews per assignment and so many days (or evenings) to do them, you can adjust your time. A study might run for one hour, days, or a Saturday or Sunday, or extend over a period of weeks. Note for those with math proclivities and the ability to work a tabulating machine: you can do coding, sorting, and counting data in questionnaires completed by interviewers, working full days at a time or a few hours a day.

How Much You Earn You're paid by the hour or the work unit, and rates vary according to companies, difficulty of assignments, and time work is done. All out-of-pocket expenses are reimbursed. Hourly rates for general interviewing range from $2 to $3 an hour, averaging about $2.50. Market Trends, Inc., a survey company, estimates their telephone interviewers earn $200 a month, part-time, depending on the consistency of the need for interviews in an area. An average assignment could take four hours a day, three days, and pay $40 plus travel time. Specialized or in-depth interviews can pay from $5 to $15 an hour, depending on the difficulty of assignment, and require a high level of intelligence. Working by the day, covering three such interviews, one can earn anywhere from $25 to $50 a day and average $200 a week. Pay is higher in large cities and suburbs because standards of living are higher. If you progress to field supervisor, you may be put on a retainer basis and paid a flat fee.

How You Get Started • Send for the survey research handbook, ASKING QUESTIONS, published by the Marketing Research Trade Association; it tells you everything you should know about the work. Send $1.00 to cover costs to Box 1415, Grand Central Station, New York, New York, 10017 • Watch the help-wanted ads in local papers • Use the INTERNATIONAL DIRECTORY OF MARKETING RESEARCH (Green Book) in your public library to find all marketing research houses and services. If it's not there, ask them to order it. Or buy it ($12.50) from New York Chapter, American Marketing Association, 60 East 42nd Street, New York, New York, 10017 • Bradford's DIRECTORY OF MARKETING RESEARCH AGENCIES also gives a complete listing of companies, and the classified section of your phone book will help you to locate nearby research people and interviewing services • Visit office temporary agencies; they place women in these jobs, too.

Every so often, one stumbles onto a forward-looking executive who adjusts his thinking and business to take advantage of the untapped talents in the womanpower around him. Such an administrator is Theodore Karger, president of The Nowland Organization, Inc., a consumer-research company in Greenwich, Connecticut, that does in-depth studies of life activities. At this writing, twenty women at Nowland work on what he calls customized schedules, giving their available time to meet company needs. Paid by the hour, they deal with a wide range of projects allowing them to use all their considerable creative and administrative abilities. No preconceived plan, this flexible arrangement evolved spontaneously, and Mr. Karger, for one, couldn't be happier. It has all been so outstandingly successful for Nowland and the women that he fervently wishes that other employers everywhere would benefit from his company's example.

12

Office Work —
Your Foot
in the Door

Office help of one kind or another is a must-have for practically every type of business going, and no other kind of work can make that claim. For this reason, it's the open-sesame to almost any type of job or career a woman might have in mind. For example, someone with art or music training may wonder how she might break into some special area of her field when a frontal or headlong approach is likely to be fruitless. The answer—an office skill can get you into the milieu. The rest is up to you. This same circuitous approach can be used for any work you've set your heart on. Try it. But first, acquire those skills—or at least one of them.

TEMPORARY HELP SERVICES

These are a blessing to the woman with or without business experience. If you've been out of it all for a while, even years, they offer brush-up courses in old skills, training courses in new ones in shortage jobs (bank tellering, for example). Through them, you can try out different kinds of business settings and roles until you light on just the one for you. If office work just isn't for you, office temporary services also find jobs that don't demand special skills (see list). With over five hundred temporary-help services flourishing all over the United States, you should have no trouble finding one. Major companies include Manpower, Inc., Western Girl, Inc., Kelly Services, Inc., Employers Overload Company, Inc., Stiver's Lifesavers, Inc., and Task Force Service. Mature Temps specializes in placing retirement-age applicants and has offices in the large metropolitan areas.

Advantages Offered by Temporary Help Services • Someone else does your job-hunting for you, finding one to fit your time, abilities, interests. If you're a retiree, they find work with salaries that stay inside your Social Security limits • The age range is almost as broad as life itself—from an eighteen-year-old college student to a great-grandmother in her eighties • You have only one employer (the service) but enjoy a variety of places, people, kinds of work (all kinds of travel is broadening) • You can accept or refuse jobs at will, and work hours and days best for you (there's usually a four-hour minimum stretch) • You're covered for Social Security, workman's compensation, and unemployment insurance, as with any full-time job • You can be sure you're paid because the service pays you • If you like a job enough to make it permanent, some services will arrange for the company to put you on their payroll. Inquire. And if you want to work in another city or part of the country, larger services will transfer you through their branch offices.

Temporary Help Service Jobs—Office • Typing • Stenography • Key punching • Credit checking • Clerical • Telephone and reception • Filing • Accounting • Business machines • Billing machines • Teller service (banks) • Transcription • Statistical typing • Secretarial (including special secretaries, e.g., medical, legal, engineering, etc.) • Mail-room work • Data processing • Bookkeeping

Temporary Help Service Jobs—Nonoffice Possibilities • Demonstrating • Hostessing • Survey tabulating • Merchandising • Survey taking • Tour guiding • Modeling (conventions, businesses) • Writing and editing • Food tasting • Personal correspondence • Market research • Personal shopping • Inventory checking • Telephone work • Assisting professionals • Trained professional work such as engineering, etc. • Media research • Plus almost any type of fillable business situation

Temporary-help service giants have compiled long and entertaining lists of the many different kinds of jobs they've offered—interesting, unusual, and often glamorous. So if you have no special office skills, ask about other assignments.

What You Need Personally • A pleasant manner • Good grooming • Punctuality • Adaptability • Enthusiasm • Interest • Accuracy

What You Need Materially An adequate wardrobe or simple (preferably tailored) clothes and accessories.

What You Need Educationally Whatever training

or schooling you've had can be adapted to either office or non-office type jobs. According to a 1972 profile survey of Manpower, Inc., female temporary office workers, 93 percent are high school grads, 42.7 percent have attended college, 17.6 percent have gone to business or technical schools. And if you agree that marriage is part of life's education, 70 percent are married, 60 percent have children. Most of the skills needed for office work are taught in academic and vocational public schools. What you can't or didn't get in school, you can learn now in a business school or an adult-education course, or through courses arranged for or offered by temporary help services. Most of the latter are free; occasionally there's a nominal fee. They also give refresher courses, so ask about these. Help services have found that making the transition from manual to electric machines is usually done quickly—just a little practice, perhaps an hour or so, and a woman is off and running like an old pro. You also can practice at home and sharpen up your shorthand and transcription by taking down TV dialogue.

How Much You Earn Your skills and how well you apply them, your geographical location and the local supply-and-demand will affect your pay rate, highest in the biggest cities, lowest in small communities. Per-hour rates have been going up five cents and ten cents each year, and the average range for general office skills is $1.60-$3.50 an hour. Specialized work pays more.

How You Get Started Had previous training? Brush up. If you have a new job goal in mind, decide how your skills and previous experience can help achieve this. Explain your background and aims when you apply to the service, so they can place you accordingly. If you've had no previous training, follow learning suggestions above, or apply for a non-office job.

BANK JOBS

Tellers Nearly always openings for this work. Takes a head for math and detail, and someone who enjoys contact with people. You need to know elementary banking methods, negotiable instruments, and commercial arithmetic for which the bank trains you—usually a school program with on-the-job training, all of which takes several weeks.

Other Bank Jobs • Drivers • Messengers for mail room • Bookkeeping clerk • Receptionist • Telephone operator • Transit clerk • Typist • Stenographer • Secretary • Tabulating record control clerk • Office machine operator. **And these**

newer jobs (thanks to electronic data-processing equipment): • Card-tape converter operator • Coding clerk • Console operator • Data typist • Data-converting machine operator • Data examination clerk • Tape librarian • High-speed-printer operator • Teletype operator • Verifier operator

What You Need Educationally A high-school diploma is enough to begin a clerical job. Any office skills put you ahead of the game. Banking offers special training in their field: College Tuition Reimbursement Plan, on-the-job guidance and training by supervisors, management development to train those who show promise for administrative jobs, and special-training programs for minority groups.

Hours You Work The needs of the community dictate these—early morning hours near railroad stations, late evenings in shopping centers, and the like. Ask when you apply.

How Much You Earn The location and size of the bank, services offered, and type of community served determine your pay. Some banks have a system that breaks down each job category into minimum, midpoint, and maximum salaries based on the person's experience and period of service. Most prefer to promote from within.

How To Get Started Apply to banks in your area. Your past experienc, if any, and any skills or special knowledge will help to determine your job, along with your interests. If you start as a clerk or teller, you can train to advance.

WORK-AT-HOME OFFICE SUGGESTIONS

Some office skills can be done easily at home—typing, billing, bookkeeping, for example. Accounting can be done independently, too, if you're so trained—limiting the number of clients to suit your personal schedule, working at home or on a part-time basis.

Typing All kinds of businesses, organizations, and individuals use this type of help—churches, health and charity groups, ad people, retail stores, large companies, direct mail houses, suppliers, mail order companies, and many others. Depending on their needs, you could type: • Business letters • Theses and manuscripts • Statistical reports • Envelopes • Labels • Speeches • Term papers (high school and college) • Year-end, progress and other reports • Professional papers (doctors, lawyers, researchers, etc.) • Postcards • Index cards • Income-tax forms for accountants (this can be quite profitable during the tax season) • "Thinking" typing is compilation work done for directories, using a special yardstick (a particular area or profession, homeowners only or such).

Hand Writing (including calligraphy, Spencerian, other) Dusica Karsanidi of Dobbs Ferry, New York, works for a large radio-TV organization that calls on her each year to address approximately four thousand invitations to their Christmas affair. This, in turn, has led to hand-addressing engraved invitations for other affairs outside the company. She expanded on this demand by making up a personal folder with samples of her penmanship which she left with printers, engravers, art shops, and others. For a few hours work in the evening she has extra spending money. She also took a course in calligraphy to expand her sphere, bought a book on it and needed materials, and practiced until she perfected this skill. An elegant touch for wedding and very special invitations, it can earn as much as $1.25 per set (inside and outside envelopes). Suggested helpful text: CALLIGRAPHIC LETTERING WITH WIDE PEN & BRUSH by Ralph Douglass, 3rd edition, Revised & enlarged, Watson-Guptil Publications, 1967.

How to Get Started in At-Home Office Work • Take brush-up or beginner courses in whichever skill(s) interest you • Once you're proficient enough in these, solicit home assignments from those needing such abilities (there should be no difficulty in finding them) • Invest in business stationery and cards, once you've gotten a foothold (some clients). Distribute these at club meetings, service organizations, community affairs, and among friends who might use your help • Take samples of your work along when you call on office managers, personnel directors, or whomever you see on solicitations • Send a sales letter to local business and professional people including those whose practices don't warrant full-time office help—to small companies such as garages, plumbing shops, contractors, retail stores, and groups involved in health, urban planning, child care, education, etc. Watch newspapers for announcements of new businesses • If you live near colleges, universities, or other schools, list your name and skills with the office to fill student needs for typing or helping the office crew • Set rates for each type of work you do. These will vary according to region, town, employer, type of assignment • If you type manuscripts or theses, be sure to include value of time spent in double-checking copy • Also, transcribing from handwriting can be laborious and time-consuming. Check copy in advance with your client for errors in grammar, spelling, punctuation.

The Massachusetts Department of Commerce suggests the following fees for metropolitan areas and college communities.

(Best, though, to test your own section on fees before you quote any hard-and-fast figures yourself.)

Thesis typing 75¢ a page, double spaced. No charge for carbon. You supply both paper and carbon.

Business letter 75¢ a page, extra 5¢ for envelope.

Statistical typing 75¢ a page, double-spaced, with tabulations.

Mimeographing should start at $7.50 because of time involved in cutting stencil, setting up machine.

Dictation and transcription $4 an hour; $5 for technical, legal, and specialized material.

Addressing envelopes (typing) $15 a thousand.

Record-keeping Accounting $5 an hour. (A premium price should be charged for rush jobs.)

Keep good records to help analyze your costs, including time spent, rent, cost of equipment, maintenance, supplies, gasoline for deliveries, light, heat, etc.

Girl Friday Service This offers secretarial skills, telephone answering, conference space for small business meetings, and small but valuable conveniences such as keeping appointment books in order, making travel and hotel reservations.

Home Mimeographing Service If you can type, and your town warrants your service, this can be another healthy home business.

What You Need Materially • A mimeograph machine. A secondhand one or a rebuilt machine with a guarantee would be your best bet (New ones run a few hundred dollars) • Typewriter • Stencils • Printing paper • Tubes of machine ink • Small supplies (paper clips, tape, stapler, and the like) • File cabinet (eventually) • Space to work in your home • If you work with graphics, you may want to invest in a tracing machine (Scope) that lights up.

What You Need Educationally Enough typing ability to cut a perfect stencil and the know-how to work a mimeo machine (this can be learned from the salesman or company representative where you buy it—secondhand or new). Previous layout and art training are helpful but not essential.

Hours You Work Once proficient, you should be able to cut a stencil in about ten minutes and run off a hundred printed sheets in another ten. After that, it's all hinged on how many clients you have and the time you have to give it.

How Much You Earn Overhead, costs of pick-up

and delivery, any advertising, cost of supplies, and value of your time all figure in your rates. Also, since your home is your office, estimate accordingly. Mimeo services charge so much for the stencil and first one hundred sheets, so much for each additional one hundred—less, if the stencil is prepared. Three different services charge as follows: $5 for the first three hundred sheets or less with stencil prepared, $1 for each one hundred over the three hundred—$3 for the first one hundred sheets, stencil prepared, ninety cents each additional one hundred—or $6.35 for the first stencil, including stencil and typing, $1 each additional one hundred. Letter-size charges are less than for legal-size paper. Since you'll have less overhead working at home, you can charge less, and this will help to build your trade.

TELEPHONE ANSWERING SERVICE

A telephone-answering service is to your business clients what a baby sitter is to parents. It allows them to leave the office with the comforting assurance that all incoming calls will be covered intelligently and efficiently. Its three main functions are answering clients' telephones, taking messages, and delivering these messages. The success of your service depends on just how quickly, accurately, and cheerfully you perform all three. (Although the use of mechanical answering devices has grown, there are still many people who need human response to their incoming calls—plumbers, doctors, dentists, etc.)

What You Need Personally • You should be pleasant, courteous, natural, alert, tactful, and poised • Have an understanding of your clients' needs • Know the vocabulary peculiar to the different types of business and professions you cover • Have a well modulated voice, clear diction

What You Need Materially • Your own home. (An apartment is less feasible since walls and floors must be broken through to install wiring; other tenants may object) • Enough room to set up answering and line-terminating equipment, and floor strength sufficient to hold it. In some states you must have a minimum of ten or more customers before the telephone company will install—check • Cash for initial outlay (varies considerably by area, number of customers) to cover advance payment and deposit, installation, outgoing lines, taxes, carrying charges (equipment rental) until you're established (probably six to nine months), plus sums for any advertising. Installation prices differ according to locality. A small service to accommodate about twelve clients and no desire to expand, could probably do it for about $25 each line • A relief person in case you go out or are ill (a member of your family or, for after-school hours, a teenager)

What You Need Educationally • A general education • Any previous business training or experience will help you to appreciate your client's needs, and may stand you in good stead when the board is quiet. For example, Dorothy Podesta of Bronx, New York, who has done billing for a few of her small-business clients once a month at a fee, typing and mailing their invoices, has also done leatherwork, selling her products.

Hours You Work As a one-woman switchboard, you'd function best working from 9 A.M. to 5 P.M., five days a week, and 9 A.M. to noon on Saturdays. However, with adequate relief help, you can run a twenty-four-hour service for all-nighters such as doctors, plumbers, dentists, and other emergency-prone clients.

How Much You Can Earn Your monthly charges may range from $25 to $45 a month per answering line, depending on the type and extent of service offered. The base rate covers the handling of a specific number of messages. Extra charges are made for calls exceeding the contract. Thus, if you take seventy-five calls per month for a client, you might charge $25; beyond that number, you'd earn more. Any special services such as making outgoing calls would also cost the client more.

How You Get Started • Call your local telephone-company business office • Tell them you want to rent telephone-answering-service equipment and would like to talk to their representative about all phases of the business. This representative will tell you, among other facts, whether your home location has existing telephone lines available • Check your area for zoning rules (call your city clerk) • Determine whether there's room for a service where you live and what its client potential is. Call small businesses, tell them your plan, find out if they'd be interested in subscribing. If you get at least twenty-five to thirty yes answers, you have a market • Preferably, your clients should be located near the serving central office of the telephone company, since most phone companies make a monthly mileage charge to the answering service for distances covered from the central office. Each client pays for his own secretarial line. • Be careful whom you accept as a client; check each one out with your Better Business Bureau and your chamber of commerce.

Telephone Service Operator Any woman who can

run a telephone switchboard and has the required qualifications should have no difficulty finding this type of work. A part-time schedule probably can be arranged. If you have no experience but show high potential and interest, many services will train you. Earnings around the country vary.

If you have any questions not answered by your phone company, write to Associated Telephone Answering Exchanges, Inc., 1725 K Street, N.W., Washington, D.C., 20006.

FREELANCE SHORTHAND REPORTER

A good, uncrowded field that's interesting, educational, and lucrative, if you work fast and accurately. You record, by hand or machine, convention speeches and make verbatim reports of proceedings and statements at conferences, meetings, private or public hearings, and similar situations. Today, about 50 percent of the shorthand reporters are women.

What You Need Personally • Speed • Command of the language • Native intelligence • Good vocabulary • Intellectual curiosity. If you're already a good typist, machine shorthand should be a natural for you.

What You Need Educationally The ability to sustain an accurate machine shorthand speed of 180-200 words a minute. Speedwriting, regular or machine shorthand (stenotype or stenograph), courses are given in high schools (some night adult courses), colleges, and business schools. Or you may study and build speed on your own. Law and legal stenography courses are valuable aids.

Hours You Work When called. You may do several jobs a day and can accept or refuse assignments.

How Much You Earn You work on a fee basis, so much per page. In the northeast part of the United States, this would be about $1.90 for one or two copies, reporting and transcription. Thus, a fifteen-page job would earn you about $30 to $35, forty to fifty pages close to $100.

How You Get Started Learn your skills. Then, get in touch with your chamber of commerce, city court, and school counselors to learn about work possibilities in your town.

13

Author! Author! (That Could Be You)

Ask most people, and they'll tell you they could write if they wanted to. Maybe so, but the trick is to **want** to—enough to apply the seat of your slacks to the seat of your chair and **do** it. As a field, it has some distinct advantages, which screenwriter Mary McCall has described well:

"Writing is one line of work which is open equally to men and women. There are no racial barriers, no religious restrictions or prerequisites, no age limit up or down, and nobody cares what a writer looks like. Its tools are, I think, the cheapest of any of the arts. It can be done anywhere in the world, any time, any day, any season. It can be done alone until it is ready for market. Except for its lack of guaranteed financial yield, plus the discipline, concentration, and even selfishness it requires, it combines well for a woman with marriage and the raising of children. In writing there is no monotony. I've been disappointed, I've been broke . . . but I've never been bored."

If you write commercially, you'll meet all kinds of people and touch on different spheres—manufacturing, retailing, communications, among others. As a published author, you're likely to make radio and TV appearances and talk to groups and find yourself conquering lifelong shyness (and most authors are basically shy). If you're the hub of a household, don't let this deter your resolve to write. Ideas can come any time, and though they might not always hit the paper pronto, they get there—often more polished for the waiting.

And if, for any reason, you must stop writing for a period of time, even years, no formal brush-up is needed, for once a writer, always a writer. Nor is it ever too late to make it in the writing world. Ida Cowen, a retired schoolteacher, had her first book published at age seventy-three. She took writing courses at New York's New School for Social Research, traveling between studies to collect material for her nonfiction books. She also took courses in typing and photography to help her work, and at this writing is taking a class on China, preparing to travel there for material for another book.

WHERE TO FIND WRITING JOBS

Newspapers Mass media, trade, weeklies, special interest, shopper papers, organizations • Do news reporting, special-interest articles, rewrite work, fillers, book reviews, shopping and advice columns, captions.

Books (Adult, children; mass market, fiction, nonfiction, educational, specialized). Copy-editing (grammar, punctuation, typos), first reading and reporting on submitted manuscripts, jacket copy, press releases, captions for photos, illustrations, reviews. Possibly start with publicity letters, planning book exhibits, helping an editor. Typing essential.

Magazines Adults' and children's, slick, literary, trade, pulp, comic book, specific age group markets, special interests (sports, pets, art, etc., guides). Stories, articles, columns, photo captions, articles on personalities, news of related interest, special events, other.

Corporations House organs, press releases, company bulletins, interdepartmental communiques, speech and ghost writing, year-end reports, advertising and publicity writing.

Greeting Card companies

Ad agencies TV and radio commercials, print ads, sales promotion, presentations, technical materials.

Record Album companies Writing cover material. (Music or drama background.)

Public Relations companies Press releases, bulletins, correspondence.

Retailers Advertising copy, bill enclosures, display copy.

Buying Offices and Marketing companies Style and market reports.

Mail Order, Direct Mail, Art Studios Catalog and directory copy; sales-promotion materials of all kinds.

Specialized Associations and Organizations (Charities, banks, museums, health groups, insurance, etc.) Reports, newsletters, magazine work, brochures, educational information, more.

TV and Radio (Stations and Package-Show Producers, Ad agencies)   Continuity, interview scripts, special interest programs, feature programs, comedy, publicity, news commentary, cue cards, script girl work.

JOBS RELATED TO WRITING

Some Writing Possibilities   You can find at least one of these—probably more—even in smaller towns. Most can be done freelance: • Typing, editing, copy editing, proofreading of term papers, presentations, commercials, speeches, reports, other • Research, taping, filming, collating, and checking out reference material for wide variety of projects—community, educational, civic, etc. • Writing, organizing and editing organizational newsletters, book reviews, announcements, flyers, booklets, posters, as well as publicity releases to newspapers, and other PR material, meeting reports, writing and scheduling local radio material. Note: Community volunteer groups need someone to put things in writing—plans, observations, progress reports, and the like. A great way to learn.

What You Need Personally • Literacy • The will to write and the initiative to do something with it • Love of language and desire to express yourself with it • A sharp eye and quick ear for the world around you • Self-discipline • A researcher's instincts • An ear for word rhythms • A sense of drama and timing ? Ability to be self-critical and to take criticism from others who are more knowledgeable • Patience to rewrite and polish your prose • Adaptability (commercial writing requires writing to fit clients' needs) • Imagination

What You Need Materially • Paper, pencils • Also, a good dictionary, ROGET'S THESAURUS, a book of correct usage and style (WORDS INTO TYPE) • An accessible public library is helpful • Subsequently, a typewriter, small office supplies

What You Need Educationally No set prerequisites. Most writers are self-taught. Self-discipline comes from a strong will to do, and doing it, or from holding down a structured learning job on staff somewhere, part- or full-time. You should know how to research subjects—collecting facts, interviewing people via phone or in person, calling for information, and any other called-for methods. Whatever special interest or particular knowledge you have can be grist for your writing mill—used for articles, stories, books, ad copy, on and on. Dorothy Uhnack, a bona-fide detective until a few years ago, now writes detective novels, using all her past experience with New York's Transit Authority Police, plus knowledge gleaned earning her B.A. degree from John Jay College of Criminal Justice. Her first full novel, THE BAIT, won critical acclaim and an Edgar for the "best first mystery of '68" from the Mystery Writers of America. Her later books established her reputation in that field.

Hours You Work For a staff job or a temporary job, probably 9 A.M. to 5 P.M. or a variation of the eight-hour day. Freelance, you work against a deadline, and most successful freelancers work at least a full day sometime between one dawn and the next; they just happen to do it at home. Writing with no assignment, you're on your own, but you must set aside an hour or so each day to write if you expect to produce.

How Much You Earn The important thing for you, as a beginner, is to get your work published, even if they pay you in Plaid Stamps. This can open other doors for you, since it lifts you out of the novice stage—your printed material is proof-positive! You may find yourself doing more than one kind of writing, so it's helpful to know there are big differences in pay scales among writing fields. For example, a TV script or an outlined idea for a TV series pays far more than a magazine story. Advertising copy pays disproportionately high rates compared to publishing company editorial work.

There are also variations within one area, depending on your reputation as a writer (or whether you've been published before), the size and economic status of, say, the company buying your work and the subject you write about. A big-name magazine will pay several thousand dollars for something from a "name" writer, whereas a small one may be able to afford only, say, $100, no matter who the writer is, and is liable to pay a newcomer as little as $5 or $10.

Magazines pay by the word, the line, or a flat fee for the finished job. Currently, story buying is at a minimum with concentration on nonfiction. Freelance copy jobs pay by the page (such as catalog work), by the time spent, or a flat fee for the whole assignment, and just how much depends on the employer or the client, type of account, and account's budget. You should have an idea how much you're worth by the day (this will climb with experience), and try to get paid something approximating this, if you can. However, freelancing calls for flexibility in fees as well as writing; you walk a fine line between outpricing yourself and selling yourself too cheaply.

One more thing: contrary to popular opinion, having a book published does not automatically make you rich. The time and energy expended is rarely repaid in dollars and cents: only the super bestsellers make that. (If photography is one of your hobbies, combine it with your writing as a sales package; it will probably earn you more.)

How You Get Started (Articles, Stories, Books) • Write constantly; practice makes polish. The hardest part of any written piece is the beginning—the first line, paragraph, or page • Read magazines, newspapers, good books • Try to work removed from distractions • Learn who buys what; look up publishers in THE LITERARY MARKETPLACE and in writer's magazines and guides (THE WRITER, WRITER'S DIGEST) • Write, then find a market for your work, or write for a specific market • Send queries to editors on articles before actually writing them or sending them in. Sell the subject by giving an idea what you plan to include.

Some magazines like a sample beginning and rough outline; some book publishers do, too. The query should give all your qualifications plus any published writing you've done • Plan ahead. Magazines work from three to six months ahead, books at least a year ahead • Enclose a self-addressed, stamped envelope for query replies • Look for ideas unique to your surroundings and not easily available to a magazine's staff writers • Complete any assignment with an accurately research-ed and carefully written manuscript, properly typed. Mail with return postage included. (Check your post office for the current special 4th class rate for manuscripts; be sure to mark this on your envelope.) Note: Book rate delivery takes at least as long as parcel post to reach destination. If you enclose a letter, add necessary extra postage, mark envelope "Letter Enclosed." Once you've mailed it, get busy on something else; a watched-for postman rarely delivers.

Once you have something on paper, something you think is good and publishable, don't just stash it away. Some people write, then, squirrel-fashion, bury their work in a box some-where. When Sydney Taylor wrote down the stories she'd told her young daughter about her own childhood on New York's lower East Side (where they were poor but happy), she tucked them all away. When her husband read about the Follett Publishing Company's contest for children's books, unknown to her, he mailed them in. They won first prize and were published as the first ALL OF A KIND FAMILY book, a series that's earned Mrs. Taylor a large, affectionate readership, a special niche in the children's book world, and considerable income.

You can bolster your determination to write with Marilyn Durham's saga. An Evansville, Indiana housewife and mother,

Marilyn had never written a thing before she worked on her first book, THE MAN WHO LOVED CAT DANCING, a Harcourt-Brace-Jovanovich novel that took years to complete and polish, reached third printing fast, made paperback and foreign editions with equal speed, was snatched up for a movie, and named Book-of-the-Month Club alternate. An omnivorous reader all her life, she says, "I read out the library before I had an adult card." She feels that writing's a nice occupation. "If you write a flop, no one needs to know about it."

How You Get Started (Commercial Writing—Ads, Radio, TV, PR, etc) • You need a resumé that includes everything you've ever done related to writing, plus writing samples. If you're an eager neophyte with no samples, make some up; select ads from newspapers and magazines, note product details, then rewrite them. (If you want to concentrate on a particular field, go ahead, but be sure you have potential customers for it.) Or plan an ad campaign with a theme and follow-up ads or commercials. Or do sample publicity releases on a book, an event, a project—to show versatility and open another job door • After writing, let your copy sit for a day or two, then reread to see if it still scans right and rings true. (Keep in mind that copywriters also dream up themes for print, radio, TV as well as ideas for layout, illustration, headlines, test, and dialogue plus action) • List all possible potential clients, phone their creative supervisors or copy chiefs for appointments • Believe in yourself. I've watched people with limited talent make it on sheer brass • The story-article-book writer's bête noir is the rejection note. The copywriter's is the "road block" or "company obstacle course."

If you start as a retail print copywriter, then head for ad agency work, they all too often tell you a retail writer can't do agency writing. And an agency print writer can't do radio. And a radio writer can't write TV commercials. 'T ain't so! A writer is a writer for all that, and if she's worth her creative salt, can pick up the differences in technique on exposure. (See Publishing, for other suggestions.)

How to Segue Into Copywriting from the Sidelines • Take a job in retailing (see When Persuasion Pays Off chapter) to learn about products, merchandising, the consumer's viewpoint. (Department-store advertising departments are ideal training grounds for copy) • Or take a nonwriting job in a writing spot—typist, receptionist, anything short of weight-lifting (and maybe even that!), then learn like crazy • Be nicely nosey so someone will tuck you under wing, play teacher, and give you trial writing assignments • Or take a job as an assistant or apprentice to a big cheese in a small stall for minimum pay, to start. (A local weekly newspaper is one such place.) If you prove yourself, they'll feel lucky, you'll get experience • Take any kind of a fashion job as a foundation for fashion copywriting (yes, department-store selling, too). Ditto mail-order catalog work, which includes nonfashion • Work for the local radio or TV station to learn how they tick and what writing they use. The same goes for any other writing arena.

Literary Agentry Big contact job. You're the middle man between writer and publisher with ability to deal with all kinds of people. You need practical knowledge of contracts, markets, and how to protect authors' rights plus editorial astuteness to judge saleability and merit of work. You may also work out new book ideas with editors and assign work to one of your stable of writers. Best ways to learn agentry—work for an established agent (they all need office assistants) or as an editorial assistant in a publishing house.

Work as a Translator Combine language skills with secretarial work to do correspondence translating or verbal interpreting. Your chamber of commerce should be able to give you a list of businesses involved in foreign trade—banks, publishers, transportation concerns, insurance, advertising, legal firms, art museums, export departments of manufacturers and international organizations. Nancy Diggs of Cleveland, Ohio, knew only French when a company's confidence that she could also handle Spanish prompted her to enroll in a once-a-week course and read Spanish reference books. The company was pleased with her subsequent work. After that, requests for her help in German, Portuguese, and Italian came rolling in, too. Nancy came through on all of them. She has fifteen clients, charges by the word, and has earned enough to finance a trip to Europe.

Poetry Therapy In the past few years, poetry, like filmmaking, has emerged as a strong youth medium. It also has joined art, dance, drama, crafts, and music as a way to help children to communicate their inner feelings. Joy Shieman organized a volunteer poetry therapy team for the psychiatric wing of El Camino Hospital in Mountainside, California. It was so well received, the hospital put her on salary. And so it has been going with other poetry therapy volunteers. They work with many different groups in nursing homes, drug-abuse centers, prisons, homes for the mentally retarded, in ghettos with the poor, in hospitals with the handicapped.

Most poetry therapists working now have no specific training for the work—just a love of literature and people. For information and inspiration, read POETRY THERAPY (1969) and POETRY THE HEALER (1973), both by Dr. Jack Leedy for J. B. Lippincott Company, publishers. Dr. Leedy is a leader in the poetry-therapy movement. Or write to him at Poetry Therapy Center, 799 Broadway, New York, New York, 10003. Also, send for the MADEMOISELLE magazine pamphlet MENTAL HEALTH JOBS* (35¢); Box 3389, Grand Central Station, New York, New York, 10017. It includes a section on poetry therapy.

Greeting Card Messages Write these freelance for greeting-card companies. One woman I know turned out a prodigious number of verses to make time go faster while waiting for her baby to be born. In two months, she'd earned over two hundred dollars, enough to help pay layette expenses.

What You Need Personally • A flair for verse and/or a bright turn of phrase • A perfect sense of meter or rhyme for the former • A keen ear for current colloquialisms • A contemporary style (Auld English is definitely old hat) • Objectivity • Ability to visualize a card idea and describe it or rough-sketch it

What You Need Materially Four- by six-inch plain index cards or paper on which to submit your work; a file box for records of submitted verses, phrases—which publishers, dates, etc.; a rhyming dictionary.

How Much You Earn This depends on the type and size of company; large ones pay more, buy less, as they have their own writing staffs. You may make anywhere from a low of 75¢ a line (four to eight lines each verse) to $40 for a studio-card idea. Make rough sketches to help sell your ideas: stick figures or magazine cutouts are okay. A novelty card or elaborate mechanical can bring in as much as $75 to $100, but unless you get a brainstorm, stick to the $1-a-line, $5-an-idea range and make up the amount in quantity.

How To Get Started • Write to the National Association of Greeting Card Publishers, 200 Park Avenue, Pan Am Building, New York, New York, 10017, for their booklets ARTISTS AND WRITERS MARKET LIST and DIALOGUE.

*College and Careers series.

The first lists all companies who buy art and verse ideas; the second explains in a conversational format how to think up and write greeting-card sentiments. Each booklet, fifty cents (no stamps or checks, please, coins or bills only) • Learn your market; haunt card shops and do personal surveys on friends, family, acquaintances to learn which cards sell. Make certain your work is legible, neat, clean • Type verses double-spaced, one to a card, a carbon for each • Follow all rules and suggestions outlined by the NAGCP • Always include a stamped, self-addressed envelope for returns

OTHER WAYS TO USE YOUR LOVE OF THE WRITTEN WORD

Read to shut-ins, the handicapped, the aged, the blind—to all who can't read themselves or will benefit from this shared experience. Or conduct a children's hour, reading in the public library or in the park in good weather, to community groups of children—e.g., in school. Work as a library aide. Write letters for those who cannot.

14

If You're a Go-Go Person, Try Travel Work

Even if you lack the wherewithal and/or freedom to travel, your mind and spirit can be constantly on the move working in this field, for helping others to plan their trips can initiate you into the sacred rites and mysteries, the life and lingo of the world traveler. Any number of these jobs offer you the real thing, travel for yourself, as well. Besides those described here, many others throughout this book involve some kind of travel, so after reading these, roam through other chapters for ideas, too.

THE TRAVEL AGENT
You plan itineraries and accommodations for individuals and groups, as well as package tours offered by travel wholesalers. It helps if you're a joiner, know many hometown people, and they have faith in your travel knowledge. Work on staff in a travel agency or bird-dog,* bringing in clients on a freelance basis.

What You Need Personally • Accuracy (you can't afford to goof on tickets and reservations) • An understanding of varying human tastes and values • Math ability to figure costs, distances, time, etc. Roz Sobel of Yonkers, New York, adds the personal touch. She gives clients a bottle of champagne

*Flushes out the game, i.e., finds prospects.

164

on departure or wires ahead to hotels to place flowers or a fruit bowl in their rooms.

What You Need Educationally The more you've traveled, the better, since you'll be expected to be an expert on transportation, touring, lodging, and restaurant facilities all over the globe. Travel agencies often arrange for attendance at travel schools, seminars, or courses in facets of this work, and the American Society of Travel Agents (360 Lexington Avenue, New York, New York, 10017) offers a home-study course (about $200). Write to your state's department of education and ask about approved school courses in travel work.

Hours You Work Frequently part-time or flexible hours can be arranged. It depends on the individual agency.

How Much You Earn You'll make a commission (which varies according to clients' modes of travel), a salary, or both. Not a highly paid field, chief attraction has been the 75 percent off given to approved agents for international air and steamship travel.

How You Get Started • Read current issues of FIELDING'S TRAVEL GUIDES, HOLIDAY magazine, and other travel materials • Watch newspaper want-ads for openings in travel agencies or offers to train people • Apply to any nearby accredited agency for a part-time trainee position and ask about training.

OTHER TRAVEL JOBS

Travel Companion Someone going along on a car trip to spell the driver or to help with the very young, the elderly or the ailing. They all need company for long-distance travel. Interested? You'll find these paid (and paid-for) trips (all modes of transportation) advertised in classified columns in THE NEW YORK TIMES, your local newspaper, and through community contacts.

Travel Counselor Works for the AAA (American Automobile Association) which has offices in all major cities. Not high paying, but varied and interesting. You plan auto trip routes for members, make up kits of maps, weather and highway conditions, sightseeing spots, etc.

Airlines Work If you live near an airport, apply for a job as ticket or reservations clerk, director of traffic or ramp agent. (Women have just broken into this last category. Southwest Airlines has Nancy Grubbs signaling on the runways and supervising baggage flow.) Or work in a city airline office.

Another recent first: a woman aircraft cleaner. DPS (Director of Passenger Service) is the title for women working as management representatives for Continental Airlines. They sell tickets, make room and car reservations via plane-to-ground telephone, and decide on a variety of customer problems—all while in flight. Women are working as commercial pilots with foreign airlines, and America is next. A few of ours are currently piloting taxi or commuter planes. Meanwhile, American age barriers have come down for stewardess jobs.

Railroad Jobs Amtrak's passenger-service representatives are somewhat similar to Continental Airline's DPS's—they ride the rails and make reports on customer reactions, suggestions for service improvement, and act as public-relations people for the company.

Car Rental companies They need agents at office counters to service clients, handle paperwork.

Big Business Companies with enough frequently traveling employees usually have a staff traffic clerk to handle all travel arrangements. Learn by working as such a clerk's assistant or reach the job via travel-training and experience. You should be accurate, efficient, speedy, and diplomatic, and be able to wangle emergency reservations in the face of resistance. Locality and company rates will determine your salary.

Buslines (local, interstate, cross country) They need office and reservations help, and if women aren't in the driver's seat yet, they will be. Sightseeing and tour buses use guides and (with youth groups) chaperones. These assignments can take a few hours or many weeks and locally based, they make a great weekend job for, say, a teacher, or anyone with applicable special knowledge (art, history, science, etc. for guide work in museums, at points of historical interest, and the like).

SOME TRAVEL-RELATED JOBS

Resort Representative Live near a resort or landmark section? Sell yourself as a built-in public-information person to the chamber of commerce to promote the area, deal with visitors, write letters, answer questions, do publicity, and hold similar responsibilities.

Club Travel Arranger Crash the travel field via contacts made with transportation companies while booking tours and trips, arranging to show their audiovisual materials. Once they know you, ask about jobs with them.

Special Interests These can send you scooting to

far corners of the globe, often with expenses paid. Katherine Lewin has done this in her quests for puzzle art, and she's also visited such far places as Patagonia and the Antarctic, working for wildlife conservation. Audrey Gluckin finds jewelry-design inspiration in her travels. And Seena Hamilton moves around the United States as a school-trips consultant. On and on. These examples and many others are in these pages.

Traveler's Aid Shop With world travel so commonplace today, there's room for the shop niche filled with all kinds of specialty articles that make travel life easier. Start small, in your home. (The Q.W. Labs, 915 West Front St., Plainfield, New Jersey, 07063, Box 3118, carries a few products; scout the stores for other products, sources.)

Jobs in Travel-Related Spots • Guide work at conventions • Hotel-motel resort travel clerk • American Youth Hostels guide or hostel house-parent • Camper-sales and camper-park jobs • Travel account work with a public-relations or advertising agency

And Transportation Work Keeps You Moving Women are at the wheel more than ever. If not the first woman truck driver in America, Emmie Peek was the first to be enrolled at the New York Transportation Training Center in Long Island City, New York, one of the largest in the United States. Paid while attending the twelve-week training program for truck drivers, she feels the possible financial rewards far outweigh any of the disadvantages; many tractor-trailer drivers earn about $25,000 a year. And the woman cab driver is no longer a novel sight; you see her everywhere these days.

SCHOOL TRANSPORTATION

Here's another job angle. Mrs. Evelyn Geldon of Yonkers, New York, has four sons, one handicapped who needed transportation to a special school. She solved that problem for herself and the mothers of other children at the same school. With one small sedan, she drove them for six months, collecting enough money from the parents to cover her expenses. From then on, her taxi service grew into a full-scale business with thirteen vehicles transporting 270 children during the school year for the boards of education of eight towns plus several day camps. Her husband soon left his job to share responsibilities. In many parts of the country, there's a big need for such services.

What You Need Personally • Driving ability •

Emotional stability • A liking and concern for children •
Enterprise • Some business acumen (if you lack it, get help) •
Bookkeeping ability (ditto)

What You Need Materially • A car or station
wagon (later, more and larger vehicles) • Special insurance •
Permit or certification to transport youngsters • Special license
from the public-service commission and your state department
of transportation • Inspection approval for your car • Chauf-
feur's license (each state has different requirements; meet those
in your state) • Later, other drivers

What You Need Educationally If you transport
children with any special disabilities, read up on these so that
you can cope properly and kindly. Know first aid; take a Red
Cross course in order to handle emergencies. Mostly, you need
common sense—and heart.

Hours You Work Distance between homes and
schools and whether or not you'll do lunchtime pickup and
delivery will determine these. A home-based office and two-way
radio system can simplify your schedule when you're in charge
but not driving anymore yourself.

How Much You Earn Add up all your costs—
labor, maintenance, special operating overhead—then divide the
total by the number of children and figure your markup at
somewhere between 15 percent to 30 percent over each child's
carrying cost. That's your fee per child. One service owner
estimated 40 percent for labor, 20 percent for maintenance, 10
percent special operating costs—and pockets $30 out of every
$100.

How You Get Started • Call school systems
(public) and private schools in your county to learn if they need
transportation for any students. Tell them to put your name on
the list of services bidding for contracts for the new school year
• Ask your public-service commission about laws and requirements covering your territory • You and/or your drivers should
pass physical exams for approval by the state department of
education or whoever passes on such matters • Take care of all
other fringe needs—insurance, car inspection, and the like •
Limit your routes by common sense (it doesn't pay to take just
one child to a distant point) and don't take on more
assignments than you can cover reliably and efficiently.

15

Help the Harried Homemaker

Are you a housewife with skill in any or all facets of homemaking—cooking, buying (consumerism is ver-r-ry big these days), sewing, organizing, decorating, laundry and ironing, care of clothing, home maintenance? Have you had any home-economics training? Are you a private-household worker? Or do you simply enjoy keeping house? If your answer to any of these is yes, there are numerous ways you can turn these capabilities into income.

HOMEMAKER-HOME HEALTH AIDE

Sooner or later, families in all economic and age groups run into problems too big to handle. When the going gets rough, when a serious injury, a long illness, or extreme poverty threaten to disrupt a home drastically, the professional home-maker-home health aide steps in to give the love and help needed to prevent this. As such, your work is a specialty within the healing and helping vocations, and your role is vital as an important tool in the war on poverty. You are a substitute mother who assists in the care of children or those who are aged, emotionally disturbed, mentally retarded, or chronically ill, either during the period of emergency or through prolonged illness. As a homemaker-home health aide, you also manage a household when members are unable to do so—planning meals, cooking, shopping, doing light cleaning, and laundry. All this is done under the supervision of a social worker, nurse, or other professional personnel connected with the sponsoring agency. If you are a mature woman with no special vocational training but a sincere desire to do something worthwhile and earn at the same time, this job could be just what you're looking for.

What You Need Personally • The ability and stability to assume responsibility for jobs assigned to you • Good health • Good character • A warm personality • A liking for people and concern for their welfare • Tolerance • Adaptability • You also need the ability to function alone in an upset household, the ingenuity to cope with limited resources, and the articulateness to share your observations and problems with those in charge at the homemaker office.

What You Need Educationally Among over thirty thousand practicing HHH Aides in the United States, many have had no more than eight-grade education, a few have had less, while others have attended college. The most important requirement is experience in caring for one's own home (or someone else's) and raising a family. Beyond this, your homemaker agency will train you in their own methods.

How Much You Earn Variations in pay levels recognize differences in knowledge, ability, and job performance. Classifications are based on your ability to work with children and adults, home-management skills, and your acceptance and use of supervision and training, or your ability as a teacher to those you help. Pay also depends on the agency's overhead and geographic location, since price and wage levels differ around the United States. Outside the big cities, you stand to make $1.80 and over per hour. Usually, there are special rates for extended service (over eight hours), and rates often vary between full- and part-time service.

How You Get Started • Go directly to your local homemaker-home health aide service, if there is one • Or contact hospitals, state or local public-welfare departments, social-service groups, state or community public-health agencies, nursing associations, child-welfare services, your Community Chest or United Fund, community council or council of social agencies, to learn where you can do this work • Watch newspapers, church bulletins, neighborhood publications, and house organs of local industry for appeals for homemaker help • To learn of established homemaker services in your area, write to National Council for Homemaker-Home Health Aide Services, 1740 Broadway, New York, New York, 10019, or U.S. Department of Health, Education and Welfare, Room 2212, South Building, Washington, D.C., 20201.

HELP FOR THE HOME

The household worker or "domestic" has had all kinds of valid gripes about working conditions in the past, but the increasing shortage of this type of help has caused concerned groups, including the government, to take a long, hard look at the situation to see how they can help. Currently, there are important new programs being set up around the country, and those already in progress are giving the entire field a fresh and far more appealing look. The National Committee on Household Employment, a government agency, has set up training and placement projects in key cities. The plan—to upgrade domestic work and give workers the dignity and status, the pay and fringe benefits, and the standards and government protection they deserve. These programs determine wages, hours, work loads, lunch and rest breaks, and all other vital factors concerning such employees. To learn about free training and placement programs—the potential for attending one or running one in your area—write to National Committee on Household Employment, c/o Women's Bureau, U.S. Department of Labor, Washington, D.C., 20210.

Private Groups People with the same goals are working with the blessings of the National Committee. One of these, McConnell Brooks Carlos, Inc., (MBC) in New York City, gives a three-hour employee-indoctrination course and two weeks of training. Workers receive vacations with pay, holidays, sick leave, a good salary, and after completing a hundred days with the company are eligible for workmen's compensation, Social Security, and health insurance.

The Cooperatives These are several federally funded or privately subsidized experiments in such cities as Washington; New York; Summit, New Jersey; Alexandria, Virgina; and Cleveland. Household Assistance, Inc., in Raleigh, North Carolina, is typical of groups that focus on specialized training, with ten to twelve week courses given to employed domestics, unemployed women, and those who plan to specialize as party aides and caterers.

Clean Teams and Home Help Services They prove that providing more than one set of hands to do household work can give a home the horde-of-locusts treatment and get a job that might have dragged on for hours done in a twinkling, tackling at least three or four homes in a day. Whether it's your own business or you're part of a team, think of yourself as a home specialist and perform as such in order to build business.

Home-help services vary. Some do private homes when called or on a contract basis—say, once or twice a month. Others specialize in disaster restoration (clean-up after fires, furnace puff-backs, etc.). Still others specialize in particular chores. And there are services that do only office cleaning—night work that's part-time or a second job for the workers.

In setting up a service, decide which of the following you will handle • Scrubbing and waxing floors • Shampooing carpets • Washing venetian blinds • General housecleaning • Bathroom and kitchen cleaning • Woodwork • Windows • Tiles • Thorough vacuuming including bedding • Light housework jobs (cleaning silver, washing, ironing, hanging curtains and drapes, cobweb chasing, etc.) • Whitewashing garages, cellars • Painting (small touch-ups, furniture, rooms, etc.) • Paneling and carpentry • Clean-up of attics, cellars, garages, storerooms, closets, etc. If heavy equipment is required, rent machines until you can afford to buy your own. Promote your services (see Promotion Hints).

Running a household training and placement service requires • Enough funds • Ability to handle people (trainees, employers) • Knowledge of the best methods for doing each type of work you offer • The proper way to use equipment needed for each • How to recruit, screen, and hire help • How to administer, advertise, do basic public relations, handle insurance, bond employees, and other details. The Women's Bureau can guide you on these or steer you to help. Write to them (see Index) explaining your goals, background, and needs.

The Entrepreneur Approach to Home Service It's exemplified by The Helpful Elf in New York City, a service started by Lila Gold which now has about sixty "elves" on call who will do anything "as long as it's legitimate" • Clean ovens (the most hated household job in America, according to surveys) • Pick up and deliver ironing • Sew hems • Write speeches • Install locks • Do market research • Address invitations • Do sitting • Shop • Cook • Tend bar and serve parties • Even build, paint, wire, or wallpaper a house (these last are contracted for with people in these fields). Fees are set for each chore. Ms. Gold is an Ivy League college grad who tired of the professional rat race and felt that providing a service would make her feel considerably more useful and just might be profitable enough to support her. She's proved right on both counts.

ADMINISTRATIVE HOUSEKEEPING

This title belongs to the woman whose overall job is to maintain a clean, safe, and pleasant environment in a hotel, motel, school or college, hospital or extended-care facility, or in a YMCA or similar environment. Specifically, you're in charge of personnel, methods of operation, supervising staff and their work, equipment and supplies for the department, as well as maintaining department records, budget, schedules, and work procedures. You may also be responsible for interior decorating. If the place where you work is large enough, some of these responsibilities may fall to others.

The National Executive Housekeeping Association, Business and Professional Building, Second Avenue, Gallipolis, Ohio, 45631, can guide you on schools giving a variety of institutional housekeeping courses. Write to them.

The Hannah Harrison School (of the YWCA in Washington, D.C.) This offers a live-in arrangement in which you get free intensive training in administrative housekeeping—a five-month course in which the school covers all expenses for a private room, board, and tuition plus laundry and kitchen facilities as well as all meals and traveling expenses related to on-the-job training.

Entrance Requirements for This Course You must: • Be between thirty and fifty-five or so years of age • Have had four years of high school or passed a high-school equivalency test • Lack funds for vocational training • Be able to make satisfactory arrangements for the care of any small children you may have

The Course This includes classroom instruction, field trips, lectures, demonstrations by experts, practice projects, and actual experience in a hotel, motel, hospital, school, or extended-care facility. The course has been certified for many years by the NEHA (National Executive Housekeeping Association).

For Further Information Write to the director, Hannah Harrison School of the Young Women's Christian Association of the National Capital Area, 4470 MacArthur Boulevard, N.W., Washington, D.C., 20007.

TEACH HOMEMAKING SKILLS

If you're adept at any homemaking skill or have home-economics training behind you, polish off your knowledge by reading up on the latest and best techniques for it, then conduct classes locally. Even long-time homemakers can be woefully unversed in these arts, and youngsters, teenagers, brides-to-be, and young adults (male or female), living on their own or in groups, offer a vast, unclaimed market for such teaching. With such a solid subject and the right promotional push, you could start a whole new field.

16

Handy Andys, Move Over!

Are you a fix-it person? When something goes blooey in the house, can you calmly and efficiently get it to work again? Only a few years ago, women hid such talents and interests under the proverbial bushel. Today, they're using them to the hilt, and not only earning with them, but earning well. In recognition of this trend, a Goucher College course, "Nuts and Bolts in Contemporary Society," has been a smash hit, teaching small-appliance repairs and auto tune-up. Y's around the country give similar classes, and a batch of new books on all facets of fix-it is flooding the market. What's more, the U.S. government, anxious to fill drastic needs (5 million more service-type workers will be needed by 1980), publishes SKILLED TRADES FOR GIRLS, a pamphlet listing numerous "men's type" jobs offering trade apprenticeships, employer training programs, vocational, trade, or technical school, or correspondence courses. (Write Women's Bureau, Wage and Labor Standards Administration, U.S. Department of Labor, Washington, D.C., 20210.)

Examples of women working in so-called men's spheres are diverse, myriad. Sandra Gourley, a divorcee with children, has used her savvy with power tools in a job touring the United States for Rockwell Manufacturing Company, a Pittsburgh-based company, demonstrating the equipment to women. Cheryl Eule and Mary Korechoff are partner carpenters in a company called Women's Woodwork. Social work and art were their backgrounds. Now they build rooms, do demolition and plastering, make fittings for stores, and do a great deal of shelf, bed, and furniture building. M & M Production Center is a women's cooperative printing company founded by Millie Margiotta who, armed with a high-school diploma and secretarial training, became production manager for a trade association where she learned about the mechanics of offset printing, trained operators, and purchased presses.

Danielle Sandow also founded her own New York printing firm and takes on jobs that Millie finds too large to handle alone. Women Can Do is a four-woman team of house painters and plasterers headquartered in a Greenwich Village apartment. They pool their profits, and their clients are mainly other women and young couples. (A classified ad for additional workers yielded sixty replies.) Women Painters is a team of two in New York (Suzanne Bevier and Louise Hart) who've become pros at their work, doing offices as well as homes.

In Orinda, California, Margaret Bodfish, a plumber for ten years, owns a swimming pool service company. Catherine O'Shea is New York City's first and only (at this writing) woman air-conditioning and refrigeration engineer. After eighteen months at an engineering school, and an official okay from the city's fire department, she works as day-shift watch engineer for the Hotel St. Regis.

Arden Scott is a metal sculptress who takes her youngest child on her rounds as an unlicensed plumber to artist friends who, like Arden, live in loft buildings. She picked up her knowledge by helping plumbers who worked on the family farmhouse in Wisconsin and was able to install a tub and a toilet when her family moved east.

In Detroit, Nancy Rutkowski is Michigan's first lady exterminator and in Webster, New Hampshire, Marsha Carlisle is "just trying to raise two kids" working as a laborer, helping to build the town's new sewage plant.

Women are climbing telephone poles all over the country as phone companies hire them as installers, and Sandra Waters of White Plains, New York, is one of New York Telephone's first female switchwomen. Dourniese Hawkins wields a ninety-pound jackhammer as a Con Ed "gum" or utility mechanic, digging up New York streets to check gas leaks.

So it goes. If a field hasn't had its "first" woman worker as yet, like the walls of Jericho, it will soon tumble. (See list of other such jobs in Let's Get Down to Basics chapter.) All this is not simply for the sake of iconoclasm—larger lures are usually the genuine interest in the work and the far-better-than-clerical pay scale.

REPAIRING AND RESTORING

Jo Elmo of Scarsdale, New York, has a steady little business working on fine antiques. The art interest was a family thing, and this, coupled with her manual deftness plus a little trial and error, have taught her what she needed to know. She points out that for those who cannot or will not leave their homes to work, repairing bric-a-brac and objects of art has singular advantages • It's fascinating, and leads one into worlds of history, art, chemistry, and crafts, to name a few • It presents new challenges with each job. One day you may find yourself handcarving a new section for a damaged picture frame, the next, you might be painting a rare papier-mâché clock • It's free of outside pressures • It's not strenuous. Anyone with a physical handicap in other than the upper limbs can handle the work • It's an open market; few do this type of work, despite the call for it.

There are a few very minor headaches. People's values are often odd. They're liable to spend a small fortune repairing a relatively worthless piece out of sentiment and not be willing to part with a solitary sou for something truly beautiful and valuable, out of ignorance. And you're not too likely to change their minds. Too, there's little available in American books to help with your work.

Kinds of Materials You May Be Asked to Work On • China • Bisque • Wood • Crockery • Porcelain • Pottery • Plaster • Leather • Cloth • Terra-cotta • Stoneware • Glass • Semiprecious stones • Wax • Clay • Metals and alloys (precious, nonprecious) • Papier-mâché

What You Need Personally • Skill and manual dexterity • Patience (a high frustration threshold) • Intelligence and common sense • Honesty (to be able to say whether a piece can't be fixed or is not worth fixing) • Interest in art and crafts • Initiative to research for the right materials or methods to repair and restore.

What You Need Materially A variety of glues and substances, and all the tools required for repairing a wide variety of objects and textures, including: • Plain wooden toothpicks • Glass fiber bundle for polishing metals • Pliers • Sculpting tools • Work gloves • Screwdrivers (all sizes) • Knives (ditto) • Cotton (make your own swabs) • Solvents to dissolve old paints (alcohol, benzine, naphtha, turpentine, etc.) • Forceps • All sorts of brushes (watercolor, pigbristle, oil, stubby, round stencil brushes, toothbrushes; Japanese toothbrushes with old-fashioned natural bristles and bamboo handles are found in jewelry supply houses—excellent for cleaning silver).

Jo Elmo's advice is to use the best grades of material available. "It may necessitate charging your customers a bit more, but the work, once done and done correctly, should last forever." Gold watercolor paints, for instance, used instead of real gold leaf, will eventually oxidize and turn color, causing the need for an entire redoing. For a few dollars, you can buy twenty-four leaves of gold leaf and, with a little flat gilder's tip brush, do the job right the first time. The "cheap is cheap" theory proves itself over and over again in repairing fine things.

What You Need Educationally • Some background in art and art objects, as well as history of art • Knowledge of what glues and solvents work best on which materials and how to use them (ask hardware-store sales people, glue manufacturers [by mail], read up on them [library books, trade journals], experiment, and learn for yourself) • Some idea of the value of all types of antiques and objets d'art (again, magazines and books will help) • Companies such as DuPont, Allied Chemical, Dow Chemical, Union Carbide, as well as local chemical labs are usually more than willing to give technical advice and send samples, and if you need a certain material (say, a particular acrylic resin), chances are they'll mail it to you free, along with printed information sheets.

Hours You Work Depends on the demand for your services, amount of work you have pending, and your speed.

How Much You Earn Calculate the value of your time and talents, plus cost of materials and intricacy of the job-at-hand, then charge accordingly. You might begin at $2.50 or $3.00 an hour, and by the time you're a bloomin' expert, you'll be worth every penny of $10 or more per hour. Or you may prefer to charge on a flat-fee or per-piece basis. If so, be certain to take all elements into consideration (estimated time it will take, value of piece, skill required, etc.). Incidentally, a piece worth only a few dollars doesn't rate $120 worth of time, so consider this, too.

How You Get Started • Learn all you can about art history, antiques, and articles of various periods in history and their materials • Do research (as suggested) on glues, solvents, tools, methods of work, and so forth. When inquiring of knowledgeable people and companies, don't forget art museums; letters to leading ones around the country—address curators most closely allied to your problem, if possible—asking specific questions or overall guidance should yield much help. Do the same with fine-art dealers, gallery owners, historians, private collectors, and appropriate editors at related magazines (home decorating, antiques, others) • Experiment with techniques, materials (Jo Elmo found, through trying, that toothpaste added to an epoxy glue will delay the hardening process when this is essential) • Learn methods, timing involved, and how to wipe away surface glues, paints, etc., without scratching or damaging delicate designs • Be on the alert for helpful new products

Other repairing and restoring work Restringing pearls, doll repairs, reweaving, handbag repairs, restoring old photographs, regilding mirrors and frames, recaning, refinishing furniture (lots of commercial help available now for this one).

TEACH WHAT YOU KNOW

Make the most of the trend and national needs (on your local scene). It's another way to use your special skills to earn. Lady Carpenter Enterprises, for instance, is not only an interior construction firm doing master carpentry for over eighteen years, it's a series of carpentry classes given by the Lady Carpenter herself—Joyce Hartwell. Small groups of women get fifteen two-hour lessons for $150 to learn how to build, panel, and decorate a wall or partitions, customize closets, assemble furniture, and seal, stain, and varnish or paint their first finished product. A shop course in grammar school set Joyce off in her interest, which grew and grew, and eventually took the form of a combined shop/studio where she designed, made, and sold her furniture, and built a carpentry clientele. Teaching came next.

17

Play Up
Your Talents

ART

Ivory towers are definitely outdated. These days, art is out where all can enjoy it, spilling over into everyone's scene—hallelujah! Crafts, fashion, interior design, display, graphics, photography, and many other spheres are part of this marvelous artistic profusion, often overlapping in delightful and unexpected ways. For anyone with any talent and/or creative drive, this spells greater and more golden opportunities.

Types of Art—Fine, Commercial and Mixed • Fine arts—painting, sculpture, printmaking, and experimenting with new media and techniques • **Graphics**—advertising, illustrating, publishing, mass communications, record albums, packaging, etc. • **Fashion illustration** for all communications carrying fashion information • **Industrial design**—anything from a safety pin to an air-space rocket • **Product design**—all kinds • **Dimensional design**—the fine craftsman designs useful and beautiful objects as end products, or as prototypes for factory production • **Fabric design**—creating patterns, textures for cloth and paper. Work with fashion and interior designers, with frequent overlap.

What You Need Personally • Strong interest or talent and imagination (even just a smidgen can take you a long way, if used right) • Awareness of trends, people, the times • Flexibility to grow and change • Self-discipline to work independently to meet schedule deadlines • Good, old-fashioned stick-to-it-iveness

What You Need Materially Tools for the medium you choose to work in. Try drawing pad/pencils or some modeling clay to get direction.

What You Need Educationally • All the living experience and art exposure you can get • Art practice • Guidance from teachers and other artists via public-school adult-education, workshop courses, art school, and college-extension classes, private lessons and/or a job in an art milieu that lets you observe and learn

How Much You Can Earn   It's always difficult to decide what to charge for any type of freelance work. If you can get some kind of guideline from other commercial artists, it helps. Otherwise, figure what the job's worth to you (time, ability, materials) and add to that, and you have your fee. It's easier and less embarrassing to come down in price than to raise it. These figures from U.S. Department of Labor's OCCUPATIONAL OUTLOOK HANDBOOK* should help. It says that **starting** salaries for artists with vocational high-school art training run about $70 to $75 a week, for graduates of one-year professional schools, $80 to $85 a week, for graduates of a four-year post high-school art course, $85 to $100 a week. With experience, this climbs to $125 to $175 and more per week. Art directors, designers, and freelancers in the art field stand to earn $15,000 to $20,000 annually. Freelancers earn within a specially wide range—from $25 for a single black-and-white fashion sketch to $750 for a figure in full color with background. You can earn $75 to $300 for a book jacket or record album, and a color cover for a national magazine brings in from $1,000 to $2,000. Artists experienced in paste-ups and mechanicals earn at least $4 to $8 an hour. Consider all these figures in the light of current salaries.

How You Get Started • Talk to other artists to learn about art study and jobs—the best classes and teachers and which companies use your type of work plus names of their art directors and kinds of presentations they respond to, how they pay, etc. • Make up a portfolio of your best work; it should show skillful execution, versatility, and imagination, be well-mounted and easy to handle, and display a distinctive flair. It will be your professional calling card, so it should say everything for you • Take a part-time job in any art department in any kind of company for experience and training—doing paste-ups, lettering, general helper work • Or to freelance, list reputable studios, agencies, stores, and other companies that are possible clients, call them, learn who buys art, and make an appointment to show your samples • If you know other capable

*1970 edition—check the most recent yourself.

artists, form a group with them. You'll each benefit from the professional unity and being able to present a variety of art styles to fill a broader range of assignments. **To Get Started Noncommercially:** • Show your work as much as you possibly can in order to build a reputation and eventually lead to commissions—(work assignments).

Where to Exhibit (and, Hopefully Sell) Your Work • Art centers • Banks • Museums and galleries • Community centers of all kinds • Hotel and motel lobbies • Coffeehouses and restaurants • Outdoor art shows • Organizational art shows • Theater and movie lobbies • Libraries • Civic centers • Building lobbies • Large corporation foyers • Student art shows • Boutiques • Professional offices of all kinds • Women's and men's club headquarters • Church and temple community rooms • Service organization offices (Elks, Rotary, Zonta, others) • Sidewalk and boardwalk exhibits • Bulletin boards and showcases (business, organizational, school, etc.) • Department stores (as merchandise background display) • Fashion shows • Ad agency and other art departments • State and county fairs.

Details about the where-and-when of art shows around the United States (including outdoor art-show schedules) can be found in the magazine, AMERICAN ARTIST, 2160 Patterson Street, Cincinnati, Ohio, 45214 (at libraries and special newsstands).

Where To Find Freelance Assignments and Part-Time Jobs • Department stores (display and ad departments) • Direct mail companies • Ad agency art departments • Paint and lithograph shops • Manufacturers with art departments • Photo studios • Greeting-card concerns • Newspapers • Record album companies • Mail-order and catalog companies • Public-relations companies • National magazines • Comic-book publishers • Animated-cartoon studios • Museums • Art-supply houses and stores • Community-center art classes (assist instructor or teach yourself) • Interior design (showroom work, designer's assistant, textile house or working with a design workshop) • TV and radio stations (sets, props, backgrounds) • Trade publications for all kinds of interests and industries

Freelance Job Suggestions • Greeting card designs are bought freelance by many greeting card companies. To learn who they are and how to sell them, see Author! Author! That Could Be You chapter, or you can design and market your own new and different line, selling directly to customers and/or to local card, stationery, book and gift stores, or to the large card manufacturers to make and market as your line. Example:

Sensitivity Cards with their inkblot designs. These first appeared a few years ago, dreamed up by a Massachusetts psychiatrist and made up and distributed by Buzzo/Cardozo, a division of Gibson Card Company. The idea behind them: When you care about someone and things are troubled between you, a Sensitivity Card gets you back in touch • Stationery designs—hand-done originals or printed—can be sold in the same way as your own greeting card designs (above). Gear yourself to a particular market—young marrieds, teens, mature citizens, or all of them • Playing card companies buy freelance designs. Learn who the companies are, then write to the art director, ask what he/she is looking for, and send in your work on the requested subjects. These should be card-sized (2¼ inches by 3½ inches) or in direct proportion to these measurements. Pay range is about $75 (two-color) to $300 (four-color) • Bookplates; design and print these for clients. Book collectors pay well for them. Sell through bookstores, small ads (classified) in literary magazines and publications • Portraits of children, pets, family members, ancestors are all possible income sources, if you're good at catching a likeness in any art medium. Find your first sittings among friends, acquaintances • Real-estate developers, contractors and architects need renderings to show how proposed buildings will look when completed. You must be able to read blueprints (take a course in it in public-school adult-education classes), have visual imagination, a good sense of perspective. Pay is on an hourly or by-the-job basis • Scrolls and diplomas are needed by schools, businesses, fraternal organizations, others. Calligraphy, manuscript, and just beautiful handwriting are used for certificates, awards, and the like. (See Hand Writing, chapter 12) • Spot drawings and cartoons illustrate all kinds of printed materials, and are used for display purposes in stores, windows. Perfect a style, find your market • Posters are used at some time or other by almost every business and organization. Make up varied samples and show them by appointment. Lettering know-how is basic • Painting fabrics is a great way to personalize accessories for clubs, fraternities, teenage groups, among others—or it can create unusual decoration. There's a special paint made for this; ask • Furniture finishing/furniture decorating—two separate but related jobs that come in for a lot of calls these days. With all the special kits and materials put out by paint companies now, it's relatively easy to do. Painting wicker is another specialty • Mural painting offers more earning possibilities than you might imagine and can sweep you into other earning spheres, as well.

Jeanne Owens, well-known display artist, has done many decorative wall murals in oils for suburban branch stores around the country. Anita Laidman Wagenvoord turns the walls of children's rooms into colorful zoos and gives as much time, free, to community projects such as hospitals and nursing homes, supplying her brand of color and fantasy, as she gives paid jobs. Her murals have led her into designing an entire line of linens for Burlington Industries, needlework kits for Bernath, skirts and smocks for children's-wear manufacturers, and a book, DECORATING IDEAS FOR CHILDREN'S ROOMS (Lippincott). She's also had fun appearing frequently on TV's Captain Kangaroo show • Charts for manufacturers and organizations illustrate statistics, require lettering, understanding figures and facts enough to interpret in this form. Solicit companies that do not have their own art departments • Mapmaking for homeowners and businesses can be simple or decorative but lettering skill is still a must.

SOME OF THE WOMEN WHO'VE WORKED IN THE ARTS

There are many. None follows any set format, and therein lies the excitement. Mrs. Bea Tobey of New York switched to art after college. She's designed women's scarves and freelanced fabric designs for numerous companies and studios, including fabric giant M. Lowenstein and Co., but her main interest is painting. She sells her work through various architects for use in office buildings, which is lucrative, and has also supplied THE NEW YORKER magazine with a number of covers.

Joan Amron of the same city read an article in WOMAN'S DAY magazine on silk screening and tried it. Her interest grew, and she took a college extension course to amplify her knowledge and technique. Working at the kitchen table "while the babies slept," she turned out Christmas cards for individuals and companies on a freelance basis. Soon after, she and a friend were selling a full line of their cards through gift and card shops.

When Mrs. Susanne Greason of Syosset, Long Island, set up a workshop in her pantry and made a bean mosaic, using several varieties of this vegetable, Elmer's Glue, and eyebrow tweezers, that was only the beginning. With no art background, she went on to oil paintings of nature miniatures (fruit, flowers, mushrooms). Her husband was just getting a foothold in a new business, and with three children to support, money was a large motivation for profitable artistry. Her miniatures sold well to individuals, then through a local boutique, and eventually, to fine New York stores. There's a funny postscript to the bean mosiac. Months later, Susanne noticed several tiny winged creatures flying out of the picture. On closer scrutiny, she observed that her carefully varnished objet d'art was covered with minuscule beige-colored insect eggs. The picture had served as a hatchery!

THERE ARE DOZENS OF OTHER THINGS YOU CAN DO WITH AN ART INTEREST OR TALENT

It's a Puzzlement But not to Katherine Lewin, a Rye, New York, housewife and mother who turned a long-time interest in art into a going puzzle business. A circular jigsaw puzzle gift proved so popular with her family and friends, it sparked the idea for her now-famous Springbok Editions art puzzles. Her search for designs has steeped her in art, from pop to classics, and turned a basically shy woman into a world traveler, public speaker, and authority on art and art-reproduction techniques.

Arty Parties (or Art Shows in Your Home!) Whether your object is to collect originals, make money, or both, you'll find that setting up your home for periodic art shows is a great way to bring people together socially in order to sell works of art. You get a percentage of whatever the artists make, or they pay you with originals for your home. You don't need mansion-sized rooms or a hush-hush gallery atmosphere. Arty parties can be held just as effectively in a small house on an informal basis. You need good lighting, enough wall space to hang pictures, and floor and table space for sculpture. Place art in every room to create a flow of traffic. If you know no artists personally, art schools, company art directors, and art teachers can lead you to them. You can show the work of just two or three artists at a time, but keep in mind that the greater the variety, the greater the viewer appeal and chance of selling. Some who have done this send out invitations, serve simple refreshments (sure lure!) and run their showings in two shifts, cocktail-party format.

Variation of the Arty Party If you have enough of an art background, can supply the art to be shown, and lecture on it, you can do this in someone else's home by appointment. The host and hostess supply the guests and are given a piece of art work gratis in exchange for their organizing efforts and hospitality. It can all be very businesslike, with you drawing an agent's commission on whatever art is sold (these run about 20 percent, usually; yours can be less).

Be an Art Tour Guide If you know your art history and artists, you can take groups of eager-to-see-and-learn children or adults around to art spots, filling them in on all the wonders and techniques they see. If you're a working artist, so much the better. Pass the word along that you're available for this to schools, clubs, convention groups, charitable organizations, PTA's, church and temple groups, colleges and universities, civic and fraternal groups and others. Decide what art periods, artists, and art mediums you want to cover, read up on them and make notes.

Or do what Sandi Gross of Jericho, New York, does. She takes about eight tours a year—four in the fall and four in the spring—to cover all the newest and/or best exhibits in New York. By following gallery and museum schedules, she can plan and study ahead for her tours, which she tries to keep to manageable groups of about seventeen to twenty women each. Sandi is a working artist. In fact, she was doing a lone tour of a Helen Frankenthaler exhibit at the Whitney Museum when an art-tour group came through, and she observed that the guide knew art history but nothing at all about contemporary painting. Remembering this a year later when she was asked to take a group, she accepted. She's paid a flat fee—about $60 for a day—and the program manager arranges transportation and handles individual fees.

Teach Art-Appreciation Classes These can save you the legwork of art tours, but you should have slides, films, and other audiovisual materials to make your subjects come alive. Can be done on a series basis. However, if given during winter months, its best to charge by the class, since illness will give you absentees. The same holds true for indoor-outdoor sketch classes for kids done on a workshop series basis. (Also, consider volunteer teaching of art appreciation in schools, done in cooperation with a community-minded gallery or museum.)

Museum or Gallery Work (You can find it in suburbia as well as the big city.) Volunteer or secretarial work will get you in, let you learn. With art exposure or training, you can try for these jobs: • Guard • Information desk • Assistant to curator • Catalog preparation • Lectures and gallery speaker • Registrar work (collections, correspondence, art shipping, etc.) • Commentator guide • Taping interviewer with living artists. They also use receptionists, and private galleries use practitioners of the subtle sell.

Work in the Media Write an art column for a weekly or daily newspaper or organizational bulletin, or do a local radio station show on newest art showings, news of artists, etc.

Community Groups Can Use Your Art Knowledge and Skills Think. What are your talents, and how can they be used to better and brighten the lives of others? Lee Litt of Orlando, Florida, teaches art at the Orange County Juvenile Home in that city. Her pupils—anywhere from twelve to twenty juvenile delinquents who are awaiting court hearing for anything from petty larceny to murder. What Mrs. Litt does is pure therapy, and for many of the children (ages eight to sixteen) the program provides them with their first real feeling of accomplishment. Most of them come from so-called good families but have parents who just don't care about them. Mrs. Litt makes sure that even the least talented can achieve something, whether it's drawing with rulers and compasses, making designs they can paint, or doing a variety of handcrafts. With her special brand of understanding encouragement, it's not surprising that she's uncovered some real and unsuspected talent among the youngsters, as well as helping them to work out many of their problems through art. There isn't a city, town, or hamlet in America that can't use the skills and services of someone like Lee Litt. Juvenile offenders are not the only ones to benefit—the handicapped or aged also stand to gain. You decide.

Run Art Shows for Shopping Malls You pay the mall manager a fee, but you get all the application fees from entering artists. It's your job to round up the latter, ensure a good show. With good weather and customers in a buying mood, it can be profitable for all concerned. With two hundred artists entered at a fee of, say, $25 each, you can do very well.

THE CRAFT WORLD

The entire craft world has been undergoing a mammoth resurgence. Crafts long neglected or almost dead have been revived with gusto and given fresh, present-day interpretations—collages, tapestries, quilting, and many, many others. And new craft forms and new combinations are constantly being devised. Martha Miller of Great Neck, New York, whose fabric and stitching designs have toured the country and won awards, now experiments with plastic sculpture in unique settings. Edith Bry of New York City has created a new art medium in fused-glass mosaics imbedded in cement and lit from below. She calls it "painting without paints." June Schwarcz of Sausalito, California, has come up with a new technique in enameling called **baise taille** in order to obtain the richness of light reflecting variations of surface. There are many hundreds more such contributing and outstanding craftswomen all over the country.

There are two types of people drawn to the crafts—those who are fundamentally creative and compelled by an inner drive to contribute fresh approaches and new techniques in their own designs and those who, though not particularly creative, nevertheless enjoy making things with their hands. The latter can develop skill to a high degree and execute the designs of others with consummate artistry. If you are one of these, there's no need to underestimate its worth. The cult of creativity has been overplayed to such a degree in recent years, people tend to forget that national folk art styles grew out of the endless repetition of certain motifs and methods by craftspeople. And then, too, there is always the possibility that you think of yourself as relatively noncreative and, through doing, learn that exactly the opposite is true.

The craftswoman who is primarily an artist does not differentiate between arts and crafts. Nor is she likely to work in only one medium, but rather she moves fluidly from one area of expression to another, working with different types of materials. This happens with the nonartist craftswoman as well. Exposure to the joy of making things creates a spirit of adventure in the maker.

Your desire to work at some form of craft can come about quite casually and mushroom into a profitable business with more than one outlet. With Jan Carter of Olympia, Washington, it was the loneliness when first moving to a small town that lured her to a nearby museum exhibition of creative stitchery (use of a variety of needlework stitches to create fresh and original designs). She was inspired. Three courses at the museum established it as her hobby. The realization that other women would love to start doing this work with ready-made kits, then go on to their own original designs, led her to create design kits sold via needlework stores and mail order. She also teaches her craft.

For Eva Kahn of Scarsdale, New York, it was disappointment with what was commercially available that prompted her to design her own pillows. Admiring friends and acquaintances insisted on giving her orders, and she subsequently made up a simple book of instructions and designs for various items—footstools, wall hangings, rugs, pocketbooks, door stops, and chair covers. She also has been teaching temple and adult education classes (how to use drawings for needlepoint) and has done custom-order work for organizational use.

Ruth Law of Hollywood, California, who hand-carves and markets charming wooden toys, trained in the biological sciences with an eye to teaching. "Nothing else creative came to me until I started thinking about children's toys when I was pregnant. I guess the baby kicked something loose, because I've been a busy handcrafter for about thirteen years with very little in the preceding thirty-two to indicate this would happen."

Louisa Jenkins, the fine mosaicist who wrote the first contemporary book on this, came to crafts at age fifty, after a nursing career and raising a family. Her childhood was one of a thwarted desire to draw and paint. Art will out! A friend helped to launch her on mosaic work, and from then on it was experimentation, long hours of work and frustration, and finally the evolving of new approaches to an ancient art. Private and architectural assignments followed.

Sophie Fenton, teacher of ceramics and jewelry making whose work has had national and international recognition, had no art background whatsoever when an eager and persuasive friend virtually dragged her to a class in copper enameling and jewelry making. She recalls, "I was all thumbs and so embarrassed I literally hid in the corner." She finally managed to finish a ring, and when she polished it, fell so completely in love with the craft, she set up a workshop in her home. The encouragement of a good teacher evoked her innate sense of design. She recalls that her very first home output—two hundred hand-hammered enameled copper ashtrays—sold for $2 to $3 each.

There are many, many stories like these of women who, for one reason or another, wound up parlaying a craft ability into a healthy, earning venture. You also can earn rich emotional rewards by volunteering your time and craft-teaching services as therapy for the physically, mentally, and emotionally handicapped in homes, hospitals, institutions for the chronically ill and aged, and houses of detention.

The craft world can be divided into two major segments—handcrafts and needlecrafts, with an occasional overlap of the two. For the sake of simplification, the rest of this section will treat them separately.

NEEDLECRAFTS

Kinds of Needlecrafts • Embroidery • Crocheting • Appliqué • Weaving • Crewel • Quilting • Knitting • Lacework • Hooking • Candlewicking • Rugmaking • Needlepoint • Smocking • Patchwork • Braiding • Cross-stitch • Machine and hand sewing

Some Things You Might Make with Needlecrafts • Sweaters • Bedspreads, quilts • Afghans • Stoles, scarves • Cushions • Footstools • Sachets • Upholstery work • Stuffed toys, dolls • Aprons (all kinds) • Coasters • Fabric and beaded flowers • Pinafores • Bedjackets • Cocktail napkins • Bookmarks • Book covers • Lingerie cases • Wall hangings • Room dividers • Jewel cases • Covered dress hangers • Gloves, mittens, caps, face masks • Doily portfolios • Place mats • Baby sacques • Handbags • Eyeglass cases • Vests • Shoe socks • Earmuffs • Skirts

What You Need Personally • Skill makes the needles fly • Style, flair, imagination—the je-ne-sais-quoi that adds a special something to whatever you make • A practical approach. All the beautiful items in the world won't sell if there's no demand for them.

What You Need Materially Once you've chosen a craft, needlework stores and library books can clarify this for you. So can any teachers. Monetary outlay is relatively small for most. Leftover yarns, etc., from previous projects will build a backlog for you and level off later expenses. If you steer for magazine or manufacturer assignments, they'll supply either the materials or the money to buy them.

What You Need Educationally Training in your chosen craft. You can be self-taught (many are) and learn from doing, from books and magazine instructions, from lessons (private, museum, guild, country workshop, art school, community-group classes, or any others). Any art knowledge will help if you plan to design your own items. Knit shops and needlework departments in stores give instructions with purchase of tools, yarn, etc. Commercial kits with color-stamped designs and matched wool are available everywhere, even in Sears Roebuck catalogs and five-and-tens; they're a dandy way to try needlework to see if you like it.

How You Get Started • Learn your craft • Then decide how you'd like to use it to earn • Work as many hours a day as you can spare. Concentrate on turning out perfect samples • If creating new designs isn't your talent, you can translate existing art into needlework as Mrs. A. Lazarus of Hewlitt Harbor, New York, has done—copying original paintings reproduced from books, fabric motifs, and other art forms. This requires reproducing the design on canvas with acrylic paints or through art-studio transposing methods. (When you make more than one of the same design, try the production-line technique, i.e., doing the same stage of each item at one time.) • When you've completed items that will wear well and meet high commercial and artistic standards, you can:

1.) Show them to friends and acquaintances and start a private clientele for made-to-order work.

2.) Take your work to gift shops and fine stores, exchanges, guilds, and privately owned boutiques. There, you'll either sell your work outright (preferable) or leave it on consignment (meaning that the shop does not pay you until the item is sold; since no money has been exchanged, it may get bottom-of-the-barrel treatment while on display, so this is not as desirable a route to sales). Most shops receive 25¢ on every dollar's worth of consigned goods sold. If the shop buys your handiwork on sight, they usually mark it up 50 percent, or twice the wholesale price (the amount they pay you). Exchanges have their own special approach to selling. The Massachusetts Department of Commerce Women's Program offers a free booklet, MARKETING YOUR HANDCRAFT, which explains exchange rules and regulations, costs and pricing techniques, marketing procedures, and cost analysis, in addition to offering other valuable guidance. Write to Women's Program, Massachusetts Department of Commerce and Development, 100 Cambridge Street, Boston, Massachusetts, 02202.

3.) Sell to manufacturers of needlecraft kits and yarns. Learn names and addresses from their products sold in department stores and knit shops, then • Write to the manufacturer, telling him no more than enough to stimulate a desire to see your work and ideas. Wait for acknowledgment of your letter and further directions • If he asks to see your work, arrange to take it to him yourself, if at all possible, to avoid plagiarism. (Most of these companies are highly reputable, but they can't vouch for every employee.) • If a personal visit is out of the question, mail your article REGISTERED and INSURED to the person who acknowledged your letter • Include a stamped, self-addressed return mailing envelope if such is large enough to hold your article, or tell them to mail it collect.

4.) Sell your ideas to magazines. They represent a giant maw that constantly needs filling with fresh ideas. Before submitting, look over various publications to see what they buy. Write each a letter (c/o needlework editor) telling about your work, your particular idea, its interest to their readers. Enclose an ordinary shapshot of your article (in color, if color is an important feature) or a swatch of the material. **Don't** waste your time and money sending in your work before making any other contacts. And **don't** send complete instructions in your first letter to them, either. These should be sent only after an acknowledgment of interest.

5.) Get your work exhibited. The more it's seen and the better known you become, the more likely you are to profit in one way or another. Submit your work for exhibition wherever possible (see art section for suggestions on where). Also, contact local arts and crafts groups, museums, craft guilds, art schools, university art departments, state fairs, outdoor art shows. Watch newspapers and read the magazine, AMERICAN ARTIST to learn about art events.

6.) Teach your craft. It pays consistently and well and can take in men, women, and children. Melindo Nix of New York City has run a class for men only, after teaching knitting to her father, two brothers, and a male friend. She advertised in a city newspaper and put up a flyer at the United Nations. Result: She enrolled a lawyer, two United Nations translators, an engineer, a social worker, a graduate student in economics, a writer, and a real-estate man—all eager to learn how to cast on stitches, knit, purl, etc. Her $20 fee for five 2-hour lessons held once a week included materials and an instruction booklet for the first lesson.

Jan Carter, whose fascination with creative stitchery led to designing and selling, has taught at the urging of friends, charging $1 an hour, with classes running up to three hours. With at least four pupils per class, she's earned about $12 in an afternoon. Put Jan in a city larger than her own, and chances are, she'd earn considerably higher fees. Individual-instruction charges should certainly be higher, no matter where—anywhere from $5 to $10 a lesson on up.

Teaching by writing, contrary to popular belief, won't earn you large sums per article or book, but it will help to build your reputation as a craftswoman. If the writing is simply an offshoot of an already established reputation, then it will automatically command higher sums as with Erica Wilson,

American high priestess of crewel work and embroidery, Mary Walker Phillips (knitting), and Nell Znamierowski (weaving and rug-making). All three are top craftswomen who communicate the how-to's of their skills through magazine articles and books. And then there are those like Jackie Shapiro of New York and her mother, Dinah Markham of Encino, California—both whizzes at crocheting squares. Jackie can do a five-incher in seven minutes flat; her mother's even faster. They've collaborated on a book, PATCHWORK CROCHET (Workman), to show the almost endless number of things that can be done with this simple skill.

How Much You Can Earn • Factors determining this will be the type of article you make, how well you've done it, its cost, size, potential market, and where you sell it. A novel idea stands to make more than an everyday kind of item • To sell well, your work must be professional looking and beautifully finished, look handmade but never homemade. Loose threads, sloppy seams, crooked corners, and the like are signs of the novice • Shops must add their own markup over and above your asking price. If this sets the item's price too high, it won't move, so you usually must take less, not the store. Equally true of exchanges and guild shops, too • Magazines usually have a predetermined idea what they'll pay for what, ranging anywhere from just a few dollars ($15 to $20) up to several hundred for anything from a design idea to the actual article with detailed instructions • Manufacturers run a similar broad range—from about $25 for a design, such as a child's sampler picture, to several hundred dollars for a quilt design with detailed instructions. (Don't forget to bill magazines and manufacturers for your expenses—materials, mailing, travel, etc.) • With a private clientele, you must feel your way on pricing; comparison-shop first, so you don't sell yourself short • Exhibition prizes (cash) have been an income source in the past but are on the wane. They've brought in anywhere from $50 to $200 per exhibit • Teaching, as indicated above, will bring in what your area and town can afford. Length of classes, number of pupils, your talent and reputation, and whether you're giving lessons on your own or under the aegis of some paying group will also affect your fees • Another thought: With the growth of interest in needlework, running a needlework and yarn shop is another way to use your skills, since you'll be required to stock needed kits and material, and give instructions, as well • One more idea: You can make up all kinds of needlework (or other handcraft) items on special assignment from interior designers to fit their plans for home and business decor. Contact them and present samples of your work. Know beforehand how these products of yours can enhance their work and be certain your output has current appeal (new designs) or antique-related value.

Two Needlework Groups to Join That Could Prove Helpful A $10 membership in the Embroiderers' Guild of America, Inc., 120 East 56th Street, New York, New York, 10022, entitles you to guild news about lessons, seminars, exhibitions, and information from the guild library. You may also rent portfolios of needlework and sets of colored slides. Booklets of needlework as well as guild transfer designs are for sale through the organization. Amateur Needlework of Today, Inc., is only for those who work in needlepoint or crewel. It shows work at the Lighthouse, 111 East 59th Street, New York, New York, 10022. Sale proceeds are not for personal profit, but go to the American Association for the Blind. Write to this organization c/o the Lighthouse; attention: Mrs. Richard I. Robinson.

KINDS OF HANDCRAFTS

The term "handcrafts" covers a far broader range of skills, materials, types of designs, finished articles and their uses, and quality of work than that of needlecrafts. Most uninformed people think of handcrafts as a vague "something you do with your hands" and, when pressed, are hard put to define more than a few. This list will help • Enameling • Glass (stained, fused, glassblowing, etc.) • Batik • Silk screening • Tile • Basketry, caneweaving, rushwork • Shellwork • Paperwork (papier-mâché, origami, découpage, quilling, gift wraps, tree ornaments, tinsel paintings, etc.) • Ceramics • Leather • Printing • Stenciling • Collage • Mosaics • Blockprinting • Plastics • Handpainting (bottles, tinware [tole], fabric, rosemaling, furniture, boxes, other) • Metals (copper, silver, gold, pewter, iron other) • Macramé (knot tying) • Pressed flowers • Beadwork • Candlemaking

For each of these craft forms you have a choice of interpretations, and the kinds of articles and their materials are almost endless.

Some Things You Might Make With Handcrafts • Letter openers • Ladles • Cufflinks • Bowls • Jewelry • Greeting cards • Notepaper • Screens • Mirrors (hand, hanging) • Doors (designed) • Candleholders • Triptychs • Room dividers • Hand-turned wooden plates • Embroidery paintings • Woven goods—clothing, wall hangings, screens, other • Portfolios (for art, doilies, papers) • Telephone book covers • Photo albums, scrapbooks • Belt closings • Napkin rings • Storage jars, herb jars • Windows • Finger puppets • Wall cabinets • Vases • Plates • Door locks, pulls • Coffee tables • Pillboxes • Ashtrays • Plaques • Trays • Wall hangings • Murals • Menorahs • Cookie cutters • Salt and peppers • Mobiles • Fountains • Toys (animals, dolls, other) • Display figures, props • Birdbaths, feeders, houses • Paperweights • Wastebaskets • Cache pots • Picture frames • Miniature chests • Christmas decorations • Tiles • Figurines • Many, many other items

What You Need Personally Same as needlecrafts.

What You Need Materially Each craft has its own requirements. Learn what they are from craft books, magazines, craft supply shops, craft teachers and practitioners. (The American Crafts Council, 44 West 53rd Street, New York, New York, 10019, prints a compilation of craft suppliers called CRAFT SHOPS/GALLERIES U.S.A. [names, addresses, what they sell]. It's $3 to members, $3.95 to nonmembers; send check or M.O. Add sales tax for city and state where required.) Handcraft costs can run from just a few dollars up to hundreds, depending on which you pursue. Before you invest more than lightly, be sure the craft really interests you; try it first.

The only craft launched with no cash outlay is collage making. All this takes is bits of paper, snips of ribbon, beads and scraps of all kinds. If you have children, they may already have introduced you to the delights of collage.

What You Need Educationally Same as Needlecrafts. To learn about craft courses given all over the United States, including Alaska, write to the American Crafts Council for their DIRECTORY OF CRAFT COURSES (ask for most recent edition); $3 to nonmembers, $2.50 to members. Subscribing membership (one year, $12.50, two years, $22.50) in the council entitles you to a calendar of regional craft events and exhibitions in each issue of their magazine CRAFT HORIZONS (six times a year) plus free admission to their Museum of Contemporary Crafts in New York. Craftsman/Sustaining membership ($18.50, husband/wife, $22) allows reduced rates for all ACC publications, slide rentals, film purchases, council-sponsored events, and other advantages, plus free subscription to both CRAFT HORIZONS and OUTLOOK (members' newsletter, six times a year).

How You Get Started Same as Needlecrafts. Also: • Locate your best supply sources and get only basic materials to start. Nonspecialized items such as paper stock, paints, wood, linoleum, glass, metal, fabrics, and wrapping materials usually can be found locally and, in large quantities, at a discount • The polyglot yield of thrift shops, secondhand stores, Salvation Army, and Goodwill Industries and the like can be incredibly inspiring to the craft artist. These places are rich in valuable castoffs that can be given a whole new life and beauty via the craft approach. For example, old jewelry and trinket parts can be set into tapestries and wall hangings to lend opulence and interest. In reverse, carpenter's nuts and bolts and other small goods have been used to create jewelry and other decorative pieces, as well as sculpture • Think. Who deals in fabrics, in paper, wood, linoleum, metal, and other materials, and has leftover and throwaways? Clothing manufacturers or jobbers, local decorator shops, printing companies and your town's daily newspaper publishers, mill-end stores and remnant counters in department and piece-goods stores will save you theirs if you ask. The same is true for paper (painters, wallpaper dealers, contractors, printers, stationery suppliers) and for every other type of material. Use the classified pages of your telephone book to help find all of these • Don't overlook things right under your nose that have craft potential—from toolbox items to paper egg cartons to brown paper bags. Many a solid business is built on this kind of ingeniousness (remember the workmen's lunch boxes that turned up a few years ago, lacquered and overlaid with collage designs and sold on boutique counters for way-up-there prices? The idea swept the country.)

Kathe Berl, a fine enamelist who's done considerable teaching offers this advice to the craft beginner: "Since everyone is not a designer, you should not be afraid to execute other people's designs. Adapt someone else's good design to your uses; a simple motif, such as a leaf or scroll, can be done many ways, adapted to many uses with fresh effect. Wallpaper and fabric swatches are a good source for these. Also, many an artist is too busy to carry out his own designs or prefers working in the abstract, leaving the actual workmanship to a skilled crafts-man." (This could be you.) "Your craft should grow from your feelings and heart—like a seed," Mrs. Berl explains poetically, and she cautions, "When you start, don't try to imitate high art forms. Do simple work at first—whatever is natural to you."

Marketing your handwork is much the same as needlecraft marketing and can encompass all, several, or just one form of outlet. In the Soho section of New York City, Laura Adasko and Alice Huberman are running a two-woman batik center where they dip and dye a variety of colorful, one-of-a-kind fabrics and make them into wall hangings, women's dresses and scarves, men's shirts and ties, which they sell to better stores or do on special order. They also teach this ancient Indonesian method of handprinting textiles in a six-week series of once-a-week classes that run about two and a half hours each. Charge—about $40 per pupil (four pupils) plus cost of supplies (the pupil supplies the fabric, chosen under their supervision).

Quilting, one of the crafts mentioned as having a big revival, is a big variety store. Some do them in modern asymmetric designs as Beth Gutcheon does, selling them anywhere from $150 to $400 each, and teaching others at $10 a session (three sessions of three hours each). Deann Murphy and Carol Reiling have a quilting business called Distlefink Designs which makes crib quilts and kits based on a nineteenth-century patchwork they found in the attic eaves of the Murphy's summer cottage. Both kits and made-up quilts are selling well to New York's better stores. And on East 70th Street, same city, Kate Kopp and her husband run America Hurrah, a tiny step-down shop crammed with antique quilts priced from $50 to $1,200 (kingsized). Hope Shoaf of Flemington, New Jersey, makes quilts to order for from $75 to $200, using, for the most part, no-iron sheets and fabrics and a Dacron filling to make the quilts puffier. And these are just a handful of approaches to just one craft.

Search beyond the previously mentioned outlets for your work, and you could be lucky enough to find one such as Craftsmen Unlimited in Bedford Hills, New York, which serves Westchester County craftspeople, including the elderly and teenagers, and keeps 25 percent of the profit in order to maintain the organization. Seek. You may find. (Remember, sharing your craft can help to heal, and to brighten the lives of others.)

If you are sixty years of age or over, live anywhere in the United States, and have craft work to sell (or if you live in the New York area and wish to study a craft), write to the Elder Craftsmen Shop, 850 Lexington Avenue, New York, New York, 10021 or the Katherine Engel Center for Older People, 23 West 73rd Street, New York, New York, 10023. There is also an Elder Craftsmen Shop to contact at 1628 Walnut Street, Philadelphia, Pennsylvania, 19103. They'll send you information about their services and application blanks. For other outlets for work of this age group, contact your own state's office for the aging.

TOY DESIGNING

"It can be done at home, requires little if any investment, is a wonderful antidote for housewife doldrums and can be very rewarding financially." This is how Helen Malsed, housewife, mother, and originator of the world-famous Slinky Pulltoys, feels about her field. All of the following advice comes straight from Helen and other women who've learned how the hard way—by experience.

What You Need Personally   Imagination • Business sense • A good memory • Persistence • A positive philosophy and emotional bounce (to take rejections well) • Some manual or drawing ability (helpful for making rough sketches or a crude model of your idea)

What You Need Materially   • Packing materials for toy models (paper, twine, corrugated board, box stuffing, etc.) • Business stationery • The help of a patent attorney, if possible • A technical artist to make sketches and working drawings • A model maker to make up toy models, if you cannot • A good market-located agent, if needed

What You Need Educationally   Just a good creative head. Any design, engineering, or business knowledge will be helpful.

How Much You Earn   Helen Malsed estimates that "an average, only modestly successful toy will bring in what a woman might have earned as, say, an executive secretary, whereas if you hit on a uniquely successful item, returns, particularly during peak volume, can be fantastic." However, there may be as many unprofitable years as there are profitable ones, so don't expect too much. Best to sell to manufacturers on a royalty rather than outright-purchase basis. Royalties range from .05 percent to 5 percent; popular-price, high-quantity items may pay a lower percentage than a high-price one. Table games can often pay 5 percent. (Royalties are considered capital gain. If you draw up the licensing agreement with this in mind, royalties will be taxed at a lower rate than regular income.)

How You Get Started   • Watch and listen to children at play. Look for interests, needs, dexterity, abilities. Helen claims her best concept to date came from her son when he was a child • When an idea hits you, put it on paper fast, in writing or a sketch. Keep looking at it and add improvements, eliminate nonessentials. Make it safe for children to use (very important). Decide which company has products like it and might be interested, and what materials they'd use for it—then make a model adaptable to the same materials • The reputable owner of a high-quality toy shop in your town might provide you with direction, advice, moral support • Make up rough models to let children try out your idea. Get their unprejudiced opinion, if you can (what Mama makes is bound to be more interesting than something from the store) • Keep a business diary with dates, sketches, witness signatures of people who've seen and understood your ideas. Write all your ideas in this book so that if ever one is stolen, your records will back you in court. (Dorathy Machado Wood, director of a speculative design firm in Van Nuys, California, suggests, "Read Edison's biography; learn about inventions and lawsuits the easier way") • Subscribe to toy trade journals: PLAYTHINGS (51 Madison Avenue, New York, New York, 10010), TOYS (575 Third Avenue, New York, New York, 10016). Get their directories and catalog issues for the annual toy fair. See which manufacturers make what; study the toy stores. If you have an idea that fits any of these companies, work it up to suit their production methods, then write an inquiry letter to find out to whom you should submit your idea. (Never send items in cold. The danger of piracy is ever-present) • Keep records of toys already on the market and patented so you don't overlap. Patent journals or files (in most big-city libraries) tell this and may even lead you to another, better idea. (Note: Patent journals require time to use; this is why patent lawyers are paid well for searching records.) Dorathy Wood says, "I find it hard to remember what I've seen, and sometimes create an item I've seen and forgotten. It won't be identical, but it won't be saleable, either. The more amateurish one is, the more this is apt to happen." • Dorathy, who develops products in many fields, maintains that "the most difficult part is to keep working at an idea until it's developed and ready to sell. A notebook full of unfinished ideas is worthless. People constantly tell me they thought of an idea before it appeared on the market. I tell them I've thought of many, but if I haven't tried to place it, I haven't done what's necessary, so can't claim the glory. That's why a good agent's fee is worth the shared royalty. One sold item is worth a thousand grand ideas waiting to be sold." • Choose! You can make and market your product locally on a small, manageable scale, or sell it to a large manufacturer for national distribution. Helen Malsed feels the latter is far safer, since a well-known manufacturer has the know-how, capital, and distribution. But Rachel Copelan, puppet designer, performer, and lecturer, says,

"There's something beautiful about working on a local level."
She began making original marionettes right after World War II
and sold well over a million of them. With $300 and the help of
neighborhood high-schoolers, she made the marionettes herself,
packaged them in clear vinyl bags, and sold them to local stores.
By demonstrating them herself and getting her viewers' reactions, she was able to simplify and improve her product. One of
her never-to-be-forgotten pleasures was seeing a child run
down the street after buying one of her puppets, yelling
ecstatically, "I got one! I got one!" For the local approach,
Rachel suggests: • If your toy sample is too difficult to make
yourself, find a model maker (carpenter or craftsman) • Get
written orders from local reputable stores, including department
stores, on the basis of your samples (it's not necessary to
mention that these are your only designs) • Then buy your
additional materials—in bulk (it can save you half the cost) •
Price your product by figuring all costs (see Needlecrafts) •
Register your product through your lawyer • On the subject of
patents, there are two kinds of toy patents, mechanical and
design. The latter gives little if any protection, as a slight change
here or there on the product can render the patent useless.
Mechanical patents usually give more protection. Dorathy Wood
maintains it's **not** necessary to get patents before submitting
toys if you're dealing with a reputable manufacturer. Helen
Malsed echoes this with "Don't waste your best thoughts,
money and efforts on the patent potential. Concentrate on the
merits of your product and placing it in the best possible
hands." And Rachel Copelan advises that a local lawyer, acting
as your representative, can make your contacts with toy
manufacturers on his stationery, which immediately sets you up
as "protected." The lawyer will work on a percentage basis. She
suggests that first you send a sketch and written description of
your idea to yourself in a sealed envelope, by registered mail.
Note its contents on the outside of the envelope for future
reference. Take this, unopened, with a duplicate sketch and
description, to your lawyer-representative for safekeeping •
Major toy companies such as Mattel, Inc. have printed guides on
submitting toy ideas—procedure, basis for judgment, etc.—free
for the writing. (Mattel, Inc., 5150 Rosecrans Avenue, Haw-
thorne, California, 90250, Attention: V.P. Product Planning) •
You're most likely to sell your ideas in person than by mail,
although there are exceptions. Reason: It's more effective to
talk up the value of an idea in person—to push every good
point, counter every objection, give the woman's (and, possibly,

the mother's) viewpoint • To safeguard your ideas, it's vital: Not to reveal your ideas prematurely or indiscriminately until the contract is signed, sealed, and delivered • To deal only with reputable manufacturers • To submit an idea to only **one manufacturer at a time** and ask for prompt consideration. Expect rejections • To telephone or send an inquiry letter first, and get name of person to whom you should submit ideas • To ask permission to submit a new idea (or, even better, a basic concept applicable to many different toys); however, DO NOT reveal the idea or the item in this first letter • When permission to submit is granted, it should be with the understanding that, if the manufacturer is interested, he'll enter into a written contract with you • DO NOT send the original sketch, just a copy; if you have a model, send only a color photo of it first; keep carbon copies of all data and correspondence; the letter accompanying your idea must sell it by covering its theory, background, specifications, outline of all details, the toy's potential, plus trade-name suggestions, where helpful • To mail all this registered to the person at the company who asked for its submission; insure models for complete replacement value, and label this on the product so the manufacturer will insure the return • To try for a guaranteed annual minimum payment in addition to the royalties, at least for the first few years • If you have no success with your ideas as toys, redevelop them as arts-and-crafts items and sell to that market instead.

Advice on Inventing Games Shop around. Be sure your idea is not already on the market. Don't believe your local games merchant when he says he'll order a gross if you get into production; it's always a gross, and he tells it to everyone. When friends try out your game, don't explain it to them. Just give them your model and written instructions, check your enthusiasm, and watch their reactions to the game and the directions. The latter, if obscure or incomplete can make or break a product. Even if a manufacturer buys your item, wait a while before you go on a spending spree. Not every game is a best seller. Some do well for a year or two, then taper off, and others never catch on at all.

Felicia Parker, a game and toy agent and marketing expert will read your inquiry letters if they give explicit descriptions, stating whether your idea is a game or toy, how it looks and works, plus names of manufacturers (if any) who've already seen it. Going by this, she'll evaluate its commercial potential and determine whether to see a model or not. (Note: No unsolicited models will be accepted.) If she agrees to be your agent, she'll handle manufacturer contacts, work out the best contract for you and other details. (You sign and approve all agreements.) For this, she earns either 35 percent of the inventor's royalties or a flat fee. Address Felicia Parker c/o I.S. Unlimited, Inc., 1123 Broadway, New York, New York, 10010. Agents similar to Felicia might be found in some big-city classified phone book pages under "Toy Consultants"—in New York City, there are a number of others.

INTERIOR DESIGN

So many people (yes, even decorators themselves) have such a hard time deciding how to dress up their homes, it's not surprising that the field has burgeoned both in numbers and artistry. The upsurge of artistic awareness has contributed to this growth. So has the fact that people no longer choose one style or period of furnishings and stick with it right down the line. Instead, the eclectic look—mixing old and new—as well as today's free and individualized approach, have made the whole business more complex and the need for help far greater.

Interior design is stimulating, rewarding, and prestigious. The work is done in two major areas: domestic (private homes and apartments) and commercial (offices, stores, hotels, similar public buildings). Usually, you specialize in one or the other. To put it in a nutshell, you talk to clients, determine how they like to live (at home or at work), and from this, plan and oversee the setting up of a background pleasing to them. You integrate color schemes using fabrics, wallpapers, carpets, paints, etc., buying the materials and doing custom designing when it's called for. You also take care of details like billing, selling, and contract arrangements.

What You Need Personally • A strong design sense (feeling for line, color, form, space) • Creative imagination • Basic business and selling ability • Physical stamina and strong arches • Know-how in getting along with all types of people

What You Need Materially • Desk space • Telephone • Personal Stationery, business cards, bill forms • Recordkeeping books, papers, small office supplies • Art materials, such as sketch pad and watercolors, are helpful if you can use them.

What You Need Educationally This depends on whether you plan to be a full-fledged interior designer or a friendly neighborhood consultant who uses local sources of supply for all aspects of work. To perform professionally, get all the art and design training and working experience that you can. Learn to read blueprints, draw up floor plans to scale, acquire a basic knowledge of construction materials, electrical wiring, plumbing, heating, climate control, even landscaping. You should know about cabinet work and how to design built-ins, all types of flooring, wall and ceiling coverings, lighting, woods and their finishes, fibers and fabrics, furniture styles and their periods, how to use color and work with space functionally, and more. Write to Allied Board of Trade, Inc., for their list of registration requirements. These are covered in detail. The address is 342 Madison Avenue, New York, New York, 10017.

You can spread out the training over a longer period or attend school at night to accommodate your home demands. Inquire when you contact schools. The American Art Directory lists schools of design in the United States and Canada by state, city, courses (in detail), requirements for admission, fees, other factors. Ask to see a copy in your public library. Also, send for A BIBLIOGRAPHY FOR INTERIOR DECORATING No. 54 for reading suggestions, free from Small Business Administration, Washington, D.C., 20416.

Hours You Work   Flexible. If you're away from a decorating center, you'll do most of your keeping-up-with-trends and ordering via mail—trade magazines (INTERIORS, INTERIOR DESIGN) and papers (HOMEFURNISHINGS DAILY). If you belong to either the American Institute of Interior Designers (AID) 730 Fifth Avenue, New York, New York, 10019, or National Society of Interior Designers, Inc. (NSID) 315 East 62nd Street, New York, New York, 10021, they will keep you up-to-date through their publications.

How You Get Started   Many a woman who's done an imaginative job decorating her own home suddenly realizes she's latched onto a good thing and heads for a decorating career. Ruth Benson of New Rochelle, New York, exemplifies this. Widowed suddenly and forced to support herself and baby daughter, she found a job as an assistant in a decorating studio. On-the-job learning and additional schooling groomed her for her present work as an independent interior designer.

Other ways to get practical experience in the field or in one closely related • Become an apprentice or assistant to a designer in an interior design company • Work in the showroom or office of a home furnishings manufacturer or with an antiques dealer • Assist the curator in the interior-settings wing of a museum • Be an assistant in a department store's decorating department • Become a shopper or runner for a practicing interior designer, contacting sources and selecting items under supervision • Get a job as an estimator, taking measurements for drapes, slipcovers, carpets, etc., and writing up the orders • Be a sketch artist, draftswoman, receptionist, saleswoman, secretary, stockroom clerk in any kind of interior-design milieu • Don't forget the possibility of working for a home-decorating publication, if there are any in your locality.

Credentials Needed To Operate as an Independent Interior Designer or Decorator • Open a commercial checking account at your bank • Register at your local county courthouse (small fee for this). They'll give you a resale number (file this for personal reference) and a certificate for doing business (make a photocopy for your files). Take them to the bank where you have your checking account, and they'll file them to validate the commercial value of your account • Write to Lyon Furniture Mercantile Agency, 185 Madison Avenue, New York, New York, 10016, and Allied Board of Trade, 342 Madison Ave., New York, New York, 10017, and tell them you want to register. They'll mail you a detailed form to fill in and return, after which they'll inquire at your bank to establish credit rating just as Dun & Bradstreet does for regular busines corporations. Both Lyon and Allied act as collection agencies for both wholesaler and interior designer • Order your business cards, stationery, billheads. Distribute the first where you think they will help the most—to real-estate people, architects, home-furnishings contacts. Sometimes your best connections are right under your nose. Gloria Menna of Scarsdale, New York, had a furniture designing and manufacturing father, but her training led her to work as an artist's representative and writer, and she came full circle to the family field almost by accident. A chance challenge from a doctor friend who needed help for his dreary, colorless office was more than Gloria could resist. Her career was off and running, with time scheduled to allow for two small children at home. With some years of experience behind her how, she's design consultant for New York's First National City Bank, the second largest in the world • Choose your method of charging clients. Charge at retail price plus an additional service or consultation fee. Since you're able to buy most things through showrooms and furniture outlets at a discount, you make the difference between this and the retail amount plus. Or—charge a flat consultation fee plus a service commission on purchases made by your client. Or—work on an hourly basis, charging for all time spent on every phase of the job. The fixed-fee approach is also used to cover the time estimated for a job after a preliminary consultation wherein the designer sells furniture to the client at the prices she herself pays wholesale. This method is often used on contract jobs such as offices or public buildings. It's usual, with these, to ask for a retainer paid prior to beginning the job (but not covering the first meeting) • Keep up with all that's happening in the fast-paced design world by reading related trade and consumer publications and visiting design centers in metropolitan areas (New York, in particular) as frequently as possible.

Promote Your Services (See Promotion Hints) If you have a specialty, play it up. It can be anything—lighting effects, charming done-on-a-shoestring homes for young marrieds or those with strained budgets, exciting ways with color—you determine, according to your talents and interests.

Some Interior Design Offshoots If you don't steer straight for a structured career as a decorator, there are many other outlets for your skills and leanings: Consultant work, designing and producing decor items, buying or illustrating furnishings, doing little-theater or TV set designs, teaching and writing about facets of decorating, relating a hobby or skill to interior design (for example, needlework of all kinds, or collections such as coral, butterflies, paperweights, others), refinishing and decorating old furniture (there are commercial kits to help you get started).

You might decorate low-income model apartments, designing something new and fun that may also meet a need. Jo Banks of New York designs custom clothes and interiors; she dreamed up a sofa made of a fifty-four-foot-long sailcloth tube (she stitched it up herself after paying about 60¢ a yard for the fabric) stuffed with kapok. The stuffing took a bit over an hour, blown in by four men, and came to over $100. Jo sold four of these without trying, at $600 per couch, each client paying for the design exclusive for one year. After that, she moved on to other creative ventures. With her apartment full of roaming children and dogs, the puffed-up canvas sofas (there are two now) do yeoman service for fun, games and old-fashioned comfort. (Kapok bought in bulk runs as little as 50¢ a pound, and seventy pounds are needed. By stuffing it yourself, you could make a couch for $35 plus cost of sailcloth.)

Growing plants go a long way toward enhancing interiors, and your design sense can be applied to helping clients to make the best selections for homes and offices. (See Go Back to Nature chapter.) Now add your own idea—then follow through on it.

DISPLAY

Designing store window and interior displays, creating backdrops, props, and accessories for display use is much like being a Broadway stage-set designer but on a smaller scale. You need an eye for overall effect, a knack for creating mood and excitement with color and arrangement, a flair for the dramatic, and/or some kind of craft or lighting specialty adaptable to these. What good scenery does for actors and dialogue, good display does for merchandise or a message. Display work takes in dreaming up the ideas, designing them, and then actually making them.

Some Possible Clients for Your Display Talents • Local shops and department stores • Caterers and party-planners (for centerpieces, decorations) • Charity and cause groups for fund-raising socials • Banks and other large corporations (as a merchandising arm of public relations and sales promotion) • Hotels (for seasonal decor) • Museums • Manufacturers of cosmetics and perfumes • All companies involved with fashion and fashion-related products and materials • Display and exhibit houses or studios • Ad agencies • TV producers • Manufacturers of display materials • Display jobbers or distributors.

Since almost every shop on Main Street, U.S.A., uses some sort of window display, you can act as a freelance service, planning their themes, making up props, creating the actual settings, working on a prearranged schedule. Or you can do this on a single-assignment basis for small stores and the display managers of department stores. The trick is to make your windows or display units so eye-catching and fun to see, they create community talk and draw crowds.

What You Need Personally • Good taste • A sense of design, texture, color and drama • Manual dexterity • Creative imagination • Some art or craft experience • Active interest in fashion and decor • Patience • Enthusiastic salesmanship (the client is usually buying an unseen idea, something not-yet-tangible, you must be able to put it over verbally)

What You Need Materially This will be based on what you design. Some basics are a staple gun, hammer and nails, special papers (tissue, flameproof, decorative, etc.). plastics, glues and pastes, wire, paints, plaster, cardboard (foam, flex, pressed). Watch for new trends in materials.

What You Need Educationally Display brings into play all the disciplines of the art field (graphics, flat design,— e.g., textiles—fine art) so courses in basic design, modern art appreciation, and sculpture are all good training. As for formal display training—you'll need to do some searching for courses that pinpoint the field, but it could be worth the try.

The best way to learn display is to work as an apprentice or part-time assistant in a display house or department store. This is how Louise Butler did it. She had alternated between two loves—art and dancing—until, one day, during a lean period for dance work, she happened to walk by a display house and, on impulse, went in to inquire about a job. She'd always been good at lettering, so they put her on staff right away, and before long, she was busy working on display units. Fascinated with the field, she gave up dancing and has been turning out creative exhibits and other art-display offshoots ever since—the Sony Company windows on New York's Fifth Avenue, Dry Dock Savings Bank displays, WOMAN'S DAY and other magazine craft projects, and a wide variety of other design assignments. A manual-arts course taken in seventh grade plus her knowledge of choreography and stagecraft have helped Louise immeasurably, giving her the three-dimensional flow required for display. She suggests: excitement sells, motion attracts (simple turntables, mechanization), and simplicity is powerful.

How Much You Earn Lots of factors influence this—the kind of display work you do, the quality of your work, your geographical location and its economic level, and so forth. It's a good idea to decide just how much you're worth by the day and try to work within that structure. Figure out how much a particular job is worth, too—it's not just the time and skill needed for making and installing the display, it's the idea, as well. **Don't ever forget the value of the idea. And don't give any away free!** If you work for a display department in a store, or a display house, you'll start at the prevailing rate of pay for beginners—unless you have something special to offer. To learn (and if no paying job's to be had) don't overlook the no-pay situation. After all, this will be your schooling. Best to ask display people and places what they pay.

Hours You Work If you're a freelance display service, this will depend on how many stores you work for. Work loads are heaviest before peak selling seasons and holidays. As an apprentice or display assistant in a store, you can work day or night shifts. Display studios work the usual eight-hour day.

How You Get Started • Work in any kind of art, crafts, or display environment to learn materials, three-dimensional techniques, trends—in the display department of a store, a display studio, or as assistant to an established freelance display person, or with television package show producers who need program backgrounds (watch those big musical specials) • Read up on design analysis and various display techniques such as paper sculpture, collage, lighting (very important), wire work, and so on • If you tackle store windows, case your potential market—look over local store windows to see which need improving. With seasonal promotions in mind, make sketches or models of these windows with your own ideas. Submit to either store owner or display director. Make certain you know what materials and techniques will be used as you'll probably make them yourself • Find your best supply sources—lumber yards, building-supply companies, paper and fabric manufacturers or jobbers, hardware and paint people, plastic companies. If you can't find something locally, write to the major national manufacturer for information and source guidance (DuPont for plastics, etc.). Also, use traveling display jobbers; they'll call on you if you offer them a chance for substantial business. Don't overlook secondhand stores—they have plenty of the makings for display magic • If you have a particular flair, develop it with display use in mind. Then take along photos of your work when you solicit assignments; they'll be your selling tool • Louise Butler maintains that, to many clients outside of New York City, she suggests that you try to put display on a marketing or sales-promotion level when you're selling your ideas and services; this takes it out of the unimportant, window-trimming context and gives it real sales value • Get your client interested in planning the next window change as soon as possible. Christmas in July is not unusual (though sometimes difficult) • Caution (Don't make the mistake of forgetting to measure the window openings, then arrive with a prop you can't get into the window. (It's happened.) • Read DISPLAY WORLD maga-zine—in your library reading room, or subscribe (140 West 57th Street, New York, New York, 10019). It issues a twice-a-year directory that gives names, addresses, and specialties of Ameri-can and international sources, and tells who is showing what and where • There are two major market weeks each year set up by the NADI (National Association of Display Industries) when manufacturers present their new wares for the four seasons: June for fall and holiday needs, December for spring and summer materials. Try to attend at least one of these, if possible. (Otherwise, use DISPLAY WORLD's directories.) • To learn which display jobber member is nearest you, write to Display Distributors Association, 2561 North Clark Street,

Chicago, Illinois, 60614. **Note:** To earn additional income, a display artist can also teach draft skills to others.

PHOTOGRAPHY AND FILMS

Look around you. Almost every printed item in sight uses photography in some way. And you can't turn on your TV set without running headlong into the world of film. These represent the commercial side of the coin. Then, there's art. Yes, art! For in the past few years, a trend has emerged and promises to grow. Photo prints have started to become collector's objects much as graphics moved into art spheres some ten years ago. Then, too, there's a real need for qualified technicians in the photo and film world, and this applies to graphic arts, photofinishing, audio-visual technicians, motion picture processors, and most of the essential related skills needed to produce top quality results. No matter how you approach it, photo or film work can grow as large as your interest, abilities, and time will allow, and take off in any number of directions.

Ways to Earn With a Camera and or Technical Skills in Processing Work for: • A commercial photographer or photo dealer • A caterer, photographing parties and special events that they service • Real-estate firms—photographing houses and other properties for showing to prospective clients, for window display • Newspapers (dailies, weeklies), photographing people and special news stories on assignment • Ad agencies and public-relations companies for their printed materials. Also, on your own do: • Portraiture (adults, children, family groupings, pets) • Christmas card scenes—houses, children, family groupings—have them made up to order for custom jobs • Candids—at all kinds of festivities—company affairs, family parties, school and club functions, beaches and beach clubs, picnic areas, private and public pools, teen-age affairs, graduation, etc. (see The Social Life: Get It All Together chapter for other possible occasions) • College-entrance application snapshots, passport and visa photos • Publicity photos of local celebrities. (People who appear in public or on radio/TV need glossy photos for newspaper and magazine articles, display) • Coverage of sporting, school, and other organizational events • Garden-club pictures of flower arrangements, gardens. (With knowledge of the subject, you can talk to groups using your own slides, and earn even more) • School-yearbook photos • Religious events (weddings, communions, bar mitzvahs, baptisms, etc.) • Special projects (science, shop, murals, etc.) are documented photographically; so are special displays • Fraternities, sororities, women's clubs and organizations, civic groups and the like require a photographer's services • Restore old photographs; learn this special technique from someone already doing it • And if you have any other special interest—travel, art, etc.—photography can be tied in with it.

There are countless other ways to work in photography. For details on these, ask your nearest photo dealer for a copy of PHOTOGRAPHY IN YOUR FUTURE, A Kodak Customer Service Pamphlet that is chockful of information, reading suggestions, and listings of free helpful booklets, as well as a list of all the career possibilities open in photographic and film work.

What You Need Personally • An artist's eye • Good taste • Patience • A sense of timing • Physical agility • An artistic point of view • A focus for your skills

What You Need Materially   To start—one camera, one light meter, film, and accessories.

What You Need Educationally • Knowledge of how to use the camera for best results. You can learn from: • Camera store personnel • Photography and film classes at community centers, Y's, other group situations and workshops • Public-school adult-education courses • Photographic professionals, photo and film teachers • Books and magazines (a must) • Camera clubs • City, county, or state recreation and park department programs • College and university classes (almost every state has these or technical schools that offer courses in some phase of photography. Many have four-year programs leading to a bachelor's degree with a major in photography; some offer a master's degree with a major in a specialty, such as color photography, and two-year colleges give certificates or associate degrees in photography.) • A job with a commercial photographer, photo lab, a film company, a TV station, or a museum or community center with frequent photo and film shows (you also learn from the exhibitors at these) • The best teacher of all is practice—experience—using a camera over and over to learn how to get desired effects. Also, Eastman Kodak Photo Information Books can be bought at your photo dealers for anywhere from 50¢ on up. These guides cover all phases of photographic work. Ask for them.

Hours You Work   You name it. A job will probably have set working hours, but if you start as a volunteer to learn while you work, in time you could very well be able to set your own hours—and get paid, to boot.

How Much You Earn Learn the going rates in your town for whichever type of work you do, then set yours accordingly. Different types of work pay differently—and in different places.

How You Get Started • Saturate yourself in photography. View as much as you can, all the while taking your own pictures to become a real pro, asking questions from those in-the-know to learn just what makes photos great, good, mediocre, poor • Decide how you want to use your knowledge and/or talents to earn; then pursue that • Find the best photo lab in town to process your work. Demand clean, high-standard processing. Even the best lab won't make real inroads into your profits if you figure your own fees right • Make up a portfolio of your best work to show prospective clients and exhibitors • If you have any kind of a photo service, promote it • Tie in with others to your mutual benefit—party-planners, bridal consultants or shops, editors, school officials, the local real-estate board, and so on • Build a file of good photos, and you can try to place your work with a photo agency that will sell them to others for you (magazines, house organs, book publishers, etc.) on commission. Look through the classified pages of the big city nearest you under "Photographer's Agencies," then write to them. Two New York City agencies are Black Star Publishing Company, 450 Park Avenue South (10016), and Globe Photos, Inc., 404 Park Avenue South (10016).

Where to Exhibit Your Photographic Work Follow suggestions for exhibiting art. Add these: • Private photo galleries • Custom labs or darkrooms (those who do special, fine-print work also frequently exhibit work of outstanding photography) • Commercial art departments • Exhibit areas of corporations, businesses, and organizations • Fine photography books • Photo magazines (these often feature photo contests, show winners' works).

The fact that creative camera work is gradually becoming considered art opens up new spheres for the camera artist. Not only have museums and other cultural centers been showing outstanding photo collections, but private galleries devoted entirely to photography are springing up. Some sell portfolios of ten to twenty-five prints for anywhere from $60 to $850, or single prints.

Share Your Photographic Knowledge You can teach individuals or groups for pay or as a volunteer. Film and photo workshops for teen-agers can be found in big-city ghettos, Y's, settlement houses, community-action groups, and the like. And if your town needs one, help to set it up. Give your teaching time to children and adults (including veterans) who are confined by handicaps of one kind or another.

FILMMAKING

This is the world that teenagers have tied onto with overwhelming enthusiasm. No way to earn, really, it makes up for that with challenge and excitement. You learn it much the same way as print photography. Start with a home-movie camera. Practice. Your nearest TV stations' film technicians may have helpful suggestions. THE AMERICAN FILM INSTI-TUTE GUIDE TO COLLEGE COURSES IN FILM AND TELEVISION lists all United States colleges and universities offering courses in film and television. $5.95 (non-members) or $4 (members of AFI). Add 50¢ to cover postage and mailing. Write for it to AFI at John F. Kennedy Center for the Performing Arts, Washington, D.C., 20566. Attention: Education Programs Department.

Show Films to Earn There are many film sources. Your public-library reference room can help you to find names, addresses of companies lending or renting films. Or write to Ms. Esme Dick, c/o Educational Film Library Association, Inc., 17 West 60th Street, New York, New York, 10023. There are free films and those requiring rental fees ranging from $5 to as high as $250 or more. If you plan to charge admission for viewing, rentals go up to assure the distributor as much as 50 percent of the take.

Film Projectionists They are used in every community these days. Learn how to work this machine, and you should be kept busy at schools, churches and temples, service clubs, youth groups, Y's, educational get-togethers, children's parties, business-group presentations, etc. Without disclosing your own plans, ask who uses film showings, how frequently, who runs the projector, and what the going pay rate is.

Two Real-Life Photographic Stories Helen Keenan of Medford, New Jersey, won a number of prizes in photo contests (these are announced in photo and special-interest magazines and company bulletins, and there are many sponsored by camera clubs and others on the home-town level). This made her realize the extent of her ability, and she raised her too-low prices to a professional middle-range level for her just-launched business. Helen specializes in photographing children and is particularly busy the months before Christmas. Her studio is set up in the garage. The extra income she's earning is being salted away to pay future college tuition for her own children. Phoebe Dunn is a big-time photographer today, creating full-page magazine ads for major companies and magazine covers for publications like WOMAN'S DAY, PARENTS MAGAZINE, BETTER HOMES AND GARDENS. She started in much the same way as Helen Keenan, photographing her own offspring, then those of friends. With enough skill, artistry, and promotion, the route is open to any woman who works at it.

18

Promotion Hints

•**Name your enterprise** Every baby deserves a name, and this is yours. Make it appealing, memorable, appropriate—and if it sparks the rest of your promotion (colors, packaging, advertising, etc.), so much the better.

•**Package it attractively** Packaging is not only how you wrap your product—it's your entire presentation—so make it effective. As for actual wrappings, materials can be as basic as plastic or brown paper bags with eye-catching closings.

•**Be official** Order business cards, stationery, and bill forms that use the name of your project to greatest advantage. If you're not able to do it yourself, let an artist design a letterhead or logo for you.

•**Notify the public** Tack your card or an announcement on bulletin boards at schools, clubs, business offices, libraries, supermarkets, city hall, etc., and leave your card with those who can refer business to you.

•**Bold posters pay off** If they fit into your scheme, give them big letters and bright colors and place them where they can't be missed—all over town and, for that matter, the county.

•**Spread the word** Talk is cheap, so use it. Tell everyone you know or meet about your enterprise. Word of mouth may be all you need in the way of advertising. A simple, mimeographed flyer will also deliver your message fast. Let teenagers deliver them door-to-door in various neighborhoods.

•**Get free publicity** Newspapers, organization and business newsletters, local radio and TV may find your project grist for their mills, so contact them by sending out either a fact sheet or a detailed description of your venture. Then follow it up with a phone call—your personal enthusiasm may fire their interest and get you a feature article or, at the least, inclusion in a column or program. And if you run any kind of a grand opening, invite the media.

•**Advertise** Choose your means of doing this on the basis of what you're selling. Back up your other forms of promotion with well-worded classified ads in your local newspaper or small-space ads in publications most likely to benefit your venture—if your budget permits.

•**Use tie-ins** Special promotions can be built a-round whatever's current or interesting—holidays, trends, seasons, special events of all kinds. And if others will also benefit, work out a joint promotion.

•**One last thought** You're as important a part of your presentation and promotion as your product or service. People usually must buy you as a person before they buy what you're selling. How you appear and how you relate to them will greatly influence your success.

Appendix of Organizations

Adult Education Association (810 18th Street, N.W., Washington, D.C., 20006), 118

Advocates for Women (San Francisco, California), 2

Albert Einstein College of Medicine (Bronx, New York), 90

Allied Board of Trade (342 Madison Avenue, New York, New York, 10017), 202, 203

Alumni Advisory Center (541 Madison Avenue, New York, New York, 10022), 15-16

Amateur Needlework of Today (c/o Lighthouse, 111 East 59th Street, New York, New York, 10022), 193

American Association of Colleges of Pharmacy (8121 Georgia Avenue, Silver Spring, Maryland, 20910), 87

American Association of Community and Junior Colleges (1 DuPont Circle, N.W., Washington, D.C., 20036), 5, 118

American Association of Retired Persons (1225 Connecticut Avenue, N.W., Washington, D.C., 20036), 12

American College of Nurse-Midwives (50 East 92nd Street, New York, New York, 10028), 72

American Council on Pharmaceutical Education (77 West Washington Street, Chicago, Illinois, 60602), 87

American Crafts Council (44 West 53rd Street, New York, New York, 10019), 194

American Dental Assistants Association (211 East Chicago Avenue, Chicago, Illinois, 60611), 89

American Dental Hygienists' Association (211 East Chicago Avenue, Chicago, Illinois, 60611), 88

American Dietetic Association (620 North Michigan Avenue, Chicago, Illinois, 60611), 29, 30

American Federation of Television and Radio Artists (1350 Avenue of the Americas, New York, New York, 10019), 101

American Film Institute (John F. Kennedy Center for the Performing Arts, Washington, D.C. 20566), 211

American Home Economics Association (2010 Massachusetts Avenue, N.W., Washington, D.C. 20036), 30

American Hospital Association (840 North Lake Shore Drive, Chicago, Illinois, 60611), 73-75

American Individual Merchants (c/o Direct Selling Association, 1730 M Street, N. W., Suite 610 Washington, D.C., 20036), 49

American Institute of Interior Decorators (730 Fifth Avenue, New York, New York, 10019), 202

American Kennel Club (51 Madison Avenue, New York, New York, 10010), 63

American Library Association (50 Huron Street, Chicago, Illinois, 60611), 121-22

American Marketing Association (60 East 42nd Street, New York, New York, 10017), 145

American Medical Record Association (Suite 1850, 875 North Michigan Avenue, Chicago, Illinois, 60611), 82-85

American Nurses Association (2420 Pershing Road, Kansas City, Missouri, 64108), 71

American Occupational Therapy Association, Inc. (Suite 200, 6000 Executive Boulevard, Rockville, Maryland, 20852), 82

American Orchid Society (Botanical Museum of Harvard University, Cambridge, Massachusetts, 02138), 127

American Personnel and Guidance Association (1605 New Hampshire Avenue, N.W., Washington, D.C., 20009), 3

American Pharmaceutical Association (2215 Constitution Avenue, N.W., Washington, D.C. 20037), 87

American Physical Therapy Association (1156 15th Street, N.W., Washington, D.C., 20005), 86

American Society for Training and Development (6414 Odana Road, Madison, Wisconsin, 53719), 118

American Society of Clinical Pathologists (c/o American Society of Medical Technologists), 76, 77

American Society of Medical Technologists (Suite 1600, Hermann Professional Building, Houston, Texas, 77025), 77

American Society of Radiologic Technologists (645 North Michigan Avenue, Chicago, Illinois, 60611), 81

American Society of Travel Agents (360 Lexington Avenue, New York, New York, 10017), 165

American Women in Radio and Television (1321 Connecticut Avenue, N.W., Washington, D.C. 20036), 142

Associated Telephone Answering Exchanges (1725 K Street, N.W., Washington, D.C., 20006), 154

Audubon Society (950 Third Avenue, New York, New York, 10022), 127

Broadcast Advertisers Report, Inc. (5th and Chestnut Streets, Darby, Pennsylvania, 19023), 142-43

Bronx Municipal Hospital Center (Pelham Parkway South and Eastchester Road, Bronx, New York, 10461), 91

Canadian Association of Radiologists (1555 Summerhill Avenue, Montreal, Quebec), 81

Catalyst (6 East 82nd Street, New York, New York, 10028), 2, 16

Catholic Charities, 11

Child Development Associate Consortium, Inc. (7315 Wisconsin Avenue, Bethesda, Maryland, 20014), 118

Child Welfare League of America, Inc. (67 Irving Place, New York, New York, 10003), 119

College Entrance Examination Board (Box 592, Princeton, New Jersey, 08540), 7

College Proficiency Examination Program (State Education Department, Albany, New York 12224), 7

Consumer Action Now (30 East 68th Street, New York, New York, 10021), 127

Correction Education Association (1611 8th Place, McLean, Virginia, 22101), 118

Council on Hotel, Restaurant, and Institutional Education (Statler Hall, Cornell University, Ithaca, New York, 14850), 32

Culinary Institute of America (Hyde Park, New York), 20

Day Care and Child Development Council of America, Inc., (1401 K Street, N.W., Washington, D.C., 20005), 119

Direct Selling Association (1730 M Street, N.W., Suite 610, Washington, D.C., 20036), 48, 49

Display Distributors Association (2561 North Clark Street, Chicago, Illinois, 60614), 207-208

Easter Seal Society (2023 West Ogden Avenue, Chicago, Illinois, 60612), 14

Educational Film Library Association, Inc. (17 West 60th Street, New York, New York, 10023), 211

Electrolysis Society of America, Inc. (701 Seventh Avenue, New York, New York, 10036), 107, 108

Embroiderers' Guild of America, Inc. (120 East 56th Street, New York, New York, 10022), 193

Environmental Protection Agency (401 M Street, S.W., Washington, D.C., 20024), 117

Equal Employment Opportunity
Commission, 8
Executive Volunteer Corps (415
Madison Avenue, New York,
New York, 10017), 2-3

Federation of Protestant Welfare
Agencies (281 Park Avenue
South, New York, New York,
10010), 11
Fordham University (Bronx, New
York), 118
Forty-Plus Clubs, 12
Foster Grandparents, 13, 110
Friends of the Earth (529
Commercial Street, San
Francisco, California, 94111),
127

Great Plains National Instructional
Television Library (University
of Nebraska, Box 80699,
Lincoln, Nebraska, 68501), 7
Green Light Program, 12

Hannah Harrison School (c/o
Young Women's Christian
Association of the National
Capital Area, 4470 MacArthur
Boulevard, N.W., Washington,
D.C., 20007), 70, 173
Headstart and Early Childhood
Bureau (c/o U.S. Department
of Health, Education and
Welfare), 119
Health, Education and Welfare,
U.S. Department of (330
Independence Avenue, S.W.,
Washington, D.C., 20201),
13-14, 119, 170
Human Resources Center (Albert-
son, New York, 11507), 14

Institute of Life Insurance (277
Park Avenue, New York, New
York, 10017), 51
Insurance Information Institute
(110 William Street, New York,
New York, 10038), 51
International Alliance of Theatrical
Stage Employees and Motion
Picture Machine Operators
(1270 Avenue of the Americas,
New York, New York, 10020),
134

International Platform Association
(2564 Berkshire Road, Cleveland Heights, Ohio, 44106),
140

Jewish Occupational Council (114
Fifth Avenue, New York, New
York, 10011), 2, 14
Just One Break (373 Park Avenue
South, New York, New York,
10016), 14

Katherine Engel Center for Older
People (23 West 73rd Street,
New York, New York, 10023),
196

Labor, U.S. Department of
(Washington, D.C., 20210), 8
See also Women's Bureau (U.S.
Department of Labor)
Leo Shull Publications (136 West
44th Street, New York, New
York, 10036), 130
Lyon Furniture Mercantile Agency
(185 Madison Avenue, New
York, New York, 10016), 203

Mailing List Brokers Professional
Association (541 Lexington
Avenue, New York, New York,
10022), 59
Manpower Education Institute
(127 East 35th Street, New
York, New York, 10016), 7
Marketing Research Trade Asso-
ciation (Box 1415, Grand
Central Station, New York,
New York, 10017), 145
Meals on Wheels (210 North Grove
Street, East Orange, New
Jersey, 07017), 27

National Association for the
Education of Young Children
(1834 Connecticut Avenue,
N.W., Washington, D.C.,
20009), 119
National Association of Educa-
tional Broadcasters (1346
Connecticut Avenue, N.W.,
Washington, D.C., 20036), 142
National Association of Greeting
Card Publishers (200 Park
Avenue, New York, New York,
10017), 162-63

National Association of Insurance
Women (1847 East 15th Street,
Tulsa, Oklahoma, 74104), 51
National Association of Real
Estate Boards (155 E. Superior
Street, Chicago, Illinois,
60611), 53, 54
National Association of Retail
Druggists (1 East Wacker Drive,
Chicago, Illinois, 60601), 87
National Beauty Career Center
(3839 White Plains Road, Bronx,
New York, 10467), 104
National Center for Information
on Careers in Education (1607
New Hampshire Avenue, N.W.,
Washington, D.C., 20009), 117
National Committee on Household
Employment (c/o Women's
Bureau, U.S. Department of
Labor), 171
National Council for Homemaker-
Home Health Aide Services
(1740 Broadway, New York,
New York, 10019), 170
National Council of Jewish Women
(1 West 47th Street, New York,
New York, 10036), 11, 119
National Council on Crime and
Delinquency (411 Hackensack
Avenue, Hackensack, New
Jersey, 07601), 110
National Executive Housekeeping
Association (Business and Pro-
fessional Building, Second
Avenue, Gallipolis, Ohio,
45631), 173
National Federation of Licensed
Practical Nurses, Inc. (250
West 57th Street, New York,
New York, 10019), 71
National Gift and Art Association
(220 Fifth Avenue, New York,
New York, 10001), 47
National Home Study Council
(1601 18th Street, N.W.,
Washington, D.C., 20009), 4
National Institute of Mental
Health (5600 Fishers Lane,
Rockville, Maryland, 20852),
91
National League for Nursing (10
Columbus Circle, New York,
New York, 10019), 70, 71
National Reading Council (1776
Massachusetts Avenue, N.W.,
Washington, D.C., 20036), 117
National Restaurant Association
(1530 N. Lake Shore Drive,
Chicago, Illinois, 60610), 32

National Society of Interior
Designers, Inc. (315 East 62nd
Street, New York, New York,
10021), 202
National University Extension
Association (Suite 360, 1
DuPont Circle, N.W., Washing-
ton, D.C., 20036), 4
National Weather Service (c/o
National Oceanic and Atmo-
sphere Administration, U.S.
Department of Commerce,
Silver Spring, Maryland,
20910), 13
New York Medical College Gradu-
ate School of Nursing (Valhalla,
New York, 10595), 70

Office of Child Development (c/o
U.S. Department of Health,
Education and Welfare), 119
Office of Environmental Educa-
tion (c/o U.S. Office of Edu-
cation, Washington, D.C.,
20202), 117
Over-60 Employment Counseling
Service of Maryland, Inc., 12

Piano Technicians Guild (1417
Belmont, Seattle, Washington,
98122), 134
Planned Parenthood-World Popu-
lation (810 Seventh Avenue,
New York, New York, 10019),
127
Project Senior Abilities (c/o
Human Resources Center,
Albertson, New York), 14
Psychiatric Rehabilitation Workers
Training Program (Department
of Psychiatry, Bronx Municipal
Hospital Center, Room 1023,
Pelham Parkway South and
Eastchester Road, Bronx, New
York, 10461), 91

Recording for the Blind, Inc. (215
East 58th Street, New York,
New York, 10022), 90
Registry of Medical Technologists
(c/o ASCP, Box 4872, Chicago,
Illinois, 60680), 77
Rehabilitation Services Administra-
tion (c/o U.S. Department of
Health, Education and Welfare),
13
Retired Senior Volunteer Program
(RSVP), 13

School of Natural Resources (University of Michigan, Ann Arbor, Michigan, 48106), 117

Screen Actor's Guild, Inc. (551 Fifth Avenue, New York, New York, 10017), 101

Senior Aides Program, 13

Senior Community Service Project, 12-13

Senior Corps of Retired Executives (SCORE), 3

Senior Personnel Placement Bureau of Norwalk, Connecticut, 12

Small Business Administration (U.S. Department of Labor), 15, 44, 46, 47, 55-57, 60, 202

Social and Rehabilitation Service (Rehabilitation Services Administration, U.S. Department of Health, Education and Welfare), 13

Special Libraries Association (235 Park Avenue South, New York, New York, 10003), 123

State-Federal Information Clearinghouse for Exceptional Children (1411 South Jefferson Davis Highway, Arlington, Virginia, 22202), 117

Teacher Drop-Out Center (Box 521, Amherst, Massachusetts, 01002), 118

Television Information Office (745 Fifth Avenue, New York, New York, 10022), 142

Union for Experiment in Colleges and Universities (Antioch College, Yellow Springs, Ohio, 45387), 6

United Way of America, Inc. (801 N. Fairfax Street, Alexandria, Virginia, 22314), 10

Veterans Administration (Washington, D.C., 20420), 77

Volunteers in Education (NCIES, U.S. Office of Education, Washington, D.C., 20202), 110

Women's Bureau (Massachusetts Department of Commerce and Development, 100 Cambridge Street, Boston, Massachusetts, 02202), 16, 21, 190

Women's Bureau (U.S. Department of Labor), 6, 7, 15, 171, 172, 174

Xavier Society for the Blind (154 East 23rd Street, New York, New York, 10010), 90

General Index

Accounting, record-keeping, 151
Addressing envelopes, 151
Administrative housekeeping, 172-73
Adult education, 118
    in public schools, 4-5
Advertising, 134-36
    writing for agencies, 156, 157, 160
Airlines, 165-66
Animals, working with, 61-65
Antique store, 45
Antiques, repairing and restoring, 176-78
Art, 179-86
Art galleries, 185
Art shows, 184
    for shopping malls, 186
Arty parties, 184-85

Baby sitting service, 113-15
    exchange registry, 114-15
Bags shop, 46-47
Banks, 148-49
Batik, 195-96
Blind, volunteer work for the, 90
Bookplates, designing, 182
Books, writing, 156, 158-59
Bus companies, 166

Car rental companies, 166
Civil Rights Act, 8
Cleaning services, 171-72
Clothes, selling second-hand, 46
Colleges, 5-7
    community, 118
    commuter-car classes, 6
    continuing education programs, 5-6
    extension courses, 5
    proficiency examinations, 6-7
    two-year, 5
    university without walls, 6
    weekend colleges, 6
Community service classes, 5
Copywriting, 160-61
Correspondence courses, for
    medical record technician, 84-85

Cosmetics
    jobs related to, 103-8
    natural, making and selling, 105
Counseling, 2-3
    for handicapped women, 13-14
    private counseling agencies, 3
Crafts, 186-88
    handcrafts, 193-96
    needlecrafts, 189-93

Dance, 134
Day care centers, 119; see also
    Nursery school
Department stores, 40-43
    advertising jobs in, 135-36
    fashion-related jobs in, 93
Dictation and transcription, 151
Dining directories, 26
Direct selling, 47-50
    cosmetics, 105
Displays, 205-8
Dog bathing, clipping and
    grooming service, 63

Ecology, 127
Education
    adult, 118
    early childhood, 118
    opportunities for, 3-7
    public school, 117
    See also Colleges; High school;
        Training
Educational research development, 118-19
Electrolysis, 106-8
Employment agencies, 17
    for married women, 8
    for older women, 12
    temporary help, 146-48
Equal Pay Act, 8
Equal Rights Amendment, 8
Exercise classes, 105
Extension courses, 5

Farm/city trips, 115-16
Fashion, jobs related to, 92-94
Fashion shopping service, 93
Fashion shows, 93
    for short, tall or overweight
        women, 102

Floral arrangements, 125
Food, health, 23-24
Free schools, 118

Games, inventing, 200-1
Gardening
    designing gardens, 128-29
    rent-a-garden service, 127
Gift shops, 45-47
Girl Friday service, 151
Greeting cards
    designing, 181-82
    writing, 162-63
Grooming service, dog, 63
Guidance, *see* Counseling

Handcrafts, 193-96
Handicapped, the
    job opportunities for, 13-14
    volunteer work for, 68
Health foods (organic foods),
    23-24
    raising and selling, 126
High school equivalency tests, 7
Home help services, 171-72
Home lunches for children, 27
Home-study courses, 4
Horse racing, 64
Hospitals, 66-91
    volunteer work in, 67-68
Household training and placement
    services, 172
Housekeeping, administrative,
    172-73

Industrial tours, 115
Insurance industry, 50-52
Interior design, 201-4

Jigsaw puzzles, 184

Laboratory jobs, 79
Leisure learning centers, 6
Libraries, 120-23
Lunches for children at home, 27

Magazines
    selling old, 46
    writing for, 156, 158, 159
Mail order selling, 55-60
Makeup application, 105
Market research, 143-45
Meals on Wheels, 27
Mending service, 99
Mental health, 90-91
Mimeographing service, 151-52
Mobile classrooms, 116
Modeling, 100-2

Mural painting, 182-83
Museums, 185
Music, 132-34

Needlecrafts, 189-93; *see also*
    Sewing
Newspapers, 138-39, 156
Nurse Training Act, 71
Nursery school, home-based,
    110-12; *see also* Day care
    centers

Office jobs
    temporary, 146-48
    work-at-home, 149-52
Older women, jobs for, 11-13, 196
On-the-job training, 4
Organic foods, *see* Health foods

Parties, arty, 184-85
Patents for toys, 198, 199
Perfumes, making and selling, 106
Personnel agencies, *see* Employ-
    ment agencies
Pet boarding, 62
Pet shops, 62
Photography, 208-12
    pet, 64
Plants, 124-29
    boutique specializing in, 125-26
    decoration with, 128
    rental and service of, 124-25
    sitting service, 124
    See also Floral arrangements;
        Gardens
Playing cards, designing, 182
Poetry therapy, 161-62
Posters, 182
Pregnant women, rights of, 8
Promotion, hints on, 213-14
Public relations, 136-37
    writing for, 156, 157, 160
Publishing, 138-39
Puzzles, jigsaw, 184

Quilting, 196

Radio, 140-42
    performing in, 131
    writing for, 157, 160
Railroads, 166
Recipes, selling, 26
Record album companies, 156
Rehabilitation, vocational, 13-14
Repairing and restoring work,
    176-78
Resumés, functional, 16

Retail stores
  jobs in, 40-43
  See also Department stores;
    Shops
Retired women, jobs for, 11-13,
  196
  employment agencies for, 12

School transportation, 167-68
Schools
  free, 118
  See also Colleges; High school;
    Training
Selling
  cosmetics, 105
  direct, 47-50
  mail order, 55-60
  by telephone soliciting, 54-55
Sewing, 98-100
  classes in, taking, 98
  lessons in, teaching, 99-100
  See also Needlecrafts
Shops
  antique, 45
  gift, 45-47
  needlecraft, 190, 192
  opening your own, 43-45
  plant, 125-26
  sick-a-bed, 45
  thrift, 46
  traveler's aid, 167
Sightseeing service for young
  people, 115-16
Sitting service, 113-14
Ski trips, weekend, 115
Small businesses, counseling for,
  2-3
Souvenir shop, 45
Stationery, designing, 182

Table coverings, 100
Tandem jobs, 8-9
Teacher training programs, 118
Teen centers, 38-39
Telephone answering service,
  152-154
Television, 140-43
  educational, 5
  performing in, 131
  writing for, 157, 158, 160
Temporary help services, 146-48
Theater
  nonperforming jobs in, 132
  performing jobs in, 130-31
Thrift shops, 46
Tours for young people, 115-16
Toys, 197-201
Training, vocational, 3-5
  for handicapped women, 13-14
  on-the-job, 4
Traveler's aid shop, 167

University, *see* Colleges

Vocational training, *see* Training,
  vocational
Vocational schools, private, 5
Voice over, 142
Volunteer work, 10-11
  blind, working for the, 90
  educational work with children,
    109-10
  in health field, 67-68
  for older women, 13
  performing arts, 130, 131
  writing as, 157

Youth service bureaus, 24-25

Job Title Index

Accounting clerk, insurance, 51
Administrative housekeeper,
172-73
Administrator, dietetics, 28-29
Admitting officer, hospital, 75
Agent, lecturer's, 140; literary,
161; talent, 137-38; travel,
164-65
Alteration hand, 99
Art tour guide, 185
Artist, 179-86; see also Designer

Baby sitter, 112-13
Bank clerk, 148-49
Bank teller, 148
Bartender, 35
Beauty therapist, 102
Bookkeeper, insurance company,
52

Calligrapher, 150, 182
Caretaker, plants and animals, 79
Cashier, insurance company, 52
Cat handler, 63
Caterer, 19-24
Central service technician, 73-74
Chemistry technologist, 78
Clerk, see specific kinds of clerks
Clinical dietitian, 28
Club travel arranger, 166
Cookbook writer, 25
Cooking teacher, 24-25
Copywriter, 160-61
Cosmetologist, 103-4
Costume designer, theater, 132
Counselor, public school, 117,
travel, 165
Cytotechnologist, 77-78

Decorator, 201-4
Demonstrator, food, 26
Dental assistant, 88-89
Dental hygienist, 87-88
Designer, display, 105-8; fashion,
94-97; garden, 128-29; greeting
card, 181-82; playing cards,
182; stationery, 182; theater
costumes, 132; toys, 197-201
Dietetic technician, 30

Dietitian, 27-30; clinical, 28
Display designer, 205-8
Dog groomer, 63
Dog handler, 63
Dog show judge, 63
Dog show superintendent, 63
Dog trainer, 63
Domestic, 170-72
Dresser, theatrical, 134

Editor, food, 27; public relations,
137
Electroencephalograph technician,
74-75
Electrologist, 106-8

Farrier, 64
Fashion coordinator, 105
Fashion designer, 94-97
Fashion model, 100
Fashion writer, 93
Film projectionist, 211
Film researcher, 142
Filmmaker, 211
Fitter, 99
Floor clerk, hospital, 73
Food company representative, 27
Food demonstrator, 26
Food editor, 27
Food service clerical worker, 31-32
Food service supervisor, 30-31
Food service worker, 32

Garden designer, 128

Haircutter, 105
Hand-finisher, 99
Hand writer, 150, 182
Histological technician, 78
Homemaker-home health aide,
169-70
Hospital aide, 73-74
Household worker, 170-72

Insurance agent, 50-52
Interior designer, 201-4
Interviewer, market research,
143-44

Jockey, 64

Laboratory aide, 79
Laboratory assistant, certified, 77
Laboratory technician, medical, 77
Lecturer, 139-40; gardening and
    related subjects, 126
Librarian, 120-23
Library clerk, insurance company,
    51-52
Library technician, 123
Licensed practical nurse (LPN),
    70
Life insurance agent, 50-52
Literary agent, 161

Materials handler, hospital, 73-74
Medical laboratory technician, 77
Medical record administrator,
    82-84
Medical record technician, 84-85
Medical technologist, 75-77;
    nuclear, 78; specialists, 78, 79
Mental health worker, 90-91
Microbiology technologist, 78
Midwife, 71-72
Model, fashion, 100-2
Music historian, 133
Music teacher, 132-34

Nuclear medical technologist, 78
Nurse, 66, 68-72
Nurse aide, 72-73
Nutritionist, public health, 28

Occupational therapist, 81-82

Party planner, 33-35
Payroll clerk, insurance company,
    51
Pet photographer, 64
Pet sitter, 62
Pharmacist, 86-87
Photographer, 208-12; newspaper,
    139; pet, 64
Photographic model, 100-2
Physical therapist, 85-86
Piano tuner, 134
Poetry therapist, 161-62
Projectionist, film, 211
Psychiatric aide, 72-73

Radiologic technologist, 79-81
Reading specialist, 117
Real estate agent, 52-54
Registered nurse (RN), 69-70
Reporter, freelance shorthand,
    154
Researcher, dietetics, 28; film, 142
Resort representative, 166

Saleswoman, cosmetics, 104;
    manufacturer's showroom,
    92-93; retail stores, 40-43
School crossing guard, 117
Shorthand reporter, freelance, 154
Showroom model, 100-1
Sketcher, fashion, 93
Solicitor, telephone, 54-55
Stable groom, 64
Stenographer, insurance company,
    52
Supply room worker, laboratory,
    79
Surgical-technical aide, 73

Talent agent, 137-38
Teacher, art-appreciation, 185;
    bilingual, 117; cooking, 24-25;
    dietetics, 28; exercises, 105;
    gardening and plants, 126;
    homemaking skills, 173;
    makeup application, 105; music,
    132-34; needlecrafts, 191-92;
    nonpublic school, 118-19;
    performing arts, 131; photo-
    graphy, 210-11; public
    school, 117; vocational-
    technical, 117, 178
Telephone service operator, 153-54
Telephone solicitor, 54-55
Television model, 101
Theater administrator, 132
Theatrical dresser, 134
Therapist, beauty, 102; music, 133;
    occupational, 81-82; physical,
    85-86; poetry, 161-62
Tour guide, art, 185; for young
    people, 115-16
Toy designer, 197-201
Translator, 161
Travel agent, 164-65
Travel companion, 165
Travel counselor, 165
Typist, work-at-home, 149-51

Underwriter clerk, insurance
    company, 51

Veterinarian's assistant, 62
Vocational-technical teacher, 117,
    178

Ward clerk, hospital, 73
Wedding planner, 36-38
Writer, 155-63; animal subjects, 64;
    cookbooks, 25; fashion column,
    93; newspaper, 138-39; public
    relations, 137
X-ray technologist, 79-81